In Good Hands

250 years of craftsmanship at
SWAINE ADENEY BRIGG

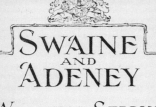

SWAINE
AND
ADENEY
WALKING STICKS
& UMBRELLAS WITH
CARVED HEADS

THE
COACH HORN:
WHAT TO BLOW
AND
HOW TO BLOW IT.
BY AN OLD GUARD.

Belohnt mit Preis-Medaillen in den Austellungen von
1851, 1855, 1862, 1867, 1873, 1876, 1878, 1889.

SWAINE UND ADENEY,
PEITSCHENFABRICANTEN
Zu der Königin dem Prinzen und der Prinzessin von Wales
UND DER KÖNIGLICHEN FAMILIE.

185, Piccadilly, LONDON.

HUNT SERVAN...
WHIPS
and other requisites
Hunting Horns

SWAINE & ADEN...
Whip Makers by Special Appointment
to
H.M. THE KING
H.M. QUEEN ALEXANDRA

Bot. of Thos. Brigg & Sons.
Umbrella & Walking Stick Manufacturers,
23. St. James's Street. S.W.
ACCOUNTS STANDING OVER 12 MONTHS 5 PER CENT EXTRA WILL BE CHARGED.

SWAINE & ADENEY.
WHIP MANUFACTURERS,
TO THE
QUEEN, PRINCE & PRINCESS OF WALES
& ROYAL FAMILY.
AN ASSORTMENT OF EVERY DESCRIPTION OF WORK ALWAYS READY.
CANES, SPORTING APPARATUS, &c. &c.

PENDRAGON

John Köhler

SWAINE & ADENEY
185, PICCADILLY, LONDON, W.
Telephone : REGENT 797.

SWAINE & ISAAC.
Whip Manufacturers,
To the Queen & Royal Family.
185, PICCADILLY,
London.

SWAINE & ADENEY,
Whip Manufacturers,
TO THE
Queen,
The Prince &
Princess of Wales
AND THE
ROYAL FAMILY.
185,
PICCADILLY
LONDON
WHOLESALE
RETAIL, AND
FOR EXPORTATION.
PRIZE MEDALS AT VIENNA 1873, & PHILADELPHIA, 1876.

Herbert Johnson
HAT & CAP MAKER,
38, New Bond Street,
LONDON, W.
Telephone: 784 Mayfair,
Telegraphic Address:
"BROWBOUND." LONDON.

WHIP · MAKERS
BY APPOINTMENT

WHIP · MAK...
BY APPOINTM...

SWAINE & ADENEY LT...
185 PICCADILLY, LONDO...
W.1.

Pendragon perfection

'STAG'S HEAD' BRAND.   "KANGAROO" BRAND.

the skilled touch of craftsmen

BY ROYAL WARRANT OF APPOINTMENT
NUNQUAM NON PARATUS
HERBERT JOHNSON
38
New Bond St.
LONDON,
W.
Frans Sauwels
HOFLEVERANCIER
S'GRAVENHAGE

THE "Jauntie"
Exclusive to Herbert
Johnson an inexpensive hat for the
"occasional" occasion. Available in
a wide range of attractive colours,
including black, white and the latest
pastel shades. Can be slipped into the
handbag or pocket, and just will not
crease.
HERBERT
JOHNSON
of Bond Street
38 NEW BOND ST., LONDON, W.I.
£1
19/6
Inclusive of postage, or
for personal shoppers, or
at ladies' salon on the first floor.
MAY. 0784

SWAINE & ADENEY, LTD.,

Mr Hinton Kelly
Bought of
(Successors)
WHIP MAKERS,
their Royal Highnesses
Dukes of York, Clarence, Kent, Cumberland and Cambridge.
No 238, PICCADILLY, LONDON.
Wholesale Retail & for Exportation
Jas Swaine
to his MAJESTY,
the Prince of Wales

In Good Hands

250 years of craftsmanship at
SWAINE ADENEY BRIGG

Katherine Prior

JOHN ADAMSON
CAMBRIDGE

John Adamson
90 Hertford Street, Cambridge CB4 3AQ, England

First published 2012

British Library Cataloguing in Publication Data
A catalogue record of this book is available from
the British Library

ISBN 978-1-898565-09-3

Designed and set in Fresco Pro, Ideal Sans
and Typonine Stencil by Philip Lewis,
LewisHallam Design

Printed on Burgo R400 gsm matt paper by
Conti Tipocolor, Florence, Italy

FRONTISPIECE A medley of printed matter from
the Swaine Adeney Brigg archive, encapsulating the
variety of businesses that have contributed to the
company over the last 250 years.
TAILPIECE The Duchess of Cambridge sporting
a Brigg umbrella on board the royal barge *Spirit of
Chartwell* on the occasion of the Diamond Jubilee
Pageant on 3 June 2012.

AUTHOR'S ACKNOWLEDGEMENTS

A book of this nature inevitably incurs many obligations and debts, both professional and personal. First of all, of course, I must thank Roger Gawn, the new owner of Swaine Adeney Brigg, who commissioned me to write this book soon after he took over the company in 2009. At the time we had no idea of how much we would be able to piece together about the company's history, and Roger has been extraordinarily tolerant and indulgent as the project and its costs have expanded with my ever-widening circles of research. I am most grateful to him for the opportunity to work on such a rewarding topic.

John Adamson has, as ever, been an incisive editor, a patient publisher, and a good friend. The book would not have seen the light of day without his guidance and oversight. To Philip Lewis, the designer, I also extend my heartfelt thanks, for he has taken an awkward, caption-heavy text, and made something beautiful of it. In this, of course, he has been aided by the superb photography of James Austin and his wife Pauline, who have, I feel, captured the appeal of the wonderful old handcrafted items featured in the book.

For access to many of the items themselves, both Roger and I are very deeply indebted to two people in particular. Dominic Strickland of Michael German Antiques Ltd was unstinting in sharing with us both his knowledge and his wonderful collection of antique walking sticks to illustrate the book. Similarly, Lindsey Knapp of the Victoria Gallery entrusted us with a large selection of hunting antiques and memorabilia and made many helpful suggestions. We cannot thank the two of them enough for their cheerful support of the project.

Archivists and library staff have been unfailingly helpful with my many queries and it seems therefore invidious to name but a few of them. But some went well beyond the call of duty in their promptitude, courtesy, and readiness to waive or substantially reduce image reproduction fees, and I would therefore like to thank Toby Wilson of the Automobilia department at Bonhams, Charlotte Heyman of the Bridgeman Art Library, Sue Martin of Cambridgeshire Archives, Robert Jones of the Government Art Collection, Max Williamson of Charles Leski Auctions in Melbourne, Jeremy Smith of the London Metropolitan Archives, Rebecca Kohl of the Montana Historical Society, Arian Sheets of the National Music Museum at the University of South Dakota, Kathryn Jones and Karen Lawson of the Royal Collection, Mike Glasson and David Mills of Walsall Leather Museum, Maggie Wood of the Warwickshire Museum Service, and Alison McCann of West Sussex Record Office. I should also like to thank the Rt Hon Lord Egremont for permission to reproduce, at no cost, documents from the Petworth House Archives.

Many other people have also contributed information, insights, and goodwill to the book and in this respect I would like particularly to mention Peter Adamson, Keith Cowie, Christopher Czilinsky, Jane Rees, Peter Tebbit, and Denise and Alan Tilley.

Lastly, I must thank the craftsmen and women and the retail and administrative staff at Swaine Adeney Brigg. Essentially, the future of this grand old British company lies in their skilled and careful work. The book is thus dedicated to them and the memory of their many worthy predecessors.

Katherine Prior
London

Contents

Foreword   7

1   Swaine Adeney Brigg – The Founding Fathers   9

2   J. Köhler & Son – Hunting, Coaching,
    and Signal Horn Manufacturers   75

3   G. & J. Zair Ltd – The Birmingham Connection   83

4   Thomas Brigg & Sons – Royal Umbrella-makers   91

5   Herbert Johnson – Hatters of New Bond Street   123

6   'Pendragon Perfection – The skilled touch of craftsmen'   135

7   Looking Ahead   148

Chronology   152
List of Illustrations   154
A Note on Sources   156
Index   157

This, then, is the formula:
honest material and the finest
craftsmanship that can be
put into the moulding of it.

Edward Swaine Adeney Jr, 1927

Foreword

THE DAY THAT I SAW the advertisement in the *Financial Times* in 2009 I knew I was committed. The opportunity to buy a company with 250 years of unparalleled trading history, a company that had enjoyed royal patronage since the reign of George III, a company with skills to make superlative products in Britain; it was all too irresistible.

Craftsmanship and workmanship have long been under threat in this country and I have for many years been determined to reverse the trend. My own history of using skilled craftsmen in the restoration of historic buildings made the transition to leather working relatively easy and at least as enjoyable. For me the fundamental principles underlying both activities are the same. Our recent introduction of leather and wood furniture continues the blending process over all skilled traditional craftsmanship.

I knew from the outset that it was going to be a challenge taking on the company, for it had had a very difficult past few years. The reality was sadly as bad as I had feared, but three years later and with a major restructuring behind us the new die has been cast. All of the very good has been retained, and with it the ability to develop further the classic skills of working leather in order that many new people may enjoy the true luxury of the best traditionally made British goods. Also it is the opportunity to re-establish apprenticeships for young people to master the skills of leatherworking in luxury goods as well as umbrella- and whip-making, thereby giving them a solid future career in uncertain times.

Using natural materials in a sustainable way to make essential but luxury products - this is the ethos that has run through the company for two and a half centuries. We have always nurtured pride in ownership and our thriving repairs department upholds the longevity of our products and supports our customers' emotional and family links with them. We continue our traditions with energy and in good heart.

Swaine Adeney Brigg has sold its goods throughout the world for many decades to connoisseurs of this particular luxury. We will soon re-enter the international stage in a way that shows the true value of tradition, understated high quality and discreet style. I believe that Swaine Adeney Brigg and all that it stands for make it truly a company of the moment.

Roger Gawn
CHAIRMAN

1

Swaine Adeney Brigg
The Founding Fathers

THE SWAINE ADENEY BRIGG FAMILY OF COMPANIES represents over two hundred and fifty years of quality craftsmanship in leather goods, equestrian equipment, and elegant personal accessories. Between them, the companies have won numerous royal warrants and international prizes. Their survival today is proof of the continuing appeal of stylish, handcrafted goods in a world of anonymous mass production, and their traditional policy of direct sales and service to customers will be maintained in the new Swaine Adeney Brigg shops in St James's, Mayfair, and the City of London. Were customers to visit the Swaine Adeney Brigg factories in Norfolk and Cambridgeshire they would see craftsmen and women cutting out leather hides and shaping umbrella components by hand much as it was done two hundred years ago. The workshops hum with quiet, industrious purpose, the air rich with the mingled odours of hides, oils, and woods. There is experimentation and innovation, but there is also respect for old knowledge and appreciation for the unique, characterful beauty of natural materials. Few manufacturers in Britain today can boast such a heritage and look to the future with such confidence.

John Ross, Royal Whip-maker, c.1760–1798

The founding father of this impressive tradition was a saddler named John Ross who set up a whip manufactory in London, perhaps around 1760. Little is known of his background, but he was probably a Scot, for he is known to have had three nieces surnamed Haig, and Ross was not then a common surname in London.

Ross's first known factory was in Marylebone Street, just to the north of Piccadilly. This street was incorporated in Glasshouse Street many years ago, but it used to form part of the old highway from the Haymarket up to Oxford Street. John Ross moved into No. 8 on the north side of the street, probably in late 1762, after the death of its previous occupant, a carpenter named William Insley. His next-door neighbour at No. 9, trading under the sign of the Golden Fleece, was Richard Warren, well-known perfumer to the nobility. Some of Warren's genteel clientele may have overflowed into John Ross's premises, for he early counted Prince Henry Frederick, Duke of Cumberland, and George Wyndham, 3rd Earl of Egremont, among his customers. Both men were enthusiastic patrons of horse racing; Prince Henry bred twenty-seven winners at his stud at Windsor between 1767 and 1781, while Egremont boasted the largest racing stud in England at Petworth Park in Sussex. Prince Henry also had a reputation as a splendid libertine. He was a younger brother of George III and the king never forgave him for introducing his eldest son, George, Prince of Wales, to the distracting pleasures of the turf and a succession of highly unsuitable consorts.

John Ross's Marylebone Street factory was lost in a fire on 26 July 1769. The blaze started at about half-past eight at night, when two apprentices were boiling pitch and rosin for making whip stocks. Within minutes, Ross's establishment had been destroyed and the flames had spread to Warren's perfumery and other neighbouring buildings occupied by a shoemaker, cabinet-maker, confectioner, and tailor. The chemicals, timber, and textiles fuelled a firestorm that twenty fire engines battled to contain, and when it was finally extinguished around dawn, eighteen buildings had been razed, a householder had died, and several firemen had been injured by falling chimney stacks. London newspapers described the event in shocked tones, conscious that the

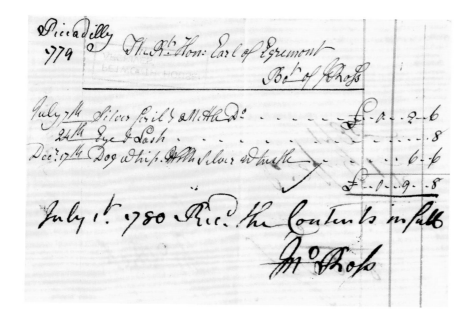

1
An invoice from John Ross's Piccadilly shop for purchases made by George Wyndham, 3rd Earl of Egremont, in 1779, which shows that Ross was in the business of supplying components as well as complete whips. The items sold include ferrules in silver and nickel, and a spare lash and the eye or loop for attaching it to a crop.

2 (right)
A Crown Estates survey of Marylebone Street and neighbouring roadways made in July 1771, two years after the disastrous fire that began in John Ross's whip manufactory at No. 8. The houses marked in yellow are the ones rebuilt after the fire, including Richard Warren's perfumery at No. 9.

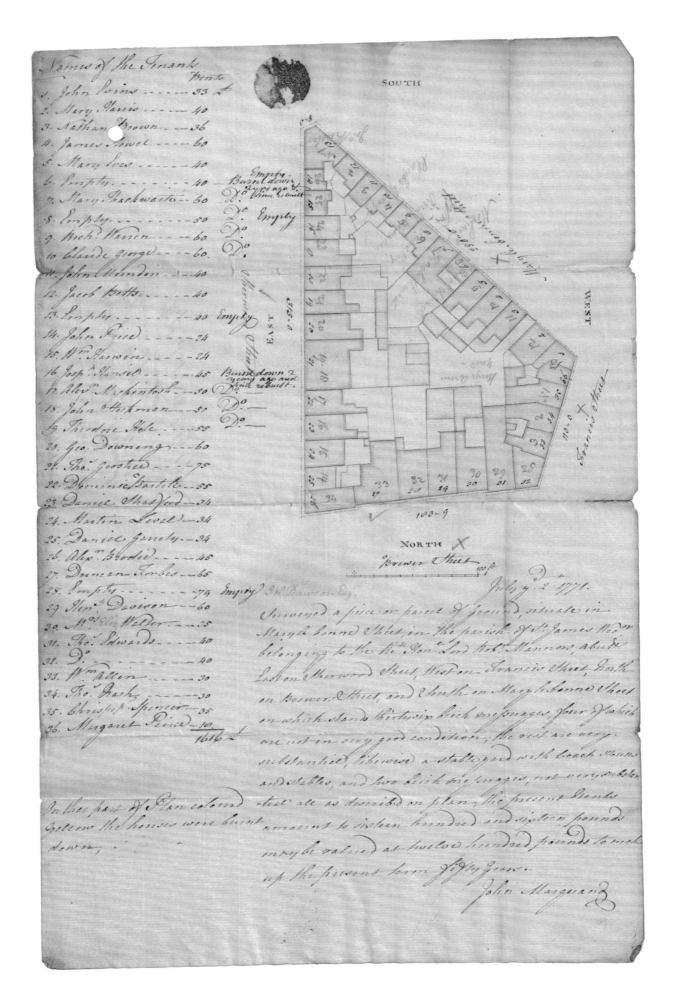

Names of the Tenants
Rents

1. John Ivins — — — — 33 £
2. Mary Harris — — — 40
3. Nathan Brown — — 36
4. James Sewel — — — 60
5. Mary Ives — — — 40
6. Empty — — — — — 40
7. Mary Freshwater — 60
8. Empty — — — — — 50
9. Rich.d Warren — — 60
10. Claude George — — 60
11. John Munden — — 40
12. Jacob Betts — — — 40
13. Empty — — — — 40
14. John Pried — — — 24
15. W.m Darwin — — — 24
16. Jos.ph Hamel — — — 45
17. Alex.r Mackintosh — 50
18. John Atchman — — 50
19. Theodore Ash — — 55
20. Geo. Downing — — 60
21. Tho.s Goostree — — 75
22. Dominic Bartok — 55
23. Daniel Shadford — 34
24. Martin Level — 34
25. Daniel Janety — 34
26. Alex.r Brodie — — 45
27. Duncan Forbes — 65
28. Empty — — — — 70
29. Her.d Davison — 60
30. M.rs Elis Welder — 35
31. Tho.s Edwards — — 40
32. D.o — — — — 40
33. W.m Allen — — — 30
34. Tho.s Bush — — — 30
35. Chris.ph Spencer — 35
36. Margaret Peirce — 10
— — — — — 1616 £

Empty — Burnt down 2 years ago &
D.o — D.o since rebuilt
D.o — Empty
D.o
D.o

£115-0

Empty

Burnt down 2 years ago and since rebuilt.
D.o
D.o

Empty

On this part of Plan colour'd yellow the houses were burnt down.

SOUTH

WEST

EAST

NORTH ✗
Brewer Street — — — 100 ft

Empty W.m Brownson Esq.

D.o
July y.e 2.d 1771.

Surveyed a piece or parcel of ground, situate in Marylebone Street, in the parish of St James West.r belonging to the R.t Hon.ble Lord Rob.t Manners, abut.s East on Sherwood Street, West on Francis Street, North on Brewer Street, and South on Marylebone Street, on which stand thirty-six brick messuages, four of which are not in very good condition, the rest are very substantial, likewise a stable yard with coach houses and stables, and two brick messuages, not very substantial all as described on plan, the present Rents amount to sixteen hundred and sixteen pounds may be valued at twelve hundred pounds to make up the present term fifty years —

John Marquand

city had only just escaped another Great Fire. 'It was so sudden, and so rapid,' reported the *Public Advertiser*, 'that the unfortunate Sufferers are supposed to have saved very little, if any, of their Effects.'

John Ross bounced back from this calamity quickly. By 10 March 1770, according to an advertisement in the *Gazetteer and New Daily Advertiser*, he was trading at 238, Piccadilly. His illustrious client list probably helped him start afresh. On 11 April 1777, he advertised himself in the *Daily Advertiser* as 'Whipmaker to the Royal Family'. He had more than replenished his stock by this date, for in September of that year one of his journeymen, Thomas Knowland, was found guilty of stealing from him 100 horse whips, 30 gross of silk lashes for whips, 300 silver caps for whips, and 100 whip handles. With a product made up of essentially small components, pilfering must have been as great a hazard as fire.

Ross's new factory was on the south side of Piccadilly, close to the Haymarket. It was an excellent location for a whip-maker. Whereas the north side of the street featured several imposing residences, such as Burlington House and Devonshire House, the south side was the working half, and was lined with shops, manufactories,

and coaching inns. Ross was just a few doors east of one of the largest coaching inns of all, the famous White Bear Inn at No. 235. Behind the White Bear's frontage was a double row of stables running all the way through to the north side of Jermyn Street. It was the embarkation point for daily coach runs to Dover, Margate, Ramsgate, Canterbury, and Rochester, and a pick-up point for numerous coaches from the City heading for the West Country. The shop itself perhaps left something to be desired. In 1797 surveyors acting for the Crown described it as dilapidated and unhygienic and ordered the landlord to carry out £120 worth of repairs. Desperate to off-load the responsibility, the landlord shortly afterwards advertised it for sale as 'a convenient house and excellent shewy fronted Shop'.

In 1798 Ross sold up to a whip-maker named James Swaine and his financial partner, a brewer named Benjamin Slocock. An invoice headed 'Jas. Swaine & Co. (Successors to Mr. Ross)' survives from September of that year, but the transfer was only formally announced on 19 January 1799, when a pair of advertisements appeared in the *Courier and Evening Gazette*. In the first one, 'John Ross, Late Whip-Maker to His Majesty' begged leave to

WEST COUNTRY MAILS AT THE GLOUCESTER COFFEE HOUSE, PICCADILLY.

4
A plan from a Crown Estates survey details six houses on the south side of Piccadilly, near the junction with the Haymarket, in 1811. James Swaine and Benjamin Slocock, successors to John Ross, are shown at No. 238.

5
An invoice issued by James Swaine & Co., 'Successors to Mr. Ross' and 'Whip Makers to His Majesty', to Frederick Booth, dated 26 September 1798. The item Booth purchased, a servant's velvet hunting cap, suggests that Swaine & Co. retailed at least some accessories along with their whips. The invoice's letterhead was engraved by James Swaine's younger brother, John (1775–1860), who had a studio at 80 Margaret Street, Cavendish Square, and afterwards in Queen Street, Golden Square. He had been apprenticed to Jacob Schnebbelie and then Barak Longmate, and in 1797 he married Longmate's daughter Elizabeth. He was a prolific producer of fine facsimiles of old plates, as well as scientific illustrations, and was to contribute plates to the *Gentleman's Magazine* for some fifty years.

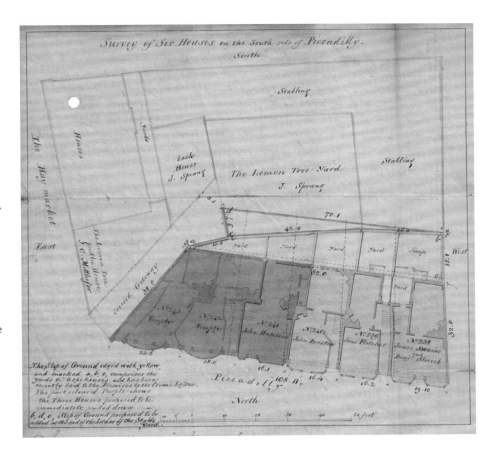

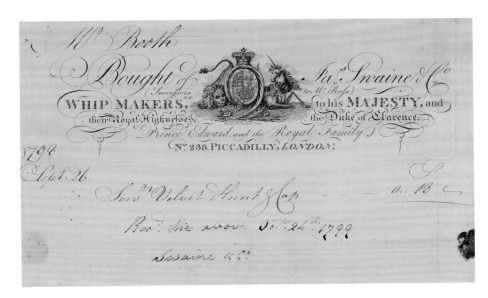

3 (left)
West Country Mails at the Gloucester Coffee House, Piccadilly, an engraving by Christian Rosenberg, after a painting by James Pollard, 1828. The print gives an idea of the volume of horse-drawn traffic passing through Piccadilly in the early nineteenth century – and the customers this brought to a whip-maker. There are four coaches bound for Poole and Exeter and four pony traps engaged in ferrying parcels and passengers to them; seven whips can be seen.

'return his most grateful Thanks to the Nobility and Gentry for the past Favours' and requested that 'their future Commands may be transferred to Swaine and Co., his successor in Trade, at his late Shop, No. 238, Piccadilly'. In the second, 'Swaine and Co., Whip-Makers to His Majesty' asked for the continuing patronage of John Ross's customers, noting their determination to preserve the reputation he had acquired for 'goodness of Articles and moderation in price'. The new owners also promised variety, modishness, and improved technology: 'Whips of every kind for the Country, and exportation also, fashionable Black Whips that will retain their colour, and not soil the gloves of the wearer.'

James Swaine's purchase of John Ross's business was the first association of the name Swaine with the company we know today as Swaine Adeney Brigg. John Ross died not long after the sale; his will was proved in September 1800. Susanna, his widow, died in 1802. They had no surviving children.

Swaine & Co. (1798–1825)

James Swaine was born on 30 July 1766, in the village of Stanwell, near Staines on the south-western outskirts of London. He was the eldest surviving son of the nine children born to John Swaine and his wife Margaret French. One of his brothers was the artist and engraver John Swaine (1775–1860).

In June 1782, just before his sixteenth birthday, he was apprenticed to Benjamin Griffith & Co., whip-makers of High Holborn. Benjamin had been entered as a Freeman of the Saddlers' Company in 1747, and since then he had built up a substantial business. One of his older sons,

Thomas (1754–1820), was already trained up and working alongside him. Another son, Charles (1765–1843), was apprenticed to him at exactly the same time as James Swaine. James and Charles grew up in the business together and remained good friends after James struck out on his own. In years to come, James Swaine would license Charles Griffith to produce some of his whips, and in 1850, when Charles Griffith's son was ready to retire, he would sell all his stock to James's son.

James could not have had a better introduction to the whip trade than at Griffith's. Thomas and Charles took over the running of the company in 1787, after their father's death, and within twenty years they had made Griffith the biggest name in the business. Details of it are preserved in a trial held at the Old Bailey in April 1799, when Charles Griffith charged one of his former employees with stealing the company's stock. In his evidence Charles revealed that he employed one hundred and thirty workers at his barn-like factory at 322, High Holborn, which was actually the shell of a hall built c.1500 for the Earl of Southampton. These workers performed highly specialized tasks in separate departments or workshops, including thong-making, braiding, binding, buttoning, and finishing. Indeed, argued Charles, it was no longer possible for one person alone to make a quality whip because of the range of skills involved. There was also a considerable amount of mechanization in the industry, especially in the braiding of the whip stocks and the winding of threads around the stocks. At around the time James Swaine left Griffith, the company had thirteen braiding machines and at least one 'raising engine' for threadwork on the handles. More than anything else, the size and complexity of

6
A trade card for Griffith & Son, Whip Manufacturers, of No. 322, Holborn, London, engraved by Henry Thomas Green, c.1825–40. James Swaine was apprenticed to Benjamin Griffith in 1782; by the time this card was made, Benjamin's son Charles ran the family company along with his own son, Charles Jr.

7
An invoice issued by James Swaine & Co.
to Mr Hinton Kelly in November 1802 for
two four-horse whips. Like the bill at fig. 5,
dated 1798, this one was engraved by James
Swaine's younger brother John. But there are
some important differences between the
two invoices; in the space of four years, the
company is shown to have added more royal
clients and could now boast of being whip-
makers not only to George III, but also six of
his seven sons: the Prince of Wales and the
Dukes of York, Clarence, Kent, Cumberland,
and Cambridge. There is also the hint of
expansion in the line added over the coat of
arms: 'Wholesale Retail & for Exportation'.

Griffith's operations in 1799 are useful reminders
of the importance of the whip-making industry in the
era before steam trains broke the horse's monopoly
of land transport.

In about 1790, a few years before he left Griffith's
employ, James Swaine married a woman called Ann. She
was a kinswoman – possibly the younger sister – of the
brewer Benjamin Slocock (1749–1831), who put up quite a
bit of the cash to enable James to buy out John Ross. His
financial input continued to be significant; an account
dated June 1818 records a payment to him of £9 10s 4d as
interest on a loan of £2,382. In 1804 Slocock took on his
own son, Benjamin Jr, as an apprentice whip-maker. In
1810, James Swaine's only son, Edward, was also apprenticed to Slocock. Slocock was a Freeman of the Brewers'
Company, which is probably why he acted as master to
the boys. Benjamin Jr and Edward were plainly expected
to inherit the company and for a short time after Edward
completed his apprenticeship in 1817 it traded with two
identities: Swaine & Co., and Swaine, Slocock, & Swaine.
But Benjamin Jr died on 15 March 1825, aged only 35.
This seems to have been the catalyst for his father's
retirement from the partnership, for when Benjamin Sr
wrote his will the following month he described himself
as a gentleman of Camden Town, who had been 'formerly
in partnership with James Swaine of Piccadilly, whip-
maker'. He had two daughters, but neither of them
married into the business, and when he died in 1831
the Slocock family's connection with the whip-making
industry came to an end.

A lone account book survives today in the company archives from the latter years of Benjamin Slocock's involvement with Swaine & Co. It is a squat, sturdy production, bound in parchment, with pages of double-entry bookkeeping accounts recording receipts and outgoings for the years 1818–25. Although brief, these entries are remarkably informative about the nature of the company's business. Most striking is the fact that until 1825 the company still retailed only whips; there is no sign of the walking sticks that Swaine would be selling by the middle of the century. This is additional proof of the large size of the whip market in the pre-railway era. Receipts in the month of May 1821, for example, totalled £592, which in retail price index terms would be about £43,000 today. The accounts also bear out reports of the seasonal nature of the trade. In London and other cities, April to July was the busiest time of year for sales of driving whips, as the smarter households renewed their equipage for driving out and making calls during the social season. Then August to October saw a burst of sales in riding whips, as the gentry took to their horses for the hunt season. November to March was traditionally the slack time of year, although as the century advanced Christmas was to assume more importance in the sales calendar. Compared with the May 1821 figure of £592, receipts in January that year were only £285.

On the right-hand pages of the account book, the lists of outgoing sums reveal the variety of materials involved in whip-making. Regular suppliers were Mr Tinning, who provided hides on a weekly basis, and William Isaac, who delivered holly and yew sticks by the dozen almost as frequently. Both woods were used for the long stocks or shafts in driving or carriage whips. The best holly was said to come from Kent, although Sussex and Hampshire also supplied the market. Of the sticks, 'rabbit-bitten holly' was especially prized; hungry rabbits who gnawed the holly bark in barren winters left a textured, mottled pattern on the sticks that polished up beautifully. Other woods supplied in quantity included bamboo and cane; these strong but lightweight sticks were often used for the shafts of hunting whips. Whalebone was another vital material. Properly called baleen, it is a cartilage-like substance from the mouth of a sperm whale that combines strength with flexibility, which made it perfect for the stocks of riding crops. Long, angled strips of whalebone were glued and bound together to form the core of the stock. This was then covered with a sleeve of 'catgut' which, despite the name, was usually sheep's or lamb's gut. It was supplied in great quantities to Swaine & Co. by a Mr Scasebrook. This in turn was covered with plaited pigskin or perhaps something more exotic, and finished with a handle that best suited the whip's purpose.

9
His Majesty King Geo. III Returning from Hunting, an etching with aquatint by Matthew Dubourg after a painting by James Pollard, 1820. Although published in the year of his death, this print shows George III probably about ten years earlier, before the bout of mental illness that clouded his final years.

8 (left)
An account book from Swaine & Co., covering the years 1818 to 1825. It is opened at a page for October and November 1818, which shows two of the royal brothers as clients, the Prince Regent, prosaically reduced to 'P. Regent', and the Duke of Cambridge, Prince Adolphus.

The less common supplies listed in the accounts were mostly intended for this finishing and decorating work, and included specialist leathers such as 'fish skins' (shagreen from shark or stingray) and colt or foal skins, along with red and yellow lacquers, quills, stag horns, and fawns' feet. Handles and grips could also be fashioned from gold, silver, or semi-precious stones, but these did not appear frequently in the early accounts.

The outgoings also included running costs, such as rent and coal payments. There were tips for the servants of wealthier customers if they spared Swaine & Co. a delivery cost by carrying their employer's purchases home for them. There were also annual payments to 'John Swaine, engraver'. This was James's artistic younger brother, who designed and printed the company's letterheads.

On the left-hand pages, the incoming sums reveal much about Swaine's clientele, while also providing an insight into fashionable pursuits for gentlemen. Sales to professional users such as coach drivers made up the lion's share of the company's income. For the most part, these were not made over the shop counter in Piccadilly, but through bulk sales to retailers. Several well-known saddlery and harness companies featured among

Swaine's clients in these early years, including Whippy and Gibson, both of London. There were also sales to general retailers in the provinces. Year after year, James Swaine crisscrossed the British Isles promoting his company's whips. Travelling mostly in July and August, when the roads were likely to be driest, his peregrinations took in a great number of English towns, as well as Carmarthen in Wales and Dublin in Ireland. Some of his journeys were simplified in the accounts to 'North Journey' or 'Sussex Journey', but others were detailed by town. In the summer of 1823, for example, James visited Oxford, Cheltenham, Ludlow, Shrewsbury, Liverpool, Derby, Doncaster, Hull, and Louth, bringing back with him over £850 in sales income. In March 1824 these sales were augmented for the first time by an overseas shipment to Monsieur Brune, of the rue de la Paix in Paris. Over the next eighteen months M. Brune ordered £132 worth of whips from Swaine & Co.

But while these sales were the backbone of the company's finances, they were not especially glamorous. This is where the Piccadilly shop came into its own. There was no shortage of royal and aristocratic patronage. As early as 1798 Swaine & Co. had advertised themselves on their letterhead as whip-makers to His Majesty George III, an honourable connection that John Ross seems to have enjoyed before them. The account book shows additionally that Swaine's customers included George III's consort, Queen Charlotte, and four of his sons: the Prince Regent, the future George IV; the Duke of Clarence, who would become William IV; the Duke of Cumberland, who would become Ernest Augustus I, King of Hanover; and the Duke of Cambridge, Prince

Adolphus. Rubbing shoulders with the royal brothers were the Duke of Bedford, the Marquesses of Buckingham and Bath, the Earl of Blessington, Lords Melbourne, Dundas, Portsmouth, Errol, and Arden, and a host of knights, army officers, esquires, and reverend gentlemen. There was also a good sprinkling of aristocratic ladies among the patrons.

Of these, it was the Prince Regent and his dandified friends – 'Prinny's Set' – who really set the tone for the sale of the best whips in this era. The Prince himself, who had been an avid breeder of race horses in his youth and a keen rider, was quite a big spender, purchasing almost £70 worth of whips in 1818 and 1819. His boon companions who shopped at Swaine & Co. included Lord Manners, Frederick 'Poodle' Byng, and Lord Petersham. All three were renowned as fashionable men about town; 'loungers' in the parlance of the day. John, Lord Manners (1778–1857), was the future 5th Duke of Rutland. He had won early fame in high society with his extravagant coming of age party at Belvoir Castle in 1799, which had cost £60,000. The Honorable Frederick Byng (1784–1871), nicknamed 'Poodle' on account of his mop of fair curls, was seldom seen in public or caricature without the eponymous canine by his side. He was a legendary gossip who used to share Beau Brummell's table in the window at White's Club and exchange acid comments with him on the clothing of the passersby. He was also a notorious libertine, and few who remembered his dissipated youth could fathom his transformation in middle age into a campaigner for sanitary reform.

But it was Lord Petersham who encapsulated the modish spirit of Prinny's Set. Born Charles Stanhope

10

An equestrian portrait of George IV when he
was Prince of Wales, painted by George Stubbs
in 1791. In his younger years, George IV was a
keen horseman and a good judge of horseflesh.
He shopped with Swaine & Co. throughout the
Regency, and may have been introduced to
their wares back in John Ross's day, when Ross
was known as the whip-maker to his fond but
wayward uncle, Prince Henry, Duke of
Cumberland and Strathearn.

(1780–1851) and destined to become the 4th Earl of Harrington, he was the archetypal Regency buck, driven by a fastidious sense of fashion. He was also famed for a dislike of venturing outdoors before six in the evening and his passion for the theatre. Indeed, after his father was safely dead and buried, he married one of Covent Garden's loveliest actresses, Miss Maria Foote. Several contemporary illustrations portray him in elegant dress and sporting a whip more or less as a fashion accessory rather than an aid to controlling a horse. But he did in fact take his equipage very seriously – at least in terms of its stylishness. Captain Gronow, publishing his *Reminiscences* in 1862, recalled of Petersham that: 'His carriages were unique of their kind: they were entirely brown, with brown horses and harness. The groom, a tall youth, was dressed in a long brown coat reaching to his heels, and a glazed hat with a large cockade.' Apparently this devotion to brown was caused by his having 'been desperately in love with a very beautiful widow bearing that name.'

Another of the Prince Regent's companions who shopped at Swaine & Co. was Colonel William Berkeley (1786–1857), eldest of the illegitimate sons of the 5th Earl of Berkeley and subsequently 1st Earl Fitzhardinge. As long-serving master of the Berkeley Hunt he put Cheltenham on the winter season map, but his custom with Swaine was not confined to the purchase of hunting whips. In 1808 Berkeley was one of the founders of the Four-Horse Club, a gathering of wealthy gentlemen dedicated to the stylish trotting of four-horse barouches, painted a uniform yellow, through the streets of London. A favourite route ran from Cavendish Square to Salt Hill, near Slough. Other followers of this hobby were less dignified in their procession; four-in-hand races between reckless drivers were for a time a menace of English country roads. Swaine's account book records the rise of this leisure activity in the late 1810s in the growing number of four-horse whips sold. This in turn reflects a shift in the eighteenth century from driving a coach with postilions to driving from the box. Until the coachman

Pub. May 16 1823 by G. Humphrey 24 S.t James's St. & 74 New Bond S.t

A View near Petersham

W.H. fect.

11
A View near Petersham, an etching by William Heath, 1823, which shows a dandified Lord Petersham wearing the eponymous Petersham coat in a fetching shade of brown. His tiny, ineffectual whip is portrayed as a fashion accessory, which is what many of them were. When a dandy was about town on foot, he 'wore' a walking stick carefully coordinated with his outfit. Similarly, when he was on horseback, he wore a whip chosen to enhance his equestrian display.

12 (right)
Divers Drivers, an etching made by William Heath in 1827, neatly illustrates the difference between professional drivers and, on the far right, the flashy amateur or 'Out & Outer'. The undisputed king of the drivers was the long-distance four-horse coachman, the 'Long Trot', next to whom the 'Cab' and the 'Jarvey', drivers of the urban cabriolet and hackney carriage respectively, pale into insignificance.

became a common sight on the nation's roads, there was relatively little call for the long coaching whips needed to command the horses from the box.

Coaching was almost but not entirely a male sport; the few women who could command a four-horse coach were assumed to be fast, and dangerous to know. Inevitably the cost of the equipage made it a leisure pursuit for the wealthy; there was a clear distinction between the 'amateur whips' such as Colonel Berkeley who pursued coach-driving as a sport and the 'professional whips' such as mail coach-drivers who made their living from it. But the best of the professionals had reputations and skills that the amateurs greatly envied and hoped to emulate. Richard Vaughan of Cambridge, otherwise known as 'Hell-Fire Dick', was the most celebrated coachman of the day. His coach, the Cambridge Telegraph, was the only one patronized by fashion-conscious students at the university, many of whom paid extra for the privilege of riding on the box beside him. When he died in 1816, aged 65, his feats of daring

and his sulphurous temper passed into coaching lore. 'Illustrious Hell-fire Dick,' wrote a nostalgic student, 'thou wast the Shakespeare of coachmen – the Lucifer or Star of Cambridge.'

Swaine & Isaac (c.1825–1848)

The account book ends in 1825, the year of Benjamin Slocock's retirement. Soon afterwards, James Swaine invited William Isaac to become a partner. This was probably the same William Isaac who appears in the accounts as a stick supplier. From his evidence in a trial at the Old Bailey we know that he was a partner in Swaine & Co. by February 1829, while the *London Gazette* reports his resignation from the partnership on 30 September 1848. This means he was part of the firm for twenty years, probably more, although the name Swaine & Isaac was apparently not routinely used until 1835. Details are scarce, but in the company's received history William Isaac is credited with broadening Swaine's

13
John Tallis's view of Piccadilly, published as
no. 23 in his *London Street Views* in about 1838,
includes a vignette advertising Swaine & Isaac
as 'Whip Manufacturers to the Queen'
(see fig. 15).

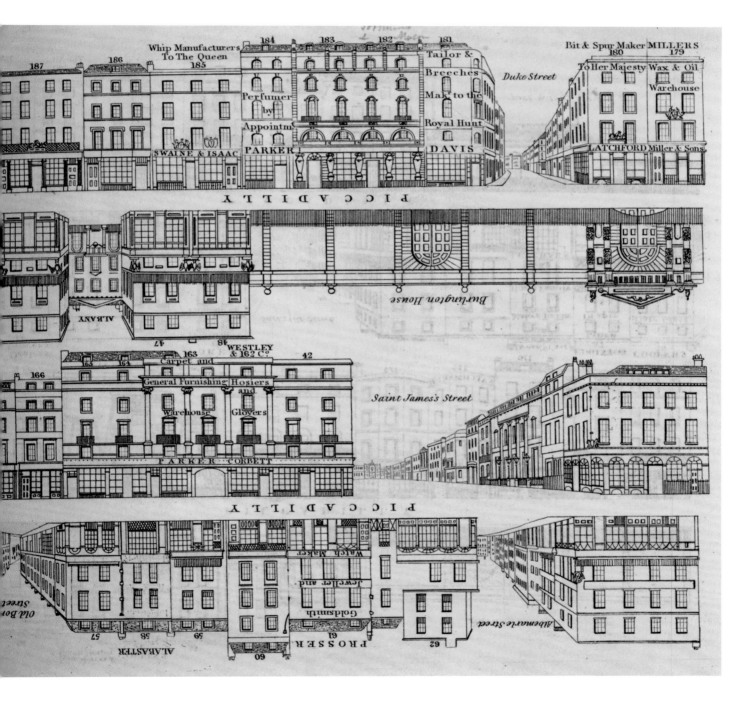

14
A trade card for Swaine & Isaac, which probably dates from soon after the company's appointment as whip-makers to Queen Victoria in December 1837.

15
The Swaine & Isaac vignette from John Tallis's view of Piccadilly, published in 1838 (fig. 13). This is the earliest known image of the company's shop at 185, Piccadilly. Today the shop forms part of Fortnum and Mason's department store, the edge of which is just visible on the far right of the vignette.

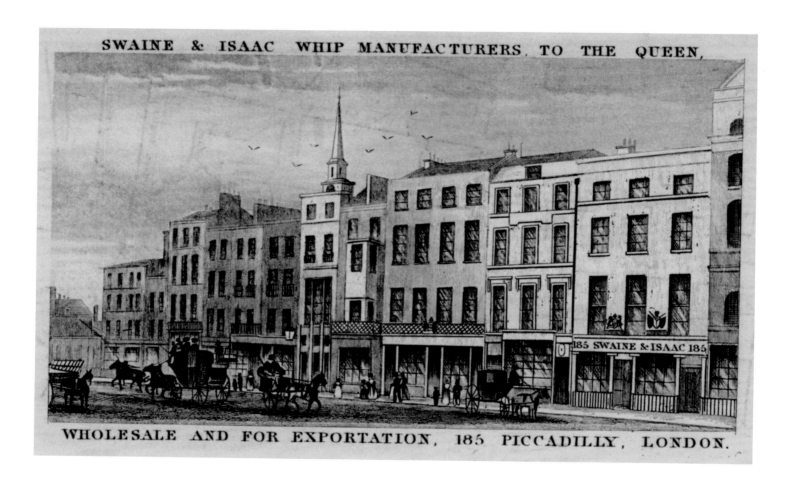

horizons and winning new, distant markets. Evidence of this appears in an advertisement in the *Sydney Monitor* of 27 April 1831 announcing the arrival in Australia of a shipment of whips from Swaine & Co. The following year, the company widely advertised its new, patented invention of the 'Arab Whip', a riding whip with a flywhisk attached, which was 'particularly commended to the notice of Gentlemen going to the East or West Indies' and promised to be 'in use not less amusing than serviceable'.

The account book is silent on the subject of Swaine's premises, but contemporary trade directories show that by 1822 the company had shifted a few doors west from 238 to 224, Piccadilly. It was to remain there until a further move west, to 185, Piccadilly, in 1835. Swaine announced this change of address in the *Morning Post* on 4 July 1835, expressing the hope that their customers would approve of these 'more eligible' premises. The new shop was next door to Fortnum and Mason's grocery and opposite the Albany, which offered a smart residence to gentlemen who found themselves without regular accommodation in London. It placed the company in the midst of the gentlemen's clubs of St James's, and suggests that James Swaine and William Isaac had decided to concentrate their business on the elite end of the whip market. Yet, despite its smart location, 185, Piccadilly, was eminently suited to manufacturing. Behind the shop's elegant façade, the building stretched back 100 feet. In parts it was five storeys high, on top of a basement, although most of the workshops were to be concentrated on three floors only. Moreover, Swaine & Isaac had secured the building on a long lease at a near-peppercorn rent from its landlords, the Governors of the Bethlehem Hospital. It was ideally suited to the company's needs and would remain its home for the next one hundred and sixty years.

In 1837 Swaine & Isaac consolidated their elite reputation with a coveted appointment as whip-makers to the new queen, Victoria. The *Morning Chronicle* of 11 December 1837 additionally reported that they had lately created a whip of a 'beautifully novel and elegant pattern' for her personal use. The appointment was perhaps not unexpected; after George IV's death in 1830, Swaine & Isaac had been reappointed royal whip-makers by his brother, William IV, the former Duke of Clarence. A ledger which was unhappily removed from the Swaine Adeney Brigg archive in the 1990s records several pages of sales to William IV, suggesting that the royal patronage was lucrative as well as prestigious (see text box: 'Whips for a King' overleaf). But winning Victoria's patronage was special. The image of her as an older, stouter woman in widow's weeds is now so pervasive that it is easy to forget how her accession in 1837 seemed like a breath of fresh air after the reigns of three increasingly elderly and decrepit kings. She was the first young monarch since George III had come to the throne in 1760, aged 22. She was also a fine horsewoman and coped admirably with the precarious side-saddles then available for genteel riders of her sex. Several of her advisers found this nerve-wracking, and would have preferred that she conduct troop inspections and other outdoor duties from the safety of a carriage, but her wishes prevailed and she was often seen in public on a horse.

James Swaine did not live quite long enough to see the new royal appointment. He had celebrated his seventieth birthday on 30 July 1836 surrounded by his family, who serenaded him with a hymn composed by his son Edward for the occasion. James was a staunch Christian, so he presumably took his son's sentiments about 'merging shadows' and 'the coming, darker night' in the kindly spirit in which they were intended. He died a little over a year later at his residence in Stanwell, on 10 September 1837, just a few weeks before Victoria's coronation. His obituary in the *Gentleman's Magazine* described him as 'a man of considerable intelligence and observation' whose loss was 'generally deplored' in Stanwell. For a

Whips for a King

The Swaine Adeney Brigg archive apparently remained reasonably intact until the 1990s, when unfortunately a number of old account books and antique manufactures were removed from it. One of the missing items is a sales ledger from the Swaine & Isaac era. A double-page entry in the book records the company's sales to King William IV from July 1831 to Christmas 1833. It provides valuable information about the style and quality of whips manufactured by Swaine & Isaac in these years, as well as the materials they used and the amount of repair work they did. It also reveals the commercial value of an enthusiastic royal patron. Some of the whips purchased were clearly intended for the king's personal use or else as gifts from him to friends and favoured courtiers. But there was also a lesser class of whips and equestrian accessories ordered for use in the Royal Mews; they did not cost as much as the finest examples, but the company sold more of them.

Interestingly, there are no walking sticks listed on the two pages. This may be because Swaine & Isaac kept separate ledgers for whips and sticks and umbrellas, or it may indicate that they had yet to branch out into this line of business. Such diversification may not have happened until the early Victorian era.

The principal items from King William's pages in the ledger are listed here. This is a modified transcription of the original, in which some abbreviations have been spelled out in full for ease of comprehension. The sums are given in pounds, shillings, and pence.

His most gracious Majesty Wᵐ IVᵗʰ

		£	s	d
1831 July 30	2 Green Shagreen Handle Jockeys, silver Gilt Buttons & lash as before 4.14.6	9	9	–
1831 Sepʳ 10	1 Large Jockey braiden with rich blue twist gilt silver wire lash	1	15	
	1 Rich gold bullion string and tassel	2	12	6
	1 Stout Jockey whip braiden with rich black silk Twist & gilt silver lash	1	15	
	1 Crimson morocco case lined with Crimson silk velvet	2	10	
		18	1	6
1832 May 17	By Cash (Lord Chamberlain's office)	9	9	–
June 22	By cash (Lord – /Master Horse's ditto) 8.12.6	8	12	6
1832 June 25ᵗʰ	1 very richly solid silver treble gilt chased mounted Arab whip with green plume Settled by cheque Novʳ 19ᵗʰ 1832, Sir H Wheatly, Privy purse	10	10	–
	to the King's Mews			
25	1 Gilt silver buttoned Arab whip ordered by R.W. Spearman, Esqʳᵉ By Cash Feb: 1. 1833	2	12	6
1833 Janʸ 18–25	Accᵗ to R.W. Spearman Esqʳᵉ Goods (8)	3	2	
Feb 11	½ points to 2 post whips	–	1	6
	Lashes to 2 horse whips	–	1	
23–26	Ditto (22)	–	9	9
Mar 4–22	Ditto (28)	–	17	–
28	Ditto (26)	–	3	6
	Settled by Cash & Stamp 2ᵈ	4	14	9
	Point to a break whip		1	
April 26	Eyes & lashes to 4 Break whips & 4 nails Foster	–	6	–
May 13	repairs and new nail to a Jockey Mʳ Lennox	–	3	6
18	Thong tied & ½ point to post whip	–	1	6
20ᵗʰ	new thong to a crop	–	2	6
30ᵗʰ	1 Bone handle Lancewood buggy whip	–	12	–
	1 new bone handle post whip to old buttons & thong		15	
	14 new bone handles, 5 new wire buttons, repairs to old buttons, etc. 7/6	5	5	
	11 bone Handle nc 3 size Jockey, or groom whips 3. 3 silver gilt 12/6	6	17	6
	4 bone Handle nc outriders whips with brass wire 3 sash and buttons 28/-	5	12	
June 8–18	Goods	8	14	
25–27	Ditto	–	11	6
	£	29	1	6
	omitted repair a pair horn whips		2	
	NB date the a/c the same as the orders are dated at the top	29	3	6
	Less stamp 1/- Paid Novʳ 27ᵗʰ 1833 WI [?]			
July 16	points to 2 post whips	–	2	
Julʸ 24	1 Gilt silver mounted Equerry's whip	1	4	
Aug 1	2 outriders' whips 28/	2	16	
9	1 Bone handle Brass mounted standard polished Coach whip & repairs 2/6	–	16	6
10	Repairs to 2 whips	–	4	
13	Ditto Phaeton whip	–	2	6
16	1 Ivory mounted Buggy whip for M. H.	–	15	
19	2 Bone handle brass mounted post whips 28/	2	16	
	1 Ditto – ditto outrider's whip	1	8	
30	Point to post whip	–	1	
Sep 3	Sew thong to Buggy Crop	–	2	6
12	Repairs to pair horse whips	–	6	6
20	Ditto pair horse whips	–	7	6
25	Ditto to postⁿ whip and outriders whip	–	5	
	Paid Feb 8. 1834	11	6	6
Octʳ 4	Eyes & lashes to 3 riding horse whips Foster	–	3	–
	New thongs to 2 coach whips J Blow		5	
11	Lashes to 4 Jockeys Sticks	–	3	
Nov 9	New Thong to horse whip Foster	–	3	6
12	Points to 2 ditto Mainwaring	–	2	
Dec 25	New thong and handle Wayland	–	3	6
	Point to coach whip Wayland	–	2	6
	Paid June 13 1834	1	2	[6]

A leather crop, with an onyx knop and
silver-gilt mount in the form of a claw (detail),
made by Swaine & Isaac. It was a gift to
Queen Victoria at Christmas, 1843.

time a reminder of his presence survived locally in the form of several cast-iron road signs with weather-proof lettering; he had been awarded a silver medal by the Royal Society of Arts for this invention in 1813.

James Swaine left his business to his son Edward, who, as we have seen, had been working with his father from a young age. The second but only surviving son of James and his wife Ann, he was born on 21 September 1795. He was a frail child, who always regretted his inadequate and unsympathetic schooling at an establishment in Peckham. At 13 he left school to learn his father's trade, but he was determined to continue his education in his own time. He also threw himself into the religious and philanthropic life of the business community in St James's, Piccadilly. These interests shaped his whole existence and also that of his company and workers.

James and Ann Swaine had nominally been members of the Anglican Church, but when James bought John Ross's business in Piccadilly, they began attending the Dissenters' Chapel in Orange Street. Edward became a teacher in the Sunday School there when he was 15, and thereafter was a zealous though amiable Nonconformist. His faith helped him through several personal tragedies, including the loss of his first wife in childbirth in 1820. In 1822 he became a founding member of the independent Congregationalist church at Craven Chapel in Foubert's Place, just off Regent Street, and served there as a deacon for over forty years. In his spare time he wrote hymns, prayers, and poetry, along with political tracts and lectures on topics such as national free education, church rates, and the extension of the franchise. In common with many other Dissenting manufacturers of the time, he was a Whig rather than a Tory, and advocated a complete separation of Church and State. He also took an interest in the wider world, supporting the abolition of slavery and the education and evangelization of Britain's colonial populations. Thus it is no surprise to find that he was a director of the London Missionary Society, or that his company made regular donations to bodies such as the British and Foreign School Society. In 1839 he had a substantial collection of his poems and hymns printed for circulation to family and friends under the title *The Hand of God: A Fragment*.

It might be thought that with all these interests, Edward Swaine would not have had sufficient time to devote to the family company, but he was a man of immense energy and application and prided himself on being able to say 'I never neglect my business.' Also he wove his beliefs into the conduct of the company and how he treated his workers. It was clear to him that honorable labour was ennobling and one of the cornerstones of a civilized, virtuous society. As an employer he believed that he had a Christian duty to care for the material and moral wellbeing of his workers and to assist them in times of genuine need. As early as 1826, this thinking inspired him to help found the London Aged Christian Society. He was joined in the venture by his brother-in-law, William Adeney, a tailor of similarly evangelical outlook, and several other local businessmen. Their new society sought to provide for the 'permanent relief of the decidedly Christian poor of both sexes, who have attained sixty years and who reside within seven miles of Saint Paul's Cathedral'. Initially its members collected charitable donations and disbursed them to approved recipients in their own houses, but in 1885 the society began a programme of building almshouses, whereupon it became one of the major providers of aged care in Inner London. Its work continues today in the form of a charitable trust that offers grants to groups working with older people in London.

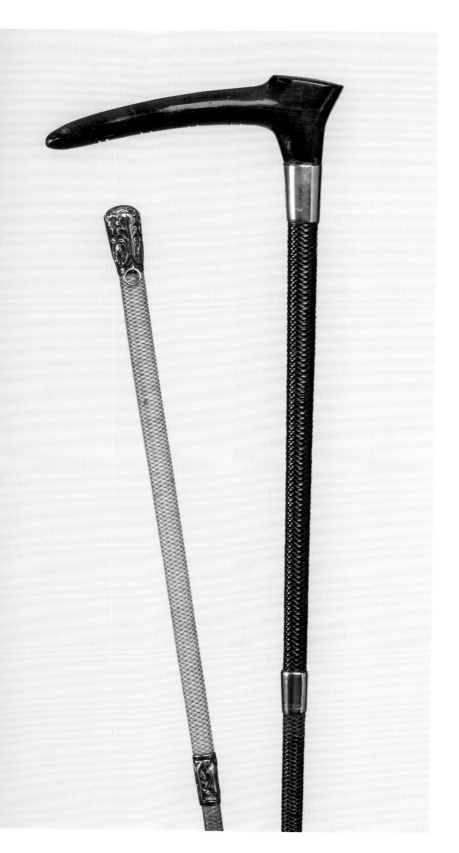

17
Two side-saddle whips by Swaine & Adeney. Both whips are very small and delicate (the horn handle is only 3½ inches long) and seem unlikely to have been of much use in directing a horse. The whip on the left is stamped SWAINE & ADENEY LONDON on the silver grip, and has a cover of braided natural baleen or whalebone on the handle and braided brown thread on the lower shaft, with a gut keeper and thread lash. It was probably made between 1860 and 1880. The whip on the right is apparently a later creation, for the mount is stamped ESA, a maker's mark for Edward Swaine Adeney Jr that was not registered until 1902. The mount is also marked SWAINE, but the date stamp is rubbed. The upper shaft appears to be braided in black-dyed baleen and the lower in black thread; it has a gut and thread lash.

18 (right and detail overleaf)
An equestrian portrait of Queen Victoria painted by Alfred, Count d'Orsay, in about 1846. Victoria carries a side-saddle whip with a braided stock and chased gold handle topped by an imperial crown and cross. The early whips that Swaine & Isaac made for Queen Victoria's personal use were almost certainly like this one: fashion accessories rather than instruments of equestrian control. This remained the case with ladies' whips until about the 1860s, when the development of the two-pommelled side-saddle revolutionized the lives of genteel women riders, enabling them to run at a gallop and to jump safely. With a two-pommelled saddle, both of the rider's legs are braced against padded curved horns or pommels, giving her as much security and stability as a rider sitting astride a horse. Following this invention, women's whips gradually became functional objects as well as things of beauty; the woman held the whip in her right hand and used it on the horse's flank where a male rider would be able to exert pressure with his right leg. As the new saddles allowed aristocratic women to participate fully in hunts without breaking conventions of modesty, many of the antique ladies' whips that survive today are hunting whips, with an L-shaped handle of antler or horn which was used for opening and closing gates.

19

A Swaine & Isaac walking stick of Malacca cane with a knop of carved coral mounted on a silver collar by the London goldsmith William Fitchew, 1845 (detail). Queen Victoria bought this stick as a present for Prince Albert on his twenty-sixth birthday, 26 August 1845. The knop depicts an amorous Centaur making away with a bare-breasted Lapith maiden. The erotic subject matter and fleshy pinkness of the coral create a surprisingly intimate object and it requires some imagination to see how the sober Edward Swaine would have handled its sale to the young queen. The stick's survival in the Royal Collection is a helpful indicator that, by 1845 at least, Swaine & Isaac had branched out into the sale of very fine quality walking sticks.

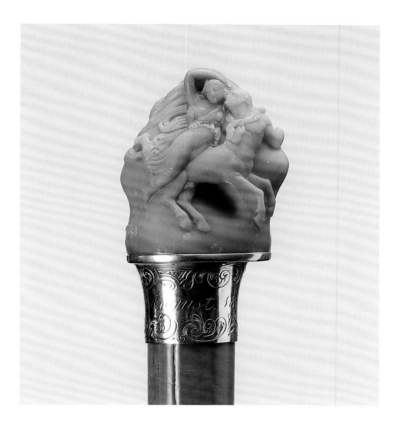

20

Prince Albert in riding costume, a water-colour portrait painted by William Drummond in about 1839–40. Queen Victoria's beloved consort is shown holding a crop which, though sketchily drawn, is identifiable as having a braided stock with a tau-shaped handle of chased silver or silver gilt. The portrait illustrates perfectly the ability of fine quality whips to act as fashion accessories for men.

Left, fig. 18, detail

21 (left)

Four prize whips with elaborate silver and silver-gilt mounts created by Swaine & Adeney for display at international exhibitions. The 1862 'Exhibition Whip' is seen third from the left. Besides the magnificent mounts, the whips illustrate the skill involved in braiding stocks; the second one from the left is braided in twist, while the others are braided in baleen. Regrettably, these superb examples of the whip-maker's craft were removed from the Swaine Adeney Brigg archive in the 1990s.

22

Whip Mounts, Messrs. Swaine, Piccadilly, an engraving from the *Illustrated Exhibitor,* 6 December 1851, p. 510. The central whip mount, shown in two views, was created by Swaine & Adeney especially for the Great Exhibition and was said to be emblematic of the Exhibition's promotion of international and peaceable trade.

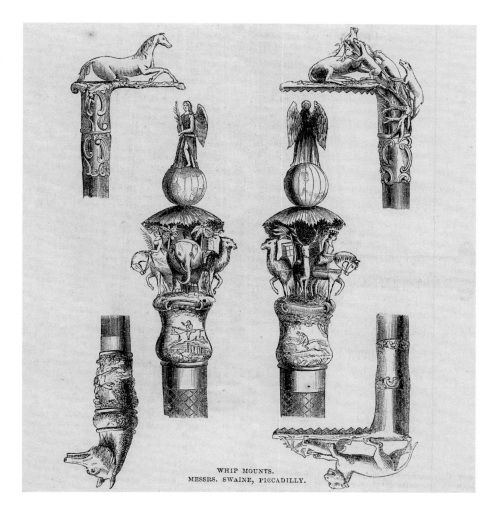

WHIP MOUNTS.
MESSRS. SWAINE, PICCADILLY.

23

Case of Whips and Canes. Prize Medal. Messrs. Swaine and Adeney, an engraving from Cassell's *Illustrated Exhibitor,* 20 September 1862, p. 144. The whip mount shown on either side of the central case was Swaine & Adeney's 'Exhibition Whip' created especially for the 1862 Exhibition.

CASE OF WHIPS AND CANES. PRIZE MEDAL. MESSRS. SWAINE AND ADENEY.

24
A portrait of the Prince of Wales in shooting costume, painted in 1875 by Frank William Dicey. The future King Edward VII's passion for rural sports and racing was matched by his pretty bride's love of hunting. Denied a meaningful political role by Victoria, they indulged these pursuits to the full, particularly at Sandringham, their country retreat in Norfolk.

25 (far right)
Princess Alexandra's Arrival Procession Passing Temple Bar, 7 March 1863, by Robert Charles Dudley. The wedding of Albert Edward, Prince of Wales, and Princess Alexandra of Denmark was the first royal wedding really to engage the British public's imagination. Following Prince Albert's early death and Victoria's retreat into widowhood, it signalled the Prince of Wales's emergence as the approachable face of the monarchy and provided a welcome boost to retailers such as Swaine & Adeney who catered to the Prince's large household and wide circle of friends.

With his own workers, Edward had a reputation as a firm but fair employer. In return, however, he expected them to be honest, hardworking, and of good Christian conduct. In this latter respect, an advertisement the company placed in 1841 for an apprentice is telling. It was published in the *Evangelical Magazine and Missionary Chronicle* for July of that year, and read:

> WANTED, a respectable Youth from a serious Family, as an Apprentice to a Saddler in a large City, where he will have a favourable opportunity of acquiring a thorough knowledge of the Trade. None need apply who cannot conform to the rules of a Dissenting Family. Application for address to Messrs. Swaine and Isaac, 185, Piccadilly.

This advertisement was probably not for Swaine & Isaac themselves, but for one of their contacts in the trade. Nonetheless, it gives a flavour of the rather earnest environment in which a youngster might find himself working at Swaine & Isaac, and we can readily see why one young man in particular did not long survive there after he made an international laughing-stock of himself. This was Benjamin Ellam, who was described in various newspaper accounts in 1847 as a 'shopman' at Swaine & Isaac and, rather more woundingly, a 'short person of

very juvenile appearance'. Ellam appears to have been something of a dandy, and, having made the acquaintance of a pretty young Frenchwoman of reputed wealth, he set out to impress her with a story that he was a nephew of the Duke of Wellington and an officer in the Queen's Guards. He squired her about town, treating her with champagne and pointing out where his famous relatives lived, and showered her with gifts, mostly of the sort that might have come from an esteemed whip-maker in Piccadilly. He also wrote the lovely Leontine some unfortunate billets-doux protesting that he was of 'respecktable famely' and born with 'noble hart'. When, however, it transpired that Mademoiselle was just as poor and just as much on the make as he was, Ellam launched a prosecution against her to retrieve his gifts. He lost, of course, but not before the judge and the press had had a field day with the case. The satirical magazine *Punch* (14 August 1847) was scathing, devoting a piece to the genealogical marvel of the Duke of Wellington's family tree that had seeded so many of his nephews in shops like Swaine's. Perhaps, *Punch* opined, it had something to do with the luxuriant moustachios cultivated by the 'young aristocrats' who manned the metropolis's shop counters. The story was printed around the globe,

including in even such far-flung titles as the *Maitland Mercury* in rural New South Wales. And every account gleefully repeated that the hapless Ellam worked for Swaine & Isaac, whip-manufacturer to Her Majesty the Queen. Edward Swaine's reaction must have been a thing to behold. It comes as no surprise to find that Ellam was soon working for himself. He established a rival whip-maker's a few doors away, at No. 213, Piccadilly, and went on to enjoy considerable success as a racehorse owner. He had just not been right for Swaine & Isaac.

Swaine & Adeney, 1848–1910

In 1845, some three years before William Isaac's resignation, Edward Swaine took his nephew and son-in-law, James Adeney, into partnership. Thus for a short time the firm was known as Swaine, Isaac & Adeney. After that, for almost a hundred years, from 1848 to 1943, the branding was Swaine & Adeney. There was one change in 1910, however, when the business was incorporated as a limited company. The addition of the 'Ltd' is helpful in dating catalogues and some products. But the absence of the 'Ltd' on a whip or stick is not by itself proof of a pre-1910 production date. The branding

varied considerably in the first decades of the twentieth century and some products produced after 1910 were simply labelled 'Swaine'.

James Adeney was born on 15 August 1821, the son of William Adeney, a tailor of 16, Sackville Street, Piccadilly, and Edward Swaine's older sister, Mary Ann. The two families were close and in 1845 young James married his cousin Caroline, Edward Swaine's only child. She was the daughter of Edward's first wife, Caroline Boot, who had died a few days after giving birth on 9 November 1820. At the time, Edward had swallowed his grief and lavished his affection on the baby, writing poems to assure her of his love if he too should be suddenly taken away. He married again, on 10 October 1822, to Sarah Westbrook of Cannon Farm, Cookham. Her brother Zachariah was married to Edward's other sister Sarah. There were no surviving children of Edward's second marriage and the family business eventually descended to the sons of James Adeney and Caroline Swaine.

James was apprenticed to his uncle Edward on 30 March 1836, less than a fortnight after Edward had been entered as a Freeman of the City of London on the Brewers' Company rolls. At 25 years of age, he was almost certainly well-trained in the business already and

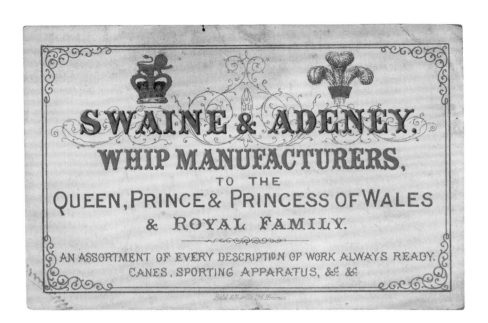

26
A Swaine & Adeney trade card, c.1865, accords equal billing to the Queen and the Prince and Princess of Wales as valued customers. The card was printed by Abraham Field & Andrew White Tuer, stationers and engravers at 136, Minories, forerunner of the Leadenhall Press, an innovative publisher that did much to raise printing and publishing standards.

27 (below)
A Swaine & Adeney advertising card, published probably for the Exposition universelle in Paris in 1889. Inside it repeats the information on the front cover in French, Spanish, German, and Italian, while the back lists the great variety of whips to be had at Swaine & Adeney, along with riding and walking canes, drinking flasks, hunting and post horns, and horse measuring sticks.

this process was probably more of a formality. He too was admitted as a Freeman of the Brewer's Company in April 1844, immediately after he had completed his seven years of 'training'. It is an unexpected quirk of history that, thanks to Benjamin Slocock's trade as a brewer, the Swaines and Adeneys do not appear on the rolls of the Saddlers' Company.

Under Edward Swaine and James Adeney, the company grew in size and fame. Already in the 1830s European royals were joining its list of esteemed clients, such as Louis Philippe, King of France. But the real take-off in the company's domestic and international reputation happened in the 1850s, beginning with the Great Exhibition in 1851. Swaine & Adeney won a prize medal in the exhibition's Leather section for 'a large assortment of Whips and Canes, showing much taste in the manufacture, and superiority in the workmanship'. It was indeed a large assortment. In its issue of 6 December 1851 the *Illustrated Exhibitor* reported that:

> England, France, Belgium, Spain, America, all contribute specimens of whips and sticks, but perhaps the best show of them all is that made by the firm in Piccadilly, from whose trophy the whip-heads in our engraving have been chosen. Amongst the articles exhibited by the Queen's whip-makers are a Prize Racing Whip, richly mounted in silver gilt, the mounts being illustrative of the universal and pacific character of the Exhibition, and also of equestrian sports, value, 35 guineas. A Gentleman's Riding Whip, of superior workmanship, mounted with gold, set with brilliants and rubies; value, 50 guineas. Ladies' Riding Whips of novel construction, with fan, or

sunshade, or parasol attached. Ladies' and Gentlemen's improved Patent Arab or Chowrie Riding Whips, with horse-hair plumes; especially adapted for India, or other parts where insects trouble horse and rider. Ladies' and Gentlemen's Riding Whips, of patterns and devices entirely new, or of superior execution. State-Carriage and Postilion Whips. Ladies' and Gentlemen's Driving Whips, of new patterns or extraordinary finish. Prize or Gift Hunting Whips, with superb sporting devices. Riding Canes, with beautiful novel mountings. 'Universal Whip Socket,' registered, and possessing advantages over every other – in fact, whips and sticks of all kinds in great variety, for which Messrs. Swain [*sic*] have obtained the prize medal.

This was splendid publicity, and probably half of the work generating it was done by the whip 'illustrative of the universal and pacific character of the Exhibition'. It was a show-stopping object, which featured a globe topped by an angelic figure, beneath which was an umbrella sheltering four animals emblematic of Europe, Africa, America, and Asia. Ten years later the company created a worthy successor to it for the 1862 International Exhibition in London. Boldly entitled the 'Exhibition Whip', the mount this time featured costumed personifications of Europe, Africa, America, and Asia who were seated around a globe surmounted by a benign British lion and cherub. These showpiece whips came with a huge price tag, but they did not need to sell to justify their creation, and indeed many were preserved in the company's archive until very recently. Whips and walking sticks were not ordinarily objects of glamour; by investing in these splendid mounts Swaine & Adeney forced

28
A splendid carriage whip made by Swaine & Adeney for the French aristocratic house of Doudeauville-Rochefoucauld, probably for vicomte Sosthène II de La Rochefoucauld, duc de Doudeauville (1825–1908), who was a great horseman and from 1884 until his death president of the Paris Jockey Club. It has a silver knop in the form of a crown surmounted by a cross and a lower silver collar engraved with the Rochefoucauld-Doudeauville crest and a ducal coronet. The handle is braided in purple, red, and silver twist, while the blackthorn shaft is ornamented with eight rings of silvered copper.

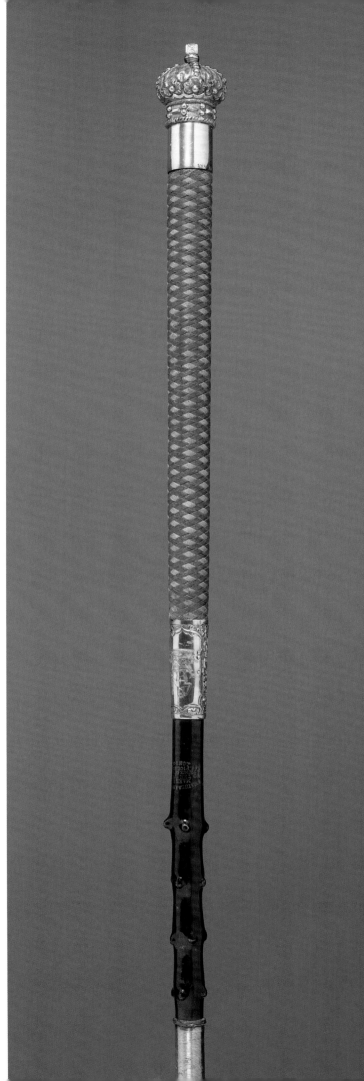

the press to pay attention to their displays. Thus the company received a page's worth of publicity, complete with engravings, in Cassell's *Illustrated Exhibitor* of the 1862 exhibition. A similar illustrated page, with letterpress in English, French, and German, appeared in the *Catalogue of the British Section* of the Paris Universal Exhibition of 1867. Moreover, Swaine & Adeney's stockists around the empire were only too happy to spread this publicity. Thus John Burnett, a saddler in Adelaide, quoted the entire article from the 1851 *Exhibitor* in his advertisements in the *South Australian Register*. Swaine & Adeney's Calcutta stockists, Thacker, Spink & Co., similarly referenced the 1851 triumph in their advertisements in the *Friend of India*.

Besides the prize medals at the London exhibitions of 1851 and 1862, Swaine & Adeney also won awards at a host of international exhibitions and world's fairs, including Paris (1855, 1867, and 1889), Dublin (1865), Vienna (1873), Philadelphia (1876), and Chicago (1893). In 1900 they carried off the Grand Prix at the Exposition universelle in Paris. They augmented the publicity from these successes with modest advertisements in papers such as the *Sporting Gazette, Horse and Hound*, and the *Field*. But the stories that wrote themselves provided their best advertising. In March 1863, for example, it was reported in the sporting press that Swaine & Adeney had been appointed whip-manufacturers to Albert Edward, Prince of Wales, and had been commissioned to make two carriage whips for his wedding to Princess Alexandra of Denmark. The man from *Baily's Monthly Magazine of Sports and Pastimes*, who had been granted a preview of the 'nuptial whips', reported that they were 'unique in

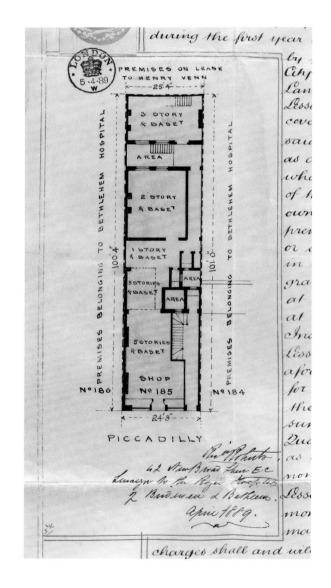

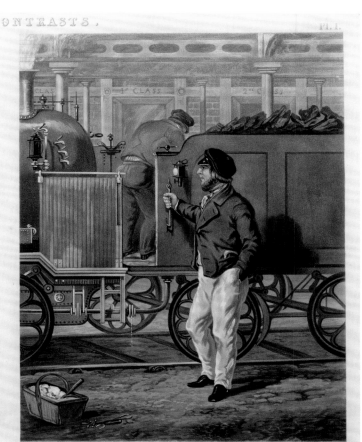

THE DRIVER OF 1832.　　　THE DRIVER OF 1852.

29 (above left)
A child's riding crop (detail), made by Swaine & Adeney in 1883 and purchased by Queen Victoria as a gift for one of her grandchildren. The crop is made from plaited horsehair and the knop of chased gold features a deer in a forest.

30 (left)
A floor plan of 185, Piccadilly, from a lease renewal signed by Swaine & Adeney in 1889. The new lease ran for eighty years, at an annual rental of £430. Swaine & Adeney's landlords were the Governors of the Bethlehem Hospital; the rent they were asking was a modest one for such commodious and well-situated premises.

31 (above)
Fores's Contrasts: The Driver of 1832. The Driver of 1852, an aquatint by John Harris, after the original paintings by Henry Alken, 1852. Remarkably, this print does not exaggerate the speed with which trains transformed British transport. In only twenty years, the long-distance coach driver was forced off the nation's roads. Coaches servicing local feeder routes continued to run and leisure coaching was kept alive by enthusiasts, but, overall, the picture was one of decline, which was gloomy news for the companies that made the coaches and their specialist harnesses, whips, and horns.

A selection of shafts from hunting whips and crops reveals a range of finishes. From the left are two covered in braided leather (probably kangaroo hide), one of stepped cane, one of flowered bamboo, and, on the right, two of braided thread. Shafts braided with linen or cotton thread were usually lacquered for shine and durability, and when done well could survive decades of use without fraying. The braiding of shafts was a different skill to the plaiting of whip thongs. The former was a woman's job, carried out at home using a hand-operated braiding machine with multiple spindles. These machines had been invented in the eighteenth century and were continued in use with relatively few modifications until the end of the twentieth century. In the 1890s, a braider with access to a machine and a regular supply of work could hope to earn about 10 to 12 shillings a week.

magnificence, as well as in good taste'. The patronage of the Prince of Wales was important for the company's future direction. As the railways ate into the market for coaching whips, Swaine & Adeney concentrated on building custom among aficionados of hunting and horse racing. Albert, Victoria's consort, had lately died, and before him William IV had been too old and George IV too corpulent to take to the saddle for pleasure. Thus, when the Prince of Wales revealed that he lived for hunting and racing, manufacturers and the sporting press alike haled him as the saviour of British equestrian pursuits, the royal figurehead they had been missing for so long.

The plight of the coaching industry was highlighted in 1856, when General Sir Henry Wyndham, the Tory MP for Cockermouth, persuaded parliament to reduce the duty on stage carriages. In retrospect, nothing was going to halt the onward rush of trains, but to the beleaguered coach proprietors this seemed like a reprieve. On 1 May 1856 a deputation of proprietors presented Wyndham with a whip by Swaine & Adeney as a sign of their gratitude. It was a splendid affair: 'a superb holly four-horse whip, with carved ivory handle and gold mounts, representing on the richly chased gold lower mount, as also in the carved ivory handle, a mail coach, with coachman, guard, &c., and four horses spanking along a turnpike road'. Swaine & Adeney often made presentation whips, although more commonly for the horse-racing industry, which usually generated helpful press coverage. In this case a report in the *Lady's Newspaper* of 10 May 1856, duly noted that 'the whip was manufactured by Messrs.

Swaine and Adeney, whip manufacturers to the Queen and Prince Albert, and elicited much admiration.' This sort of reportage shared the merits of the exhibition coverage; newspapers around the empire happily picked up the stories and repeated them verbatim.

Edward Swaine lived to see his company establish a world-wide clientele. He died on 22 April 1862, aged 66, and was accorded a fulsome obituary in the *Evangelical Magazine and Missionary Chronicle*. After his death his nephew and son-in-law James Adeney was joined in the partnership by two of his own sons, Edward Swaine Adeney (1847–1920) and James William Adeney (1849–1918). The business they joined was thriving; in the 1871 Census James Adeney was recorded as having thirty-six employees at the Piccadilly site.

The nature of these employees' work was spelled out just over twenty years later when George Duckworth called on Swaine & Adeney to ask about labour conditions in the whip-making industry. Duckworth was working for the shipping magnate and philanthropist Charles Booth, who was conducting a survey into the lives of London workers. James Adeney responded to Duckworth's queries cheerfully and helpfully, enabling him to record a surprising amount of detail about Swaine & Adeney's business. There were thirty employees, all men, working at the Piccadilly shop when Duckworth visited in September 1893. Only two were shop boys; the others were skilled tradesmen, earning between 25 and 60 shillings a week. James explained that each man specialized in an aspect of making driving whips or riding whips; there was no overlap between the two. There were

33

Two elegant vesta or match-holding walking sticks by Swaine & Adeney, *c*.1906, one with an L-shaped handle in stepped cane and the other with a crook handle in bamboo, each with gold match-holders. Both match-holders have a dark blue enamelled monogram in the form of a letter D and also an enamelled crest of a ducal coronet and demi-lion rampant with a mullet, the motto 'Semper fidelis', and the date '29.4.06'. The crook-handled stick has a maker's mark that is partially rubbed; the first two of its three letters read E H.

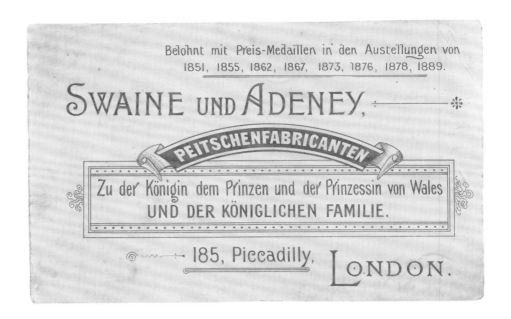

also several essential tasks done by pieceworkers in their own homes. On site, in the driving whip department, there were stick-straighteners and stick-finishers. But in between the straightening and the finishing, the sticks were sent out to dressers, a very small, specialist caste of London craftsmen, who had been handing on their skills from father to son for generations. The dressers removed the knots from the wood and peeled off the bark, smoothing as they went, except in those cases where fashion desired more knots, in which case they created artificial ones. This was highly skilled work and the dressers were regarded as the elite craftsmen in the industry, earning between 35 and 45 shillings a week in the busy season, and up to 5 shillings for a single stick with an imaginative array of 'sham knots'. The best of them had an exclusive arrangement with Swaine & Adeney and enjoyed year-round work. They were, James added, a completely different group of craftsmen to those who dressed walking sticks.

When the dressed sticks came back to the shop, the finishers stained and varnished them and did the 'quilling up' – the process of fixing the thongs to the sticks using goose quills. The thongs themselves were made offsite, a job that was often divided between two sets of workers: master craftsmen who knew how both to cut and to plait the leather, and 'small masters' who knew only the plaiting technique. If the grip or handle part of the whip was to have a finial, and possibly a collar too, of silver, gold, or wirework, this was another job to be outsourced. Duckworth noted that a specialist category of silversmiths made the coiled and plaited wire buttons that were affixed to the end and over the joints on the shaft of a driving whip. A practised button-maker took perhaps an hour and a half to make a single button.

The principal work on site work for riding whips was the creation of a flexible stock from long slivers of whalebone. This was a job requiring precision and finesse; a cross-section of a riding stock would reveal nine separate shafts of whalebone angled and bevelled so as to fit together in a cylindrical shaft and then bonded together with flax and pitch, the whole encased in gut and then a braided leather, twist, or whalebone covering. James told Duckworth that whalebone was an increasingly expensive product; in recent years sky-high prices had induced him to experiment with a mix of whalebone and cane in the core. Once the stock was finished it was sent out to women working at home with braiding machines to make the plaited cover. This was the only job that women did in the whip-making industry, but they controlled it completely. Back in the Piccadilly shop, the riding whip-finishers attached a keeper and a thong and lash, if needed, to the braided stock. If a separate handle was to be added, this usually required a metal mount, in which case the whip was sent out again to the mounters. When Duckworth questioned James Adeney about apprenticeships, he replied that it did not pay him to train up workers himself. All of his whip-finishers had learned their craft in Birmingham, which he identified as the centre of the English whip-making industry. All, he said, preferred to work very long hours during the busy season, often from 7AM to 9PM, rather than have new workers taken on and then risk lay-offs. With some pride, he added that the company was managing to weather the trade downturn of the early 1890s without putting off any workers.

In spite of the helpful details he recorded, perhaps the most striking information gleaned by Duckworth is the revelation that, as late as 1893, Swaine & Adeney were still very much a whip-making concern. While they retailed a lot of other items, and in particular walking sticks, whips remained the core of their manufacturing business. The motor car would shortly change that, but the speed of that revolution would have been hard to foresee in 1893. Unknowingly, Duckworth had captured an image of the whip-making industry as it stood on the edge of its greatest challenge.

James Adeney died on 24 March 1898. He was 76 and had lived to see his grandson trained up in the business. This was Edward Swaine Adeney Jr, born in 1875, the first child of James's son Edward and his wife, Catherine Axford. The assurance of continuity was vital as Swaine & Adeney confronted the rise of the motor car. At their first startling appearance on the nation's roads around 1895, cars were referred to as 'horseless carriages'. This was a name filled with foreboding for whip-makers and other manufacturers of equestrian goods, but rather than rue progress, Swaine & Adeney turned their leather-working skills to the manufacture of luggage sets for the new leisure activity of motoring. The car was nowhere near as democratizing as the railways; until the Second World War ownership was restricted to the wealthy. This meant that well-heeled motorists compensated Swaine &

Adeney for the falling off of trade in the coaching market. But other companies reliant on demand for horse-drawn transport were not so fortunate. In 1907 Swaine & Adeney took over J. Köhler & Son, a famous London manufacturer of coaching and post horns. Trains had already shattered Köhler's traditional market and the rise of the car dealt the *coup de grâce*. Unsurprisingly, Swaine & Adeney promptly switched the focus of their new subsidiary to horns for hunting.

The acquisition of Köhler indicated Swaine & Adeney's determination to consolidate their hold on the market for hunting whips and related accessories. They evolved a form of targeted marketing for these items, producing small illustrated catalogues that were distributed exclusively to masters of hounds and hunt establishments. The first of these to survive dates from the reign of Edward VII and proudly proclaims the company as 'Whip Makers by Special Appointment to H.M. The King and H.M. Queen Alexandra'. The catalogue begins with hunt servants' whips, which came with a two-yard thong and a distinctive L-shaped handle fashioned from stag horn. The handle was designed to facilitate the opening and shutting of gates from horse-back. The best ones were still made with a whalebone

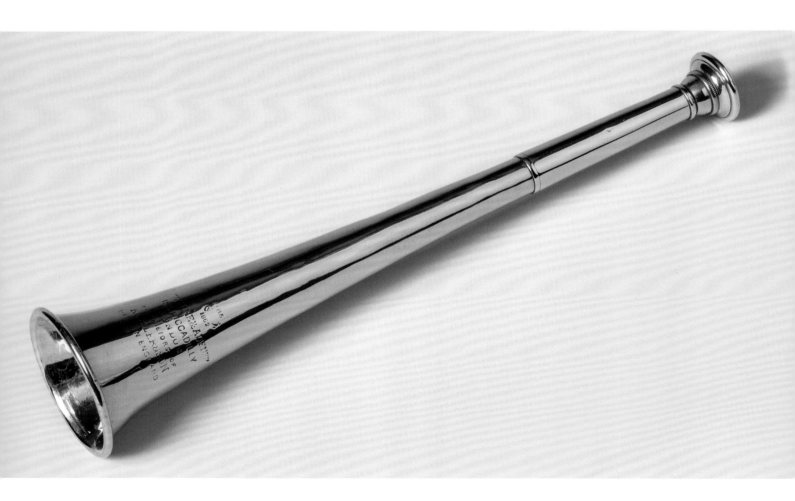

36
The Meet, an oil painting by Hermann Conrad
Fleury, c.1910. As the coaching market declined,
Swaine & Adeney turned their leatherworking
skills to the growing market for hunting
accessories.

35 (left)
A Köhler-pattern hunting horn in copper and
silver, manufactured by Swaine & Adeney after
their takeover of Köhler in 1907.

stock. But besides the whips, the catalogue offered a
large range of hunt accessories, including wire nippers,
hunting knives, dog collars, ear-tattooing forceps, kennel
whips, spurs, canteens and flasks, and Köhler hunting
horns and whistles. Many of these items came with
handcrafted leather carrying cases, and the horns, flasks,
and canteens could all be ordered in sterling silver, as
well as in a cheaper plated version. The hungry hunts-
man could even purchase a solid-silver sandwich box if
he felt so inclined, although it would set him back £13 13s.
A rarer item of hunting equipment was the otter pole,
a stout stick of ash or sometimes bamboo, about 6 to 7
feet long, with a metal-mounted V-shaped prong at the
base. The pole was the principal piece of equipment in
the formal hunting of otters with packs of trained otter-
hounds. It was not meant to kill the otter, but was used
by hunt members to harry it into shallow water where
the hounds could get to it, and also as a prop for leaping
over ditches and streams. Swaine & Adeney employed
their stick-dressing experience to produce a range of
otter poles, including ones with ornamental spirals of
brass wire, which drew upon the skills of the men who
made the wire buttons for their coaching whips.

This dual approach of consolidating old markets while
also creating new ones meant that Swaine & Adeney
were quick to see opportunities in the sport of polo,
which army officers had imported from India in the 1860s.

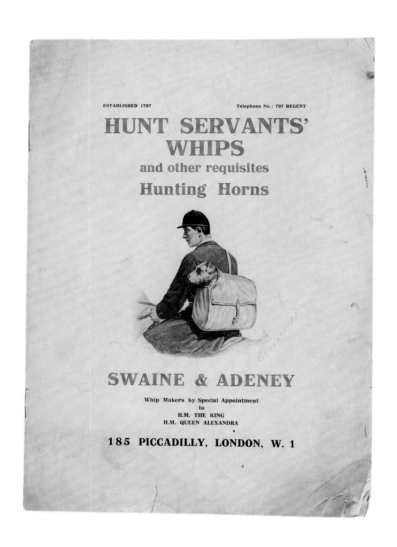

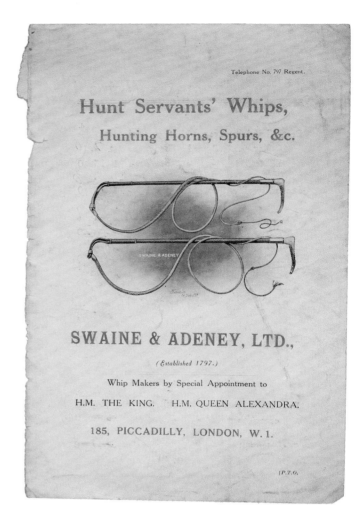

37 (above left)
A catalogue of hunting whips and 'other requisites' published by Swaine & Adeney between 1907 and 1910. The illustration shows a terrier bag. In a hunt the terrier's job was to persuade a fox who had bolted into a hole or ditch that it was better off taking its chances above ground. This bag, available in leather or canvas, enabled the terrier man to carry his dog on his back while mounted, thus keeping the dog fresh until he was set to work. Opinions, however, were divided over their merits. Writing in July 1909, when they were still pretty much a novelty, *Popular Mechanics* reported that from the bag 'the terrier contentedly surveys the surrounding landscape until its services are required', but other observers felt that the occupant had a rather cramped and bumpy time of it.

38 (above right)
A Swaine & Adeney hunting catalogue that post-dates the company's incorporation in October 1910. The artwork, as with the catalogue at fig. 37, was the work of Tillotson & Son Ltd, a well-known printing company of Bolton and founders of the *Bolton Evening News*. The reference to Swaine & Adeney's foundation in 1797 reflects a time in the company's history when no-one knew of James Swaine's predecessor, John Ross.

39 (right)
A classic Swaine & Adeney gentleman's hunting whip, with a stag-horn handle, silver collar, whalebone shaft with a braided kangaroo-hide cover, threaded wrapping around the join with the keeper, plaited thong of kangaroo hide, and red silk lash. The collar is stamped SWAINE and has the maker's mark ESA for Edward Swaine Adeney and marks for London 1935. In 1931 a whip of this calibre retailed for £16 10s.

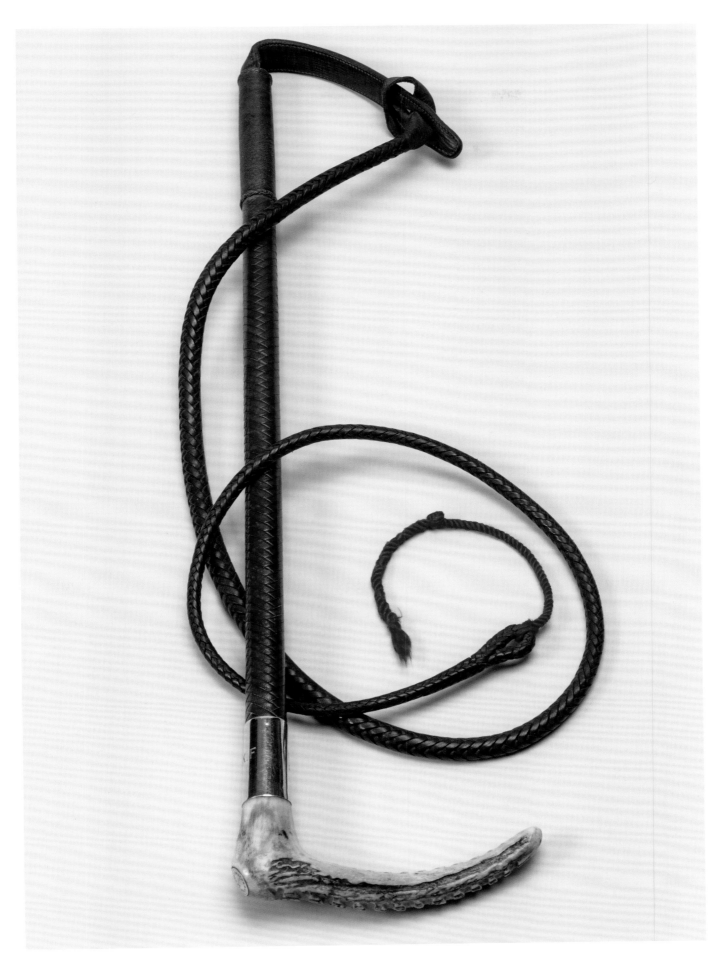

SWAINE & ADENEY, Limited, 185 Piccadilly, LONDON, W. 1

40
A page from a Swaine & Adeney hunting catalogue (fig. 37) illustrates some of the many ways in which the company could put its leatherworking skills to use in accessories for equestrian sports.

41 (right)
Polo at Hurlingham, an oil painting by Henry Jamyn Brooks, 1890. Brooks (1839–1925) was more of a portraitist than a sporting artist and specialized in complex group portraits, often based on photographs, of which this one is a fine example. The crowd of players depicted in this format reveals the value of the market for polo equipment to a stick-dressing company such as Swaine & Adeney. They produced polo whips and sticks from about 1890 until the very early 1960s.

By 1875 enthusiasts at the Hurlingham Club in Fulham, south-west London, had drawn up the first set of rules, and polo was on its way to finding a place in the English social calendar. Much like motoring, this was a leisure activity for the wealthy. The market was not a big one, but it was lucrative. One of Swaine & Adeney's polo catalogues from 1910–11 survives in the company archive. It lists not only polo whips and sticks, but also balls, belts, gloves, goal posts, helmets, caps, and spurs. These latter items were made by specialist suppliers, but Swaine & Adeney made the whips and sticks themselves, as both required only a slight adjustment of manufacturing techniques and raw materials they already knew well. The sticks or mallets were mostly made of Malacca cane (*Calamus scipionum*), a strong but light and flexible type of rattan imported from South East Asia, which the company knew well from the walking sticks it sold. The heads or mallets were made from similarly familiar woods: ash, sycamore, and bamboo root. Polo whips, which were usually carried in the left hand, had very much longer stocks than horse-racing crops, anything between 36 and 48 inches long, but they were otherwise a familiar beast. The most expensive ones had a stock

of whalebone which was covered with plaited gut or kangaroo hide, the plaiting tailing off into a short, flippy lash. Other, cheaper and more consciously modern models had a pliable steel core hidden beneath the plaited covering. Steel cores were one of the biggest innovations in whip manufacturing of the early twentieth century. Because of their strength, they quickly won favour in international horse-racing circles, and they were only displaced by the proliferation of fibreglass and nylon after the Second World War.

Swaine & Adeney Ltd, 1910–1943

In July 1910 Swaine & Adeney were registered at Somerset House as a limited company with a capital of £18,000 in £1 shares. Edward Swaine Adeney Jr was named as the managing director of the new company, although his father continued to work there until 1916. Edward Jr, who was known to his family and friends as Ward Adeney, was 35 years old and was to remain in the driving seat for almost another forty years, until his retirement in 1949. He was in many ways a remarkable businessman and it is doubtful whether the company

could have survived the upheavals of the early twentieth century without his inspired leadership. He was passionate about the company's traditions of fine craftsmanship, but at the same time he looked to the future, repeatedly inventing new product lines and improving existing ones. He committed much more funding to advertising and catalogues than before, and registered more patents for new or improved products than at any time before or since in the company's history. He also introduced incentives for his workers, including share options for key staff and tool insurance for pieceworkers, and invested heavily in a network of national travelling salesmen and international agents. These changes, although significant, are not easy to illustrate today, but one sign of Edward's business sense can be seen in some of the company's manufactures from this era. In October 1902 he had registered the maker's mark ESA with the London Assay Office; he renewed the registration in 1910 (and additionally registered it at the Birmingham Assay Office) and henceforth the silver and gold collars on the company's whips and sticks were stamped with this mark, rather than that of an independent silversmith. The mark's existence might suggest that Edward had

trained as a whip- and stick-mounter himself, but there is no independent confirmation of this.

Edward had not long been in charge of Swaine & Adeney when the First World War erupted in 1914. The war had profound consequences for the company. Initially perhaps, when people had hopes of a short, glorious, and even rather stylish war, it did not threaten to change things much. But as it dragged on, Swaine & Adeney had to develop entirely new product lines. By 1915 they were in full war-production mode. There was an element of commercial necessity in this, of course, but also a patriotic desire to be seen to be channelling production into wartime supplies rather than leisure goods. Also, the war came unhappily close to home. William Henry Adeney was a cousin of Edward Swaine Adeney Sr, who had inherited the family's tailoring business in Sackville Street. His only son, Robert Edward, was commissioned Lieutenant in the Surrey West Regiment, but in January 1917 he was seconded as a Flying Officer to the Royal Flying Corps. He survived barely three months. On 11 April 1917, a few days after his nineteenth birthday, he was shot down and killed over Douai in France.

Several of Swaine & Adeney's 'War Equipment' catalogues have survived from 1916 onwards. They include articles of kit made to War Office specifications, mostly intended for officers rather than Tommies. There were 'Officer's Design' leather haversacks, canvas or leather saddle-bags, leather and celluloid folding map cases, pigskin money belts and writing cases, oiled silk socks for combatting frostbite, and the 'National' steel bullet-proof body shield. There was also an ingenious combination mess tin and water bottle that Swaine & Adeney patented in March 1915 under the name of 'Eatanswill', which they evidently borrowed from Charles Dickens's lively description of an election at Eatanswill in *The Pickwick Papers*. It had a silver-plated nickel water bottle around which fitted the top and bottom halves of an aluminium mess tin, the whole being enclosed in a leather carrying case. The patent reveals that the inventor was Alfred Ernest East, a lace merchant who occupied the shop next door to Swaine & Adeney, at 186, Piccadilly. At £1 17s 6d, it cost more than a month's pay for the average serviceman, but it received a glowing review in the popular war magazine, *Land and Water*.

It was, however, in their traditional field of whip- and stick-making that Swaine & Adeney excelled during the war. They offered 'loaded' versions of their most popular ranges, by which they meant a knob or handle filled with lead. There were also short steel batons with lead knobs at both ends. All were discreetly covered with plaited pigskin or kangaroo hide, and some of the sticks had a traditional rattan body or whalebone centre, but there was no disguising that these were weapons designed to deliver a lethal blow in an emergency. There was also a range of military canes and swagger sticks. The latter

were made out of ebony or cane with a silver knop on which an officer's regimental crest could be engraved. The military canes were necessarily sturdy affairs; one extra-long and stout stick of hazel was specifically designed 'for trench work'.

Swaine & Adeney's wartime catalogues are incidentally illuminating about the international nature of their operations. They had long had customers around the globe, but by 1915 their suppliers were just as widely spread. Sticks of blackthorn, hazel, holly, and ash could be sourced locally, as could pigskin and stag horn, but they were also getting through considerable quantities of cane from Malacca and Manila, bamboo root from Burma and the Nilgiri Hills in India, kangaroo hide from Australia, rhinoceros horn and ivory from Africa, and whalebone from Greenland. Some supplies were coming from the Americas too, notably a sturdy black cloth used for cheaper sword and scabbard cases, kapok for military mattress stuffing, and alligator skins for luggage casing.

After the war, Swaine & Adeney faced more challenges. Despite their best efforts, the whip market was shrinking. Agriculture and local carriage of goods remained surprisingly dependent on horse power until well after the next war, but whips sold to these sectors tended not to be the high-end ones made by Swaine & Adeney. For them the future of whips lay solely in elite equestrian sports and hunting. Their response to this situation was twofold: first, to increase their hold on the quality whip market and, second, to develop radically new product lines. It was probably of small consolation that other whip-makers were facing difficult times as well, but they made the best of the situation. At the beginning of 1927 they bought out one of their biggest rivals, Zair

42
The maker's mark for Edward Swaine Adeney Jr, which was registered with the London and Birmingham Assay Offices in 1910. An earlier version had been registered with just the London office in 1902.

43
The branding S W A I N E , taken from a Swaine & Adeney hunting crop with a stag-horn handle, c.1920 (the date stamp is rubbed but an engraving on the collar dates it to 1923 or before). The company seems to have used this simplified branding in the early twentieth century. At the same time, the crop also has a metal button or pin stamped: S W A I N E & A D E N E Y Lᴛᴰ LONDON (fig. 44).

44
The pin from a Swaine & Adeney crop made in about 1920 (fig. 43). These pins or buttons were most commonly found on the stag-horn handles of hunting whips. The Birmingham whip-making company of Zair, which Swaine & Adeney took over in 1927, had dozens of these pins listed on their books, indicating that they made whips for other retail brands around the world.

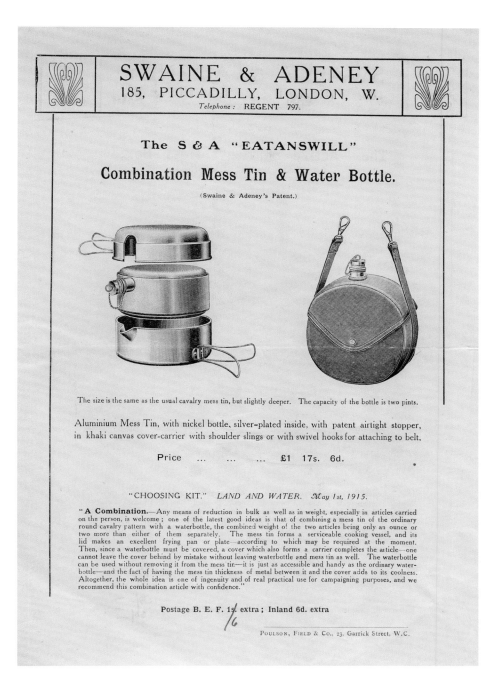

of Birmingham, which had built up an enviable international market, especially in Australasia, South Africa, and the Americas. The takeover enabled some rationalization of production and marketing between the two companies, but Swaine & Adeney respected the value of the Zair brand and did not wish to dilute it. They kept on George Percy Zair as the manager of the Birmingham factory and maintained production there until 1965.

At the same time as the Zair takeover, Swaine & Adeney decided to make more of a virtue of their preference for craftsmanship over machine-work. In 1927 Edward Swaine Adeney Jr wrote a small booklet setting out his company's philosophy. The booklet, *'Good Hands' 1750–1927*, is a lovely production in itself

and was printed by the Baynard Press, which produced many of the early lithographic posters for the London Underground. It is illustrated throughout by beautiful woodcuts of processes and tools, which Edward had commissioned as an example of fine craftsmanship in another field. Edward's approach was one which an earlier generation of craftsmen-philosophers, such as John Ruskin and William Morris, would have recognized and welcomed. 'Why "protest so much" about fine craftsmanship?' he asked and went on to say:

> Because the machine always sets out to simulate the 'signature' of handcraft. This simulation cannot be helped nor need be too harshly condemned — it must be accepted as one of the legitimate devices of eager competition.

But it is worth noting that this simulation is in itself the most significant recognition of the qualities of hand-work. It does not, and cannot, reproduce those qualities — qualities conspicuously of strength and long service. And the by no means unimportant — to many, indeed, the most important — quality of pleasantness in use: which is to say, character, texture, finish — a sort of 'freedom of drawing' as it were; an avoidance, not deliberate and mannered but natural and necessitated by the process of dull, mechanical uniformity.

Edward was, however, careful to stress that he was not anti-machine or inimically opposed to progress:

[L]est any modernist should think that Swaine's are so much behind their time as to make handcraft a fetish for its own sake, we would ask the reader to note that machines are used at certain stages of the work for the sake of speed, which means economy, but never for those processes which are essentially done better by hand and produce results more pleasing to the eye and more satisfactory in use. The machine is, in fact, used as servant—not master. This, then, is the formula: honest material and the finest craftsmanship that can be put into the moulding of it.

Edward dedicated his booklet to those who were 'concerned to see the great tradition of English craftsmanship preserved in a machine-made age'. His idealism still radiates from its pages almost a hundred years later.

Edward's booklet also illustrates the increasing diversity of the company's products at the end of the 1920s, another part of the plan to survive and thrive in the machine-made age. To the whips and sticks they added the natural bedfellows of umbrellas and sporting seat-sticks. To the motoring luggage they added hand-bags and document cases. In the 1920s they developed an extensive line in hand-made leather gloves, for which they were rewarded in 1931 with a new royal warrant as glove-makers to George V. Edward also championed the company's very great willingness to tailor goods to customers' individual requirements, such as making luggage sized exactly for the trunk of a particular model of car. This tradition of customization gave rise to the notion at Swaine & Adeney that 'two of anything' constituted a bulk order.

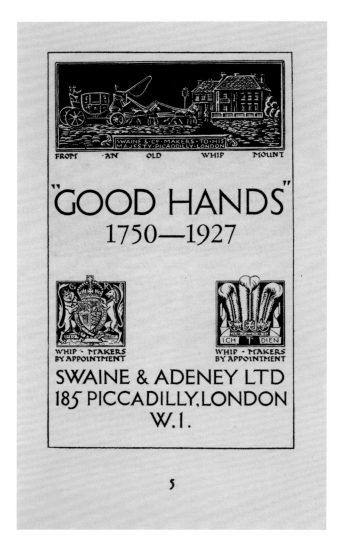

46
The title page from 'Good Hands' 1750–1927, Edward Swaine Adeney's little manifesto on the value of fine craftsmanship. The 'good hands' of the title refers to the praise commonly applied to a skilled horseman or woman; a rider who can control a horse with a light touch rather than overreliance on the whip, bit, or spur is said to have 'good hands'. The booklet's use of 1750 as a foundation date suggests that Edward had been digging into the company's past and had discovered the existence of James Swaine's predecessor, John Ross.

47 (far right)
A page from 'Good Hands' illustrating the making of a hunting whip with a whalebone stock.

'GOOD HANDS'

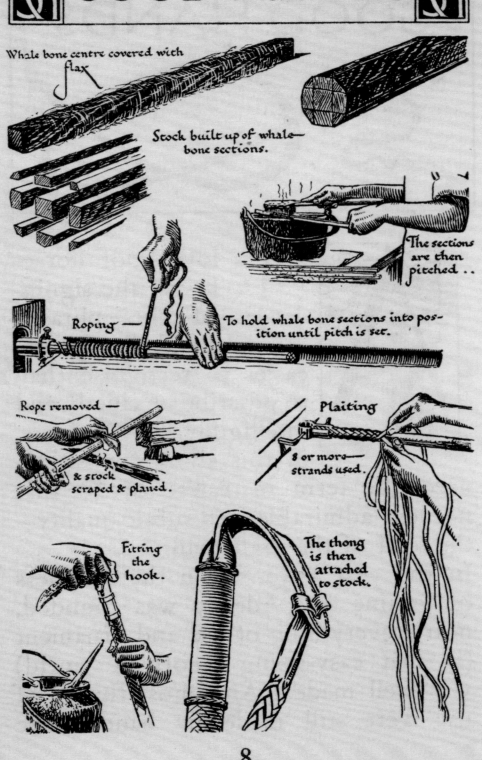

Whale bone centre covered with flax

Stock built up of whale-bone sections.

The sections are then pitched ..

Roping —

To hold whale bone sections into position until pitch is set.

Rope removed —

& stock scraped & planed.

Plaiting

8 or more strands used.

Fitting the hook.

The thong is then attached to stock.

8

48 (left)
A metal shop sign depicting a coachman
painted for Swaine & Adeney by the print-
maker and portraitist William Nicholson
(1872–1949). The painting is in the style of
Nicholson's early celebrated woodcuts, such
as his Alphabet series of 1898, but it probably
dates to around 1929 when he provided the
illustrations for Siegfried Sassoon's *Memoirs
of a Fox-Hunting Man*. This would fit with the
appearance of his design in Swaine & Adeney's
advertising and marketing materials of the
early 1930s. Sadly, the sign was removed from
the company archive in the 1990s.

49
A Swaine & Adeney hunting companion in
folding pigskin case with its original sales box
featuring the illustration of the coachman
designed for the company by William
Nicholson. The companion dates from
around 1930; an illustration of the same
model, No. A300, appears in a sales catalogue
dated December 1931, which also features
Nicholson's coachman on its cover.

50
The Swaine & Adeney hunting companion
(fig. 49) opens up to reveal two boot pulls
with ivorine handles, two jockey lifts, and
a combined shoe horn and button hook.
In 1931 it retailed for £2 17s 6d.

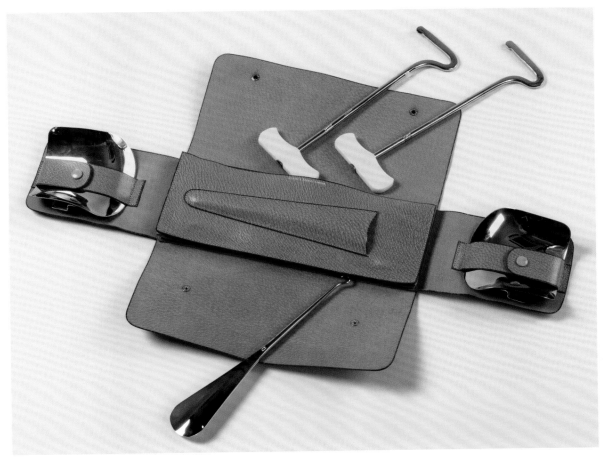

Edward kept an eye on the sporting market too. In 1927 he patented a new polo stick head, and he followed that in 1928 with a new stronger stick adapted from the thin steel core of modern racing whips. By 1931 Swaine & Adeney had made the sport of polo equipment so much their own that they bought out one of their major suppliers of polo accessories, Frederick Bedford Smith Ltd. They continued to manufacture polo equipment under the Bedford Smith name until the 1960s, but it was by then a dwindling market and they closed the company in the first half of that decade.

Of special interest, given Swaine & Adeney's eventual merger with the leading umbrella manufacturer Thomas Brigg & Sons, was their range of handcrafted umbrellas which they greatly expanded in the 1920s and 30s. All boasted frames by the preeminent English frame-maker, Fox's of Stocksbridge, and hand-woven silk covers, while the handles and shafts represented a reworking of skills honed in the making of walking sticks. There were umbrellas with crooks shaped from horn, tortoiseshell, Malacca cane, or 'whangee' bamboo root. Others were covered with plaited and patterned kangaroo, green shagreen, golden lizard, or grey alligator. Pigskin coverings could be dyed to order, but red, emerald green, navy, and royal blue were standard offerings. The 'Racing umbrella' came with a gold-plated pencil inserted in the handle, useful for filling in one's card at meets. Top of the range in the umbrella line for men was one of best hand-woven silk, with a rhinoceros horn crook, a Malacca cane handle, and a 9-carat gold collar. In 1931 it cost £15 15s. Nowadays, this would be about £800, which is not far off the current price for one of the finer Brigg umbrellas. A cheaper alternative to rhinoceros horn crooks were the carved wooden handles and knops in the form of animal heads that could be attached to either umbrellas or walking sticks. The company promised to keep a range in stock, including bull-dog, fox, otter, pheasant, and monkey, but essentially any animal head could be carved to order. Zair's supply books show that many of these were made by members of the Czilinsky family. In 1930, a dozen of August Czilinsky's 'assorted small dogs' heads' cost the company 20 shillings.

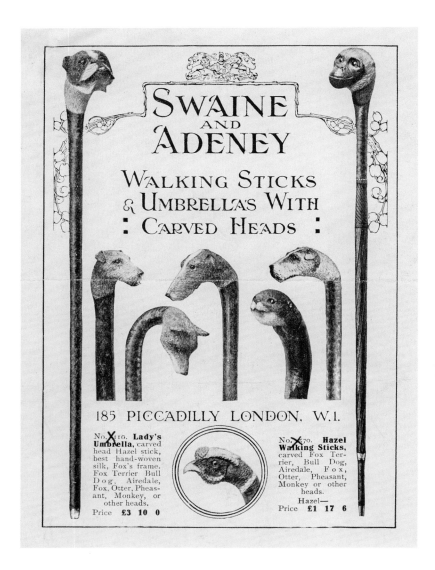

51
A Swaine & Adeney advertisement, c.1910, for walking sticks and umbrellas with hand-carved and painted animal heads. The carving of these pieces is extremely fine and distinctive and can be attributed confidently to members of the Czilinsky family, who carved animal-head handles in wood and ivory for both Swaine & Adeney and Brigg from the 1870s through to the Second World War.

52 (right)
A hazel walking stick with an integral handle carved in the form of a pheasant's head, c.1910–40. The piece is unsigned and the stick is unbranded, but it belongs in the range of animal-head carved sticks that were made for Swaine & Adeney, Brigg, and other retailers by the Czilinsky family. Coppiced hazel lent itself perfectly to this work. When it was harvested, a clump of the trunk was cut out with each stick and it was the shape of that clump that determined what sort of animal or bird the carver would fashion for the handle.

The Czilinsky Family of Ivory and Wood Carvers

It is rare for the wood carvings on Swaine & Adeney sticks and umbrellas to be signed by the craftsmen who made them. Often the shaft will be stamped with the retailer's name and a silver collar with the mark of a mounter, but the carver remains anonymous. Despite this, surviving examples show that the best work was done by master carvers, who were able to imbue their small creations with character and individuality.

The Czilinksy family produced several of these master carvers. Zair's records show that August Czilinsky supplied Swaine & Adeney with carved animal heads in the 1930s. But he was over 60 by then; if Swaine & Adeney's own records had survived they would show that the company's relationship with the Czilinskys began much earlier. Family tradition reports that August, his two brothers, and his father all carved for Swaine & Adeney and for Brigg as well. It was a relationship that dated back to the 1870s and would continue until the outbreak of the Second World War.

It was August's father, Ferdinand Czilinsky, who settled the family in London. He was born in Mainz in 1835. As a young man he worked in Paris, where a son, August, was born to his wife Maria in about 1865. Ferdinand later spoke of France as his home, but he did not spend many years there. He was a political radical and may have had to flee his adopted home after the collapse of the Paris Commune in May 1871. Certainly he was living in London by 1872 when he signed the manifesto of the Universal Federalist Council, a rival group to the International Working Men's Association, whose creation earned the scornful wrath of Karl Marx. In London he and Maria had another six children, including sons Emil Lorenz (1874–1949) and Ferdinand Jr (1879–1963). By the time of the 1881 Census, the family was settled in Hoxton, where Ferdinand earned his living as a 'carver in wood'. Fifteen-year-old August was listed as a carver as well. Later,

Emil and Ferdinand Jr would also be trained up in the craft. They worked with their father until his death in 1907. In 1897 Ferdinand registered the maker's mark FCZ with the London Assay Office, but it is not known if he ever used the mark.

In his later years Ferdinand Sr lived at 6, Tytherton Road, Tufnell Park. He had a disputatious nature and a tussle with the local authorities culminated in his conviction at the Old Bailey in February 1903 for wounding a policeman who had been sent to arrest him for unpaid rates. The trial provided snippets about his working life. His counsel described him as 'one of the most expert ebony carvers in London', and argued that much of the commotion had been caused by the police tripping over boards of pear wood stacked in the hallway. Like ebony, pear is a hard, densely grained wood; it is excellent for the carving of intricate detail and its resistance to warping makes it ideal for umbrella and stick handles. In the melee the policeman also had an unhappy encounter with something he identified as a rapier. Very probably this was one of the narrow blades typically used in sword sticks. Ferdinand's great-grandson recalls the lathes the family had for boring the cavity for the swords through the sticks.

We know that Ferdinand had a particular interest in sticks, for in July 1902 he applied to register a patent for 'Improvements in Pen and Pencil Cases for all Kinds of Walking, Umbrella and Sunshade Sticks'. This was part of the Victorian and Edwardian craze for system canes, and in particular for canes with pop-up pencils. At the time pencils were really the only truly portable writing instrument, and the handle of a parasol or cane was a convenient place for a lady or gentleman to carry one outdoors. The pencil in question was seldom the humble graphite and cedar tool of daily use, but was often titivated with a silver or gold sheath. It is interesting that Ferdinand illustrated his invention with a stick featuring an

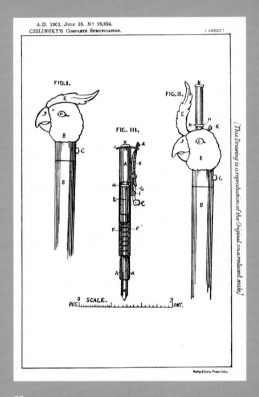

53
An illustration of an automated cockatoo's head submitted by Ferdinand Czilinsky in his application in July 1902 to patent some 'Improvements in Pen and Pencil Cases for all Kinds of Walking, Umbrella and Sunshade Sticks'.

automated cockatoo's head carved in ivory. Ferdinand was himself an ivory carver and this appears to have been intended as an illustration of his work. Identical heads were mounted on walking sticks for Brigg by the silversmith Charles Cooke and should probably be attributed to Ferdinand on the evidence of the patent drawing.

Meanwhile, Ferdinand Sr's eldest son, August, had struck out by himself. At the 1891 Census, he was working on his own account as 'a carver in wood and ivory' from his house in Mile End. With his wife, Elizabeth Mitchell, he had six children. One son was given the distinctive name of Walter Robespierre Czilinsky, suggesting that August had inherited something of his father's radicalism. By the time of the 1911 Census two of his other sons, Alfred Augustus and Percy, were working alongside him as 'carvers in wood'. His address in 1911 was 52 Parr Road in Barking, and he

was still living there in the late 1920s when he appears in Zair's account books as a supplier of carved animal heads for Swaine & Adeney. These heads were mostly for walking sticks made of Nilgiri cane or hazel, but could also be carved for tobacco jars, car mascots, inkstands, and umbrella handles.

August and his brothers and sons did not sign their animal head carvings, but Swaine & Adeney illustrated a range of them in a 1931 catalogue. All were painted 'true to life'. They have a distinctive style and can be readily matched to surviving examples today. Hazel walking sticks with integral carved dog's heads are the most common survivors. Not all of those examples, however, are branded Swaine & Adeney. Some have no branding at all; others are marked Brigg. This suggests that the Czilinskys produced these carvings for a number of retailers.

54 & 55
Two views of a painted ivory cockatoo's head automaton mounted with a silver collar on a Malacca shaft. The collar is stamped BRIGG and hallmarked for London 1899. Judging from the style of carving and the illustration Ferdinand Czilinsky submitted with his patent application in 1902 (fig. 53), this was one of his creations. It is something of a small miracle that it has survived with its delicate head feathers intact and the raising mechanism in working order. For similar ivory automatons see the sticks illustrated on pages 108-9.

56 (left)
A Nilgiri cane walking stick with an integral handle carved and painted in the form of a wire-haired fox-terrier's head, *c*.1910–40. It is stamped on the shaft: SWAINE & ADENEY. Unlike the hazel sticks, where the head is carved into a clump of trunk, on canes the head is carved into a piece of the root ball. Zair's records show that Swaine & Adeney purchased the Nilgiri canes for August Czilinsky and despatched them to him with instructions for what sort and quantity of animals they needed. Towards the end of 1929 he was producing between three and six dozen heads a month for them.

57 (above left)
A hazel stick with an integral handle carved and painted in the form of a Dalmatian's head, *c*.1910–40. It is unmarked, but plainly comes from the Czilinsky family tradition. Dalmatians are a rare find in these types of sticks; it is likely that this one was carved to order.

58 (above right)
A hazel walking stick with an integral handle carved in the form of a Scottish terrier's head, *c*.1910–40, almost certainly by a member of the Czilinsky family. The shaft has been branded in black: SWAINE & ADENEY LONDON.

59 (below)
A hazel stick with an integral handle carved and painted in the form of a head of particularly soulful hound. It is unmarked, but can safely be attributed to the Czilinsky family, *c*.1910–40. Their dog heads are always characterful and somewhat mournful as well. The light patch beneath the dog's neck shows where a piece of the bark has peeled off; once damaged like this, it is hard to effect a discreet repair.

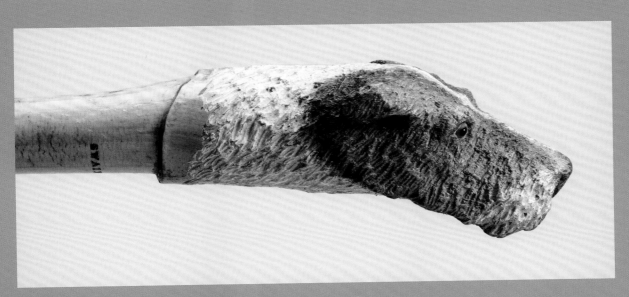

In another overlap with Brigg, Swaine & Adeney also marketed a range of sporting seat-sticks. One model that came with a concealed umbrella was patented in 1929 as the 'Swadeneyne'. Swaine & Adeney made the umbrellas for it, but Edward licensed the manufacture of the seat and stick to Juan Emilio and Albert Noirit, brothers from Argentina who had set up as saddlers and ironmongers in Walsall in the 1890s. True to Swaine & Adeney style, the stick could be purchased with a covering in pigskin, lizard, or alligator. Other multi-use items in their range included sword sticks, with razor-sharp steel blades concealed inside cane, root, or wooden sticks. Less lethal varieties might contain a long, skinny flask for a warming nip of brandy, a surveyor's 5-foot rule, or a folding horse measure, complete with spirit level.

Many contracts with selling agents survive from the 1920s and 30s. A lot of these originated with Zair and were then carried on by Swaine & Adeney until about 1950. Approved agents included Thomas, Pavitt & Co. of Hong Kong, who had the agency for China and Japan; Gordon & Gotch Ltd for India, Ceylon, and the Dutch East Indies; William Banks & Co. for South Africa; Jabez Cliff & Co. Ltd for the United States and Canada; and Everard Kerlen of Amsterdam for Holland. There were also local agents. In 1932 Swaine & Adeney signed with Eldrid Ottaway & Co. Ltd as their 'selling representatives' in England, Wales, and the Channel Islands. Usually each agreement was for a year, renewable annually if both

parties were happy. Swaine & Adeney and Zair equipped the agents with a range of relevant samples and paid a commission of between 6 and 10 per cent on any orders they placed. For their part, the agents agreed that they would market no goods from rival manufacturers and that they would restrict their canvassing to wholesalers and large retailers only. In other words, Swaine & Adeney still expected to deal with personal orders from overseas clients at their Piccadilly headquarters.

In 1939 Swaine & Adeney faced the challenge of another war. They quickly switched, as before, to retailing items of military kit. But this was a very different war from the last one and no experience could have prepared a company for the trading difficulties it would bring. Most obviously, the horse had all but disappeared from modern warfare and the cavalry officer was now only an occasional consumer of equestrian accessories. Beyond that, however, there were fundamental problems with materials. Local manufacturing was necessarily channelled into wartime needs; silk was destined for parachutes, not umbrellas. Enemy attacks on shipping and the Japanese conquest of much of Asia cut off supplies of exotic raw materials, while bombing raids in Britain knocked out many local suppliers. On 29 October 1940 John Stych & Co., leather specialists of Birmingham, wrote regretfully to Zair to inform them that 'our premises and practically the whole of our stock have been destroyed through enemy action'. This was followed by a letter from

60 (left)
A Swaine & Adeney oak hunting appointment holder, with a hunting scene carved in relief and painted and signed s J T, c.1930–5. The holder is shown with a 1931 sales catalogue advertising similar items. According to the card preserved in the holder, it last saw active use with the South Berkshire Hounds on 18 April 1955.

61
A page from a sales catalogue of 1931 advertises the Swadeneyne, a seat-stick with a concealed umbrella which Swaine & Adeney patented in 1929.

28

The "Swadeneyne" concealed Umbrella Stick and Seat
(Patent)

No. A524
HAMMOCK SEAT
metal stem covered all over pigskin, brown (dark, medium or light), blue, green or red—black, brown or navy silk umbrella £6 6 0
Ditto covered crocodile skin £8 8 0
Ditto covered grey lizard skin £9 9 0

Packing and Postage Abroad, **3/6** *extra.*

SWAINE & ADENEY, 185 PICCADILLY, LONDON, W.1

Buttons Ltd reporting that their button and buckle warehouse in London had met the same fate. Swaine & Adeney themselves came perilously close to losing their Piccadilly home, for on 14 October 1940 St James's Church took a direct hit by explosive and incendiary bombs, which left it a burnt-out shell. Swaine & Adeney must have suffered some damage in that raid or later ones, for after the war they lodged a claim with the War Damage Commission for repairs to plasterwork, windows, brickwork, roof timbers, and slates. The historic shop-front also required specialist repair work.

Even if Swaine & Adeney had been able to maintain supplies and production at acceptable levels, however, most of their Continental and East Asian customers were lost to them and they had no means of guaranteeing delivery to Australasia, Africa, or the Americas. In this they were not alone, of course. Just around the corner, at 23, St James's Street, the umbrella-makers Thomas Brigg & Sons were also struggling. Indeed, their situation was perhaps worse, as they had lost their flagship showroom in Paris to the German occupation. In February 1943 the two companies decided to join forces. From 1943 until 1990 the company traded as Swaine, Adeney, Brigg & Sons Ltd. Edward Swaine Adeney Jr was appointed chairman for life, and was one of three directors, along with his son, Gilbert Lattimer Adeney, and Bertie Walter Brigg. Brigg's gave up their shop in St James's Street, but they kept on their manufacturing premises at Newbury Street, in the City of London. The stick and umbrella manufacturing was concentrated there, while the whips and other leather goods continued to be made at the Piccadilly site and Zair's factory in Birmingham.

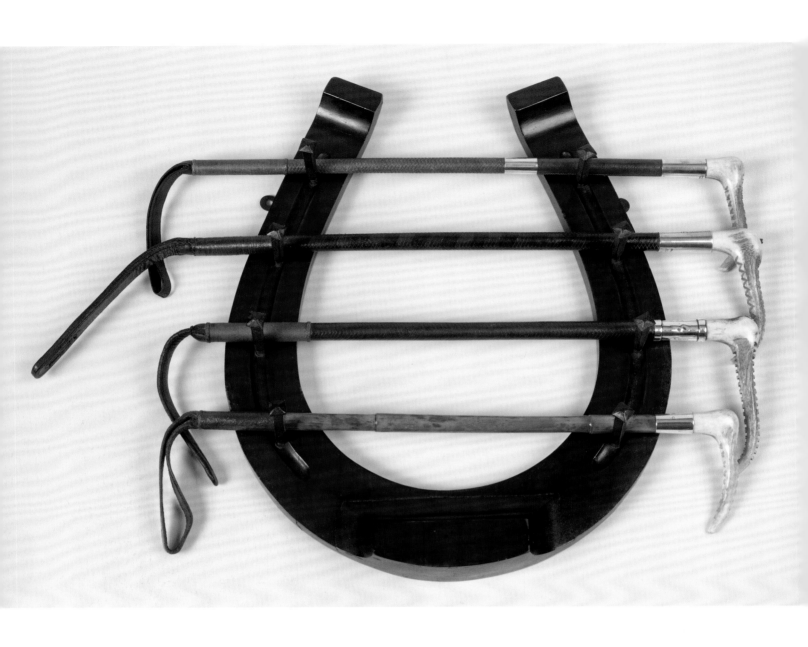

62 (and detail)
A pair of boot pulls with chromium-plated foxhound handles, an example of the extensive range of hunting accessories that Swaine & Adeney marketed in the 1930s.

63 (above)
A Swaine & Adeney whip-holder in the form of a horse collar studded with horse-shoe nails, c.1930–60. The hunting crops are from the early twentieth century, made by either Swaine & Adeney or Zair.

SWAINE ADENEY BRIGG – THE FOUNDING FATHERS

Swaine, Adeney, Brigg & Sons Ltd, 1943–1990

Having steered the new company through the final stages of the war, Edward Swaine Adeney Jr finally retired in 1949. He was succeeded briefly as chairman by Bertie Walter Brigg, who in turn was succeeded in 1950 by Edward's only son, Gilbert Lattimer Adeney (1905–1975). Gilbert had been working with his father since the late 1920s. He was the sixth generation of the family to run the company since the first James Swaine had bought out John Ross in 1798, but he inherited an economic and social climate like none that had gone before it. There were shortages in supplies, swingeing taxation rates, and a cultural impatience with the old, mannered world of the gentleman that had provided the company with so many of its customers. Mass-production techniques and cheap imitations of modernist design trends were inimical to the company ethos of traditional craftsmanship, which was in any case imperilled by a decline in workers with

specialist skills. Some of Gilbert's discomfort with this brave new world can be discerned in his chairmanship in 1959 of the newly founded Duodecimal or Dozenal Society, which listed among its objectives 'constructive opposition to any legislative proposal to extend the decimal metric base'.

The 1960s were not without their opportunities, however. Swaine Adeney Brigg prized good design, and their luggage ranges evolved to reflect the neat, clean lines and changing tastes of the decade without any compromise in quality. This was particularly apparent in the women's department, where brighter umbrellas began to jostle for attention among the serried rows of black silks, and sharply styled boxy handbags and bright red vanity cases stood out against the traditional brief-cases. New technologies compensated in part for the loss of old supplies; hand-woven silk might have become

64

A photograph of Brigg's old shop at 23, St James's Street, taken in 1963, twenty years after Brigg had joined forces with Swaine & Adeney. By this stage the building was home to a branch of Martins Bank, and in this guise it had the dubious distinction in 1955 of being the first bank in London to suffer a robbery aided by gelignite. The building was demolished soon after this photograph was taken and replaced in 1964 with a Brutalist concrete and glass tower, one of three designed by the architects Alison and Peter Smithson and erected on the site for the *Economist* magazine.

scarce and exceedingly expensive, but nylon fabric came a close second in tension, crease-resistance, and waterproofing. Nylon also replaced the increasingly rare whalebone in the core of many whips. Zair made these whips, which were trademarked 'Sabson' – derived from the parent company's name. There was also a welcome burst of publicity from the television series *The Avengers*. In 1962–4 Patrick Macnee's character of John Steed starred opposite Honor Blackman's leather-clad Cathy Gale. It was during the Macnee-Blackman partnership in the series that Steed evolved as a witty, eccentric dandy, attired in a pin-striped suit and bowler hat, twirling an impeccably furled Brigg umbrella with a distinctive whangee handle. The fact that the umbrella concealed a sword only added to its character. In retrospect, Steed can be seen as an early version of the 'young fogey', and his character helped bring about a rebirth of the umbrella as a prop for the style-conscious man. His exaggerated

Englishness was also to become a selling point for Brigg umbrellas in the United States, where the series was one of the first British television programmes to command a big following.

Meanwhile, Sean Connery's James Bond was working much the same magic for the company's luggage range. Swaine Adeney Brigg made Bond's briefcase for his 1963 outing in *From Russia with Love*; this was faithful to Ian Fleming's original novel (1957), in which it was reported that 'Q Branch had put together this smart-looking bag, ripping out the careful handiwork of Swaine and Adeney'. The briefcase was to become a classic in Bond gadgetry, a sleek black beauty with a pop-up throwing knife, folding sniper's rifle with telescopic sights, disguised tear-gas cartridge, and, tucked away in the sides, forty rounds of ammunition and fifty gold sovereigns. As Swaine Adeney Brigg did actually make a lively range of sword sticks and umbrellas and as they happily customized objects for

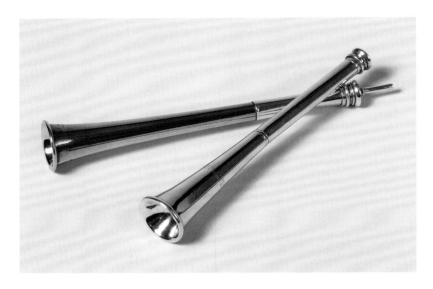

65
Two small ladies' propelling pencils in the form of hunting horns. The copper and silver one is marked SWAINE & ADENEY LONDON, and probably dates from the 1930s. The silver one is later, hallmarked for Birmingham 1957, and bearing the maker's mark V&J for Villiers & Jackson. It is stamped with the post-merger branding of SWAINE-BRIGG LONDON.

66
A Swaine Adeney Brigg hunting canteen, comprising a silver-plated sandwich box and glass flask with leather carrying case, c.1950. This late example is virtually unchanged from the version illustrated in their Edwardian catalogues. The leather case is stamped SWAINE-BRIGG LONDON, a relatively rare branding that seems to have been used from about 1943 to 1960. The cap of the flask bears the maker's mark JD&S for James Dixon & Sons Ltd of Sheffield, and the sandwich box is stamped SWAINE & BRIGG LONDON.

67 (right)
A hazel stick with an integral handle carved and painted in the form of a fox's head, c.1910–40. It is unmarked, but may well be one of the finest sticks carved by the Czilinskys. The fox is superbly rendered and easily transcends his function as a walking-stick handle.

choosy customers, Bond's murderous briefcase was probably not stretching the truth too far. Despite this, however, there is no proof that it was a Brigg umbrella that fired the fatal ricin pellet into the thigh of the Bulgarian dissident Georgi Markov on Waterloo Bridge in 1977. Neither the assassin nor the weapon has ever been conclusively identified, but urban myths persist in identifying the assailant's umbrella as one of Brigg's finest.

Gilbert retired as chairman in 1965 and handed on the baton to his 27-year-old son, Robert Edward John Adeney. Robert was to be the last of the family to run the company. Looking back, he recalled that the early years of his chairmanship were 'exciting, but harrowing'. In an interview with Stella Shamoon, published in the *Observer* on 11 February 1990, he said 'I felt duty-bound to go into the family business, but I was totally without aspects of business training which might have equipped me better.' Immediately on taking over, he faced major decisions. The lease on Zair's factory in Birmingham expired in 1965, and Brigg's old manufacturing site at Newbury Street was subject to a compulsory purchase order to build the Barbican Estate. Robert decided to consolidate the company's manufacturing at one freehold site, a factory in School Street, Great Chesterford, in Essex. The new factory opened in 1968. As well as the traditional whips, sticks, umbrellas, and luggage, the company now made saddles and bridles. A former army officer, Major John Weaver, advised Robert Adeney on developing these new lines, which were a natural and sensible extension of the company's skills in leatherworking and its long established connection with the equestrian world. John Weaver subsequently became the general manager of the Piccadilly shop, his tall frame and military bearing lending a discreet authority to proceedings there.

Other innovations were not as successful, especially those of the 1980s. These were years of conspicuous consumption, when the rise of the 'luxury brand' seemed unstoppable and when marketing men advised that customers, particularly rich Americans and Japanese, would pay over the odds for the cachet of a prized name, especially one redolent of 'ye olde England'. Tellingly, although Swaine Adeney Brigg had always prided themselves on the quality of their goods and service, they had never tried to sell themselves as a luxury or heritage brand. They were a modest, comfortably successful company. They did not charge a premium for their name or their host of royal warrants; all they asked was that their customers pay the necessary price for purchasing products that were made by skilled craftsmen and were built to last. Nor had they ever advertised their products as quintessentially English; Edward Swaine Adeney Jr did not worry whether his walking stick heads were carved by an Englishman or a German, or if his customers wanted English pigskin or Australian kangaroo hide. To him the issue was not one of selling 'Englishness', but of making what his customers around the world wanted to the best possible standards. Unhappily some of this core philosophy was lost sight of in the hubris of the big-spending 1980s. There were indeed plenty of American customers, so much so that the company found it hard to forecast accurately its sales and cash flow. After the war, about 85 per cent

68
Desmond Llewelyn's Major Boothroyd, better known as Q, hands over a Swaine & Adeney briefcase, complete with lethal accessories, to Sean Connery's James Bond, in a publicity still from *From Russia With Love*, 1963.

69 (above)
The character of John Steed in *The Avengers*, memorably played by Patrick Macnee, was a walking advertisement for Swaine Adeney Brigg long before the concept of product placement had taken root in corporate marketing minds. Seen here in a publicity still from the mid-1960s, he sports one of Brigg's classic black-silk umbrellas with a crook handle made of whangee, or bamboo root.

70 (above right)
Robert Adeney, the last of the family owners of Swaine Adeney Brigg, photographed in about 1986.

71 (right)
Princess Anne examines a riding crop at Swaine Adeney Brigg's Piccadilly premises in October 1986. Her visit was part of a week-long 'Country Fair' to celebrate the company's expansion next door into No. 186, Piccadilly. The fair raised funds for the Riding for the Disabled Association, the presidency of which the Princess had recently assumed.

of Swaine Adeney Brigg's sales were in Britain, with only 15 per cent coming from overseas. By the early 1980s this had shifted to a 50:50 weighting. Because all the sales were accounted in pounds, the company was vulnerable to currency fluctuations, especially between the pound and the American dollar. In 1985 Robert Adeney tried to tackle this problem by launching an American outlet, Swaine Adeney Inc., in San Francisco's upscale Post Street. The store won a devoted local following, but it cost the parent company too much to launch it. Looking back, Robert admitted that he did not have the capital or management resources to make the venture work quickly enough. There were also problems with advertising; since the war Swaine Adeney Brigg had not spent much money on advertising in Britain, relying largely on word-of-mouth among their loyal customers. But selling in California required a more aggressive and expensive approach. The product lines caused some problems too; 'Englishness' did sell in balmy California, but not heavy tweed riding jackets. After four years, Robert decided to surrender the San Francisco shop. He estimated that the venture had cost him £500,000, but he consoled himself that he had not tried the American experiment in New York. Failing there, he believed, would have cost him the company.

Swaine Adeney Brigg's trading difficulties were compounded in these years by an expensive expansion programme in London. At exactly the same time as he launched the San Francisco outlet, Robert was offered the lease on the shop next door, 186, Piccadilly. He had long wanted to expand the company's Piccadilly frontage, and so he took it on, despite the fact that its rent was ferociously commercial. The old shop was held in near perpetuity on a peppercorn rent of about £2,000 a year; the benefits of this had perhaps not been fully appreciated. In 1986 Swaine Adeney Brigg opened a specialist gun shop in No. 186, and they used the overall increase in retailing space to expand their range of riding and leisure clothing. In 1987 they opened a dedicated ladies' department, which carried a large range of cashmere sweaters and tailored tweeds. Both shops looked superb and the stock was of excellent quality, but the new ranges meant that they were selling an increasing number of items that they did not actually make in-house. Swaine Adeney Brigg were in danger of losing touch with the things they did best.

The expansion programme cost the company dearly. Robert Adeney looked back on it with a shudder, telling the *Observer's* Shamoon:

> I was juggling a factory, a double-fronted shop and an overseas outlet all on the same overheads. It can't be done. You need professional management and you need management controls, which I did not have. So we invested in a new computer which proved a monumental cock-up. In the event, we traded for a whole year without proper stock control.

72
The Woman who Backed a Winner with Her Brigg Umbrella, drawn by Claire Minter-Kemp for Swaine Adeney Brigg, *c.*1990, offers a gentle reminder of the failings of the cheap mass-produced umbrellas that were flooding the British market.

73
Swaine Adeney Brigg's double frontage at 185–6, Piccadilly, painted by Claire Minter-Kemp, *c.*1986. Unfortunately the rent for the new shop at No. 186, seen here on the left, was cripplingly high. Both shops were given up in the early 1990s.

The near-disaster forced a reassessment of goals and a refocusing on the company's core strengths in manufacturing quality leather goods, umbrellas, and equestrian accessories. Some financial relief was forthcoming from a Japanese conglomerate, Fukusuke, which in 1987 paid £750,000 for a 20 per cent stake in the company. They also spent a small fortune on fitting out a Swaine & Adeney shop in Tokyo's exclusive Jingumae district, which began to trade successfully in 1989. In the same year the company sold its freehold factory in Great Chesterford for £640,000; this financed the erection of a purpose-built factory on a nearby green-field site. The new unit provided 20,000 square feet of manufacturing space with room for expansion. By early 1990 Robert had nursed his company back to a small trading profit, but he seems to have been drained by the roller-coaster experiences of the previous decade. In the summer of that year he and the remaining Adeney and Brigg family shareholders sold their 80 per cent stake in the company

for a reported £4 to £5 million. The new controlling shareholder was the Ensign Trust, the investment arm of the Merchant Navy Pension Fund.

Swaine Adeney Brigg, 1990–2010

Under the new management, the company was re-incorporated as Pictology Ltd, although the shop and its goods continued to be referred to by the name of Swaine Adeney Brigg. This was perhaps the simplest of the changes facing the new owners; the recovery in 1990 had proved chimerical and for the first two or three years the company haemorrhaged annual losses of over £3 million. Rudderless, Swaine Adeney Brigg changed hands several times in twenty years, with each successive owner claiming to have worked the necessary magic on the company's fortunes. A bewildering array of company names accompanied these changes. None of these owners could be characterized as corporate raiders – far from it.

Nor, however, did any of them envisage sticking with the company for a long time. In each case, the formula was to rescue, rebuild, and sell on – a recipe that precluded the stability that the company's reputation and its dedicated customers and workers deserved.

The merchant banker Anthony Tryon, 3rd Baron Tryon, was the first chairman of the company after Robert Adeney sold up. He was followed by another banking man, Rohan Courtney, who spent a year at Swaine Adeney Brigg as executive chairman and 'corporate doctor' in 1993–4, before also moving on. After him came the Cambridge entrepreneur, John de Bruyne, who bought the company in June 1994 for rather less than Robert Adeney had sold it four years previously. His goal, as he told Guy Lesser of *Sky* magazine (August 1996), was to turn the company into a successful global luxury brand, a British Hermès or Gucci. Then, ideally, he would 'sell the company to a trade buyer, retiring as a hero'. He certainly lifted the company's profile in a short time, but perhaps inevitably much of the press coverage focused on de Bruyne himself in his role as the company's saviour, or his glamorous polo-playing wife, Tracey, the self-styled 'Queen of Umbrellas'. More controversial changes from the de Bruyne era included halving the company's labour force from about 90 to 45 and relocating from the old Piccadilly shop to cheaper premises in Old Bond Street. De Bruyne achieved big savings with this latter move, but it is questionable whether giving up a site of such historical significance for the company was worth it in the long run. As it turned out, the move to Bond Street was not a permanent one; in 1998 Swaine Adeney Brigg

moved again into a double-fronted shop at 54, St James's Street. This was not far from Brigg's old shop at No. 23, and was a location that better reflected the company's long association with St James's. As part of his programme to refocus the company on its core business, de Bruyne was keen to develop the company's luggage range. By 1996 Swaine Adeney Brigg were making 2,500 briefcases a year, and in 1997 this capacity was augmented when they bought the luggage-making department of Papworth Industries. This followed the purchase in 1996 of another venerable name, the hatters Herbert Johnson. With the purchase of the Papworth luggage-making department, de Bruyne gave up the Great Chesterfield factory and consolidated the Swaine Adeney Brigg's manufacturing at a new factory in Bar Hill, Cambridgeshire.

De Bruyne's time with Swaine Adeney Brigg has been lauded in Stephen Robbins and David DeCenzo's *Fundamentals of Management* (1998) as a textbook example of how to turn around an ailing company, but again this success appears to have been ephemeral. In 2003 the company was sold to Harris Watson Holdings PLC, a Birmingham-based company with an explicit corporate rescue mission. In 2009 Harris Watson sold it again to Roger Gawn, a Norfolk businessman with a passion for preserving and nurturing traditional craft skills. His commitment to the company's workers and customers is a long-term one and signals a return to the values of Edward Swaine Adeney Jr – the determination to make the finest quality leather goods, umbrellas, and accessories for people who appreciate the beauty, integrity, and durability of handcrafted goods.

74
Passing on time-honoured skills: one of Swaine Adeney Brigg's longest-serving workers, introduces an apprentice to the art of making a briefcase.

75

The Duke and Duchess of Cambridge
travel to Buckingham Palace after their
wedding at Westminster Abbey, 29 April 2011.
In the foreground a postilion holds one of
the whips made for the wedding by Swaine
Adeney Brigg. These whips each have
a black leather braided shaft with white
leather keeper, thong, and lash.

Whip-making was the foundation industry
of Swaine Adeney Brigg, and even though the

The company was immensely proud to be
entrusted with this commission, which brought
home to its staff how marvellous its heritage
was. As the wedding procession of the Duke
and Duchess of Cambridge made its stately
way along Whitehall and down the Mall to
Buckingham Palace, cheered by thousands
of onlookers, it seemed like an echo of the
wedding procession of Albert Edward, Prince
of Wales, and Princess Alexandra of Denmark

hn Köhler

HORN & TRUMPET MAKER

erman post horns, Bugal horn

, &c. in Silver, Brass, and Copper,

red in the best manner, and on

sonable terms, much superior to

2

J. Köhler & Son
Hunting, Coaching, and Signal Horn Manufacturers

THE FIRST INDEPENDENT FIRM TO BECOME PART of the Swaine & Adeney stable was J. Köhler & Son, a long-established horn manufacturer. Swaine & Adeney bought the company outright in February 1907 from John Buxton Köhler, who was the fifth generation of the family in the business. At the time of the purchase, Köhler concentrated on making coach, mail, and hunting horns. Until the late 1870s, however, they had been one of London's leading makers of technically sophisticated brasswind musical instruments, and it is thanks to the detailed research of the musicologists Lance Whitehead and Arnold Myers that we know so much about the company's history. Like Swaine & Adeney, Köhler could trace their origins back to an army connection and much of their success to early aristocratic patronage.

The company was founded in the 1780s by a German soldier-immigrant, John Köhler. He was born near the town of Kassel in northern Hesse in about 1754. In the summer of 1782, aged 28, he moved to England and enlisted as a musician with the Royal Lancashire Volunteers. His military career was apparently brief, for by 1786 he had set himself up in London as a French horn and trumpet maker, proudly advertising his late status as 'Master of the Band of his Majesties Royal Lancashire Volunteers'. His first shop was at 9, Whitcomb Street, but by 1794 he had rented premises at 89, St James's Street in Piccadilly. A few surviving bills and letters traced by Whitehead and Myers show that Köhler's business took off quickly. In the 1790s his customers included the Earl of Egremont's Troop of Sussex Yeoman Cavalry and the Earl of Hardwicke's Cambridgeshire Regiment of Militia. Remarkably, one of his very first instruments from the Whitcomb Street days survives today in the care of the Warwickshire Museum Service. It is a 13-inch straight hunting horn, made of copper with an ivory mouthpiece, which is stamped in capital letters near the bell rim: 'I. Köhler Whitcomb St London.' A hundred and fifty years later, Swaine & Adeney would still be making the same horns and advertising them as 'Köhler's pattern'.

John Köhler died on 3 January 1801, aged in his late forties. His only son predeceased him and his company was taken over by his nephew John Köhler, who had been apprenticed to him in the early 1790s. On 16 August 1801 this second John Köhler married Elizabeth Köhler, who was presumably a cousin, at St James's Church, Piccadilly. He died young, in April 1805, and six months later she gave birth to a son, John Augustus Köhler, who would turn out to be the musical innovator of the family. During his childhood, the business was run by his widowed mother in partnership with Thomas Percival, but in 1830 John Augustus set up his own instrument-making workshop at 35, Henrietta Street in Covent Garden. Promptly he began manufacturing brasswind instruments with novel features, and although he did not patent any innovations himself, he often won the

76
A bill from John Köhler, 'French-Horn & Trumpet Maker', which he issued for the sale of a trumpet to the Earl of Egremont's Troop of Sussex Yeoman Cavalry, 1 May 1795.

77
A trumpet in F, made in about 1838, is one of earliest instruments to survive from John Augustus Köhler's Covent Garden manufactory. A faint inscription indicates that the trumpet originally saw service in the Grenadier Guards.

76

J. KÖHLER & SON – HORN MANUFACTURERS

manufacturing rights to new patents, such as Thomas Harper's 'Improved Chromatic Trumpet' (1833). Whitehead and Myers, who have studied his instruments, conclude that he eschewed large-scale, factory-style production in favour of a small workshop that produced a limited number of instruments of high quality and intricate detailing. His prices were correspondingly high and he quickly acquired a reputation as a manufacturer of the best instruments. In 1851 he exhibited a large number of instruments at the Great Exhibition, including trumpets, French horns, trombones, bugles, and bassoons, for which he was awarded a prize medal. One of his most curious exhibits, however, was Thomas Harper's 'Walking Stick Trumpet', which he had purchased the exclusive right to manufacture in 1833. Only one of these is known to survive today. Preserved in the collections of the Royal College of Music in London, it is the length of a normal walking stick, about 33 inches, and comprises a hollow brass tube covered in leather, with a screw-on ivory cap and brass ferule. Sadly the detachable bell and mouthpiece have not survived with the trumpet body, but there is no difficulty in seeing how it would have worked. The mystery, of course, is why anyone should have seen fit to invent such a combination, although it is true that there were walking sticks that doubled up as violins, flutes, and clarinets. Perhaps Harper foresaw a time when a gentleman strolling about town would need to blast his way along a crowded pavement? Whatever the reasoning, the charming battiness of the invention seems to prefigure Köhler's eventual union with Swaine & Adeney, a company that was never short of ideas for secondary uses of walking sticks.

John Augustus Köhler married Elizabeth Sarah Mitthofer in 1835, and it was their eldest surviving son,

Augustus Charles Köhler, born in 1841, who took over the business when his father died in 1878. Instruments marked 'Köhler & Son' are therefore not likely to pre-date Augustus Charles's majority in 1862.

Soon after John Augustus's death in 1878, a drastic rent increase prompted a move from the old Henrietta Street workshop to Victoria Street in Westminster, and at around the same time Augustus Charles switched the company's focus from valved and keyed instruments to natural coach and hunting horns. Whitehead and Myers regret the loss of the musical ingenuity and adventurousness of his father's days, but the switch seems to have been determined by Augustus Charles's interests and instincts rather than any decline in family talent. In 1879 he published anonymously a booklet entitled *The Coach Horn: What to Blow, How to Blow It*, which makes clear his love of these age-old instruments and the challenge of sounding out a call on them. At the same time, however, there was something elegiac in his musings, even in 1879. The 'iron-horse', he acknowledged, had wrought great changes on the world of coaching. Coaching as a 'fashionable amusement' was in decline, while driving a four-in-hand amidst London's proliferating hansom cabs and omnibuses was now only a job for the specialist. But, as he assured his readers, there was still joy to be had on the country roads:

> for there the performer can give vent to his wind and lungs to his heart's content; his sounds, if musical, tending to cheer the spirits and enliven the journey; whilst if by chance discordant notes and queer noises are produced, the effect will be the same, inasmuch as the risible faculties and sympathies of his fellow-passengers are sure to be aroused.

80

Drags of the Four-in-Hand Club Passing the Five Bells Tavern, New Cross, by Samuel Henry Alken, c.1860–5. After the first onslaught of the trains in the 1830s and the rapid disappearance of mail and stage coaches from the highways, the revival of coaching clubs in the second half of the nineteenth century was a last flourish for the coaching industry. The Four-in-Hand Club was formed in 1856, with a nod to the much earlier Four-Horse Club. Its members' coaches, which were modified for speed, were popularly known as 'drags', whence the term 'drag racing'. It was an elite sport, as testified in Alken's painting by the presence of the future Duke of Sutherland and Earl of Lonsdale, both club stalwarts, on the drag in the foreground.

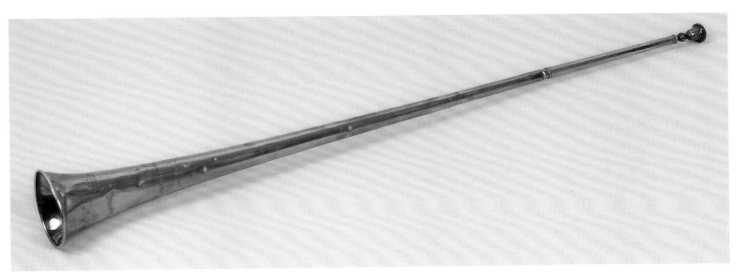

81 (above)
A 36-inch coaching horn owned by the coaching enthusiast General Sir Edwin Alderson (1859–1927). Alderson was a keen promoter of sports he believed to be threatened by the rise of the motor car. In 1934 his widow entrusted his coaching horn and whip to the 'safe care' of Swaine & Adeney, who have preserved them to this day.

78 (far left)
Detail showing the signature plate of John Augustus Köhler's trumpet in F. The 'Royal Letters Patent' refers to Köhler's agreement with the inventor John Shaw to manufacture instruments with the swivel valves that Shaw had patented in 1838.

79 (left)
Detail showing the ornate garland of John Augustus Köhler's trumpet in F. His instruments were expensive pieces, known for their intricate mechanics and fine decoration.

Augustus Charles's little book was a success and in its third edition, published in 1888, he included the musical annotation for the classic coach-horn calls or instructions, such as *Clear the Road*, *Pull Up*, and *Change Horses*. By this stage his best-known instruments were the 'Beaufort', which he had named after Henry Somerset, 8th Duke of Beaufort, who was the president of the Coaching Club, and the 'Heavy Mail', a 46-inch monster. These instruments, and Augustus Charles himself, received a ringing endorsement from Athol Maudslay in his *Highways and Horses* (1888):

> Were I asked, I think I should be inclined to say Messrs. Köhler stand pre-eminent as the makers of all kinds of horns, particularly coach-horns, to which they seem to have given a great deal of attention, and whether it be the post-horn of twenty-seven inches, the Beaufort coach-horn of thirty-six inches, the heavy mail-coach horn of forty-six inches, or the telescopic horn of unlimited length, Mr. Köhler will supply you, and, moreover, will teach you how to blow it.

82
A Köhler hunting horn in copper and silver inscribed with the name of W. Milward Jones, Rosebank, and the date 1876, with its original leather case. Jones was the head of a wealthy Anglo-Irish family with large landholdings in counties Mayo, Antrim, and Dublin. When Swaine & Adeney took over Köhler in 1907 they naturally took to manufacturing the leather cases for Köhler's horns and a great range of other hunting accessories besides.

83 (above)
Detail of the maker's signature on the 1876 Köhler hunting horn. The medallions refer to the prize medals that John Augustus Köhler won for his instruments at the Great Exhibition of 1851 and the International Exhibition of 1862.

84
General Sir Edwin Alderson's coaching whip, entrusted to Swaine & Adeney's care by Alderson's widow in 1934.

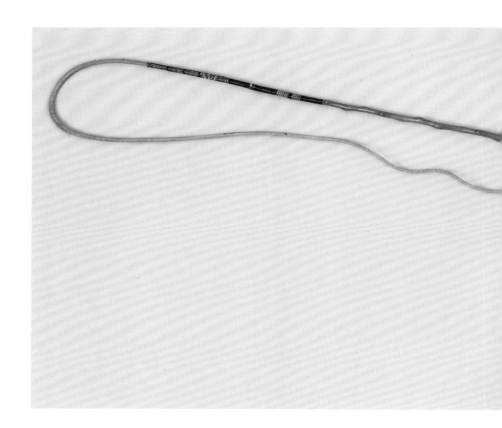

Augustus Charles had married Eliza Buxton, a banker's daughter, in 1865, and their first son, John Buxton Köhler, was born in 1869. He took over the family business when Augustus Charles died in 1890. Sadly, he appears to have suffered from mental illness, which may have been exacerbated by increasing trading and financial difficulties. The company's workshop was moved several times under his stewardship, eventually ending up in Bromley, Kent. In February 1907, he sold up to Swaine & Adeney, who undertook to retain the factory, the company name, and the company's manufacturing traditions as before. Less than a year later, on 10 December 1907, John Buxton Köhler shot himself dead. He was just 38 years of age, and left a widow and three children. It was a tragic end to his life and the family business, but the Köhler name lived on for several decades through Swaine & Adeney. Unsurprisingly, with the advent of the motor car, they increasingly focused production on hunting horns, including horns for otter hunts. And they introduced a horn with a reed 'indispensable to those who cannot sound the regular hunting horns' which almost certainly would not have met with Augustus Charles Köhler's approval. Nonetheless, he may have been mollified by the knowledge that they kept his booklet on the coach horn in print, issuing a seventh edition as late as 1963. They also reprinted many times a companion work by L.C.R. Cameron, *The Hunting Horn: What to Blow, How to Blow It*, which Köhler had published in about 1905.

85
The cover of the fifth edition of *The Coach Horn: What to Blow, How to Blow It*, which was issued by Swaine & Adeney shortly after they bought Köhler in 1907. The booklet was originally published by the natural-horn enthusiast Augustus Charles Köhler in 1879 as the revival in leisure coaching reached its peak.

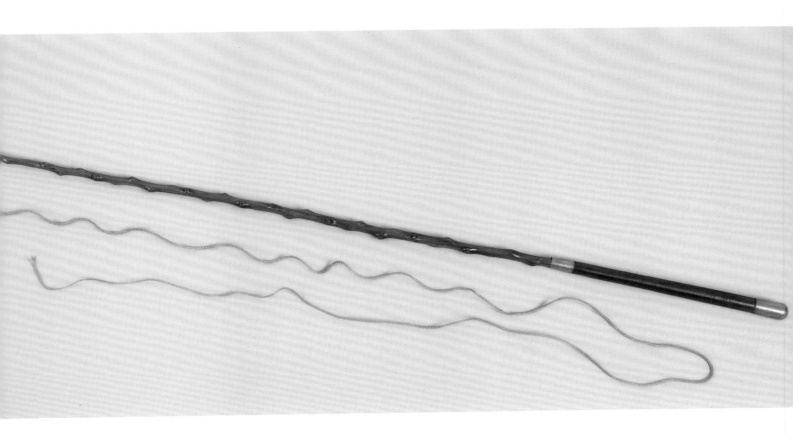

To

George Fair, Esquire

We, the undersigned Employees of the Firm of Messrs G. & J. Fair, have much pleasure in offering you our sincere and hearty congratulations on the attainment of your 70th Birthday, and ask your acceptance of this Address as a token of our high regard and esteem.

3

G. & J. Zair Ltd
The Birmingham Connection

LONDON WAS THE TRADITIONAL CENTRE OF THE English whip industry, but by the middle of the nineteenth century the bulk of production was concentrated in Birmingham and Walsall, home to most of England's saddle and harness manufacturers. One of the new Birmingham whip-makers was G. & J. Zair Ltd, which was founded in the 1830s. Zair grew to be a giant in the industry, with a long list of international clients and outlets. In early 1927 they were taken over by Swaine & Adeney Ltd, but they retained their separate manufacturing identity in Birmingham until 1965, when the lease on their factory expired and their operations were merged with Swaine Adeney Brigg.

The founder, John Zair, was born in Staffordshire, probably in the village of Gnosall, in 1809. His father George died when he was little more than a baby, and thereafter we lose sight of him until *Pigot's Commercial Directory* of 1837 lists him as a whip-mount maker trading at 8, Exeter Row, Birmingham. This was at the heart of the city's manufacturing quarter, near the canal hub at the Gas Street basin, and his neighbours included silver-plate workers, button-makers, and engravers. The 1841 Census records him at the same address, as a whip-maker. With his wife Eliza he already had one son, George, born in 1839. Another son, John, would be born later the same year. George and John Jr would become the 'G. and J.' of the family company.

By 1849, John Zair was trading as a 'manufacturer of every description of whips' at 280, Great Colmore Street. The *Birmingham Daily Post* records his occasional advertisements for 'steady workers' in the late 1850s and early 1860s, but it is his political and charitable commitments that stand out most in the newspaper coverage. Much like Edward Swaine, he was a Nonconformist and a Liberal, who supported free trade and freedom of religion. At parliamentary elections he threw his weight behind the heroes of Birmingham's Liberal and Radical tradition, William Scholefield and John Bright. A pillar of the Cannon Street Baptist Meeting House, he served on the local committee of the Baptist Missionary Society, where he campaigned for the abolition of slavery in the United States and the evangelization of Britain's colonial subjects. He was a governor of the Queen's Hospital, an annual subscriber to Birmingham's Lying-in Hospital and the Eye and Ear Dispensary, and routinely made donations to good causes, such as the Distress in Lancashire Fund.

In the late 1850s, John's sons took on similar roles. George was a founding member of the Birmingham Central Literary Association and took part in its activities for the next fifty years. He served as its honorary secretary in 1859, while at the same time putting himself through night school with the Birmingham and Midland Institute. In 1860 he was awarded a prize for French, a linguistic

86 (left)

A modern photograph of the Zair Works at 111–19 Bishop Street, Birmingham, which was built in 1865 at a cost of £1,400. It was initially assessed for the poor rates at a rather steep £139 10s, but the Zairs managed to get this reduced on appeal to £108. Whips were made at the factory for exactly a century; Swaine Adeney Brigg closed it in 1965 at the expiry of its lease and shifted the remaining manufacturing to their workshop at Great Chesterford.

87

A plan of Zair's factory from an insurance document of 1930 shows its expansive layout. Unlike other whip manufacturers, who relied heavily on outworkers, Zair put most of their craftsmen and women to work under the same roof. But they continued to work for piece rates, much like traditional outworkers.

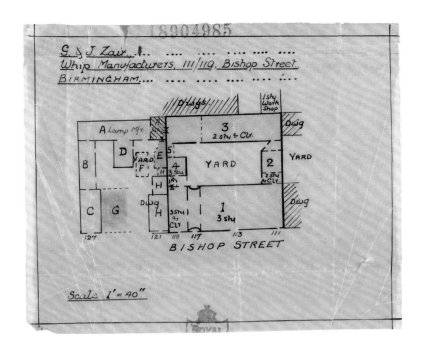

proficiency that would come in handy with the family's expanding business. His brother John was more overtly political in his associations, and in 1874 helped found the Liberal Association of Balsall Heath and Sparkbrook. Local newspapers show that there was virtually no charitable or cultural institution in the city to which the Zairs did not contribute money and support, and from the 1850s to the 1910s a Zair could always be found among Birmingham's poor law guardians, hospital governors, bank trustees, and insurance union directors.

In 1865 advertisements and notices for the company began to appear as Messrs. G. & J. Zair, suggesting that the brothers went into partnership around the time of their father's fifty-fifth birthday. This was also the year when George married Fanny Blackburn, daughter of James Blackburn, a bank manager of Walsall. James contributed funds for expanding the business, and, moving from Great Colmore Street, the brothers built their own factory in Bishop Street. (Initially the address was given as Nos. 45–6; subsequent renumbering changed it to Nos. 111–19.) The new factory, which was built around a courtyard, was a handsome, three-storey structure in sober red brick, with round-topped windows picked out in contrasting brickwork and a striking brick dentil cornice. It cost £1,400 to erect and fit out. It may have been built by the well-known Birmingham firm of architects and surveyors, James and Lister Lea. The Leas managed the building's affairs well into the twentieth century, and in 1895 John Zair Jr's daughter, Mabel Lucy, married Lister Lea's son, Montague Percy, indicating that the two families knew each other well.

Throughout the 1860s and 1870s Zair placed a steady stream of advertisements seeking stick-dressers,

braiders, stockers, finishers, and porters. As at Swaine & Adeney, braiding the stocks was the preserve of women; the advertisements always specified a 'Steady Girl'. But they did not work at home; an 1874 vacancy specified 'an experienced, trustworthy Person, as Forewoman' who could 'take charge of the Braiding Shop'. Stick-dressing, however, was a cottage industry, as it was in London. Also, as in London, piecework was the norm for both factory and outworkers until the First World War, although Zair's workers did not earn as much as Swaine & Adeney's. Wage books for the company survive from 1891. In the middle of that decade, when the company appears to have been at its peak, it was paying forty-five workers a total of £40 a week, or, on average, under 18 shillings each. This was substantially below Swaine & Adeney's average of 38 shillings for each of their twenty-eight skilled workers in 1893. The difference probably reflects Swaine & Adeney's command of the high end of the market and the corresponding skill levels and experience of their best workers. Quite a few of Zair's workers did have their earnings topped up by a five per cent bonus each quarter, but in the pre-war years there was no provision for tiding them over the Christmas and Easter breaks or the slack season.

John Zair Sr had retired by the time of the 1871 Census; he died, aged 72 years, at Hastings on 27 September 1881. After his departure his sons George and John Jr carried on the business as a partnership until John Jr retired in January 1893. George then carried on with the assistance of one of his sons, George Percy Zair, who had been born to his wife, Fanny Blackburn, in 1877.

The company's expansion, c.1865–1895, was driven by George and John's determination to provide whips for all

88
An advertisement placed by Zair in the
Queenslander, 30 December 1871. Zair
advertised widely in the Australian and New
Zealand press, always stressing that their
whips were designed for local conditions.
The company used the Stag's Head
trademark shown here from at least 1870.

89
Zair registered their Kangaroo Brand trademark
shortly after John Zair Jr's return from Australia
in 1881. Kangaroo leather was increasingly
important to their whip-making, particularly in
the braided covering of handles and the long
thongs for stock whips.

possible uses and to as many customers around the
globe as possible. Although, like Swaine & Adeney, they
made quality gift and presentation whips, the bulk of
their trade was in more humble, utilitarian whips, and
they sold these in huge quantities through their overseas
agents and outlets. They therefore devoted attention to
making whips that met the requirements and climates
of their overseas customers. Humidity affected the
'whippiness' of a whip, and the user's ability to grasp it.
Hot and sticky climates therefore needed stiffer cores in
the whips and better grips on the handles, while pliable,
flexible cores were essential in cold climates. Whips with
built-in flywhisks were popular in countries plagued by
flying insects, while very long stock whips were an essential
work tool for the cattle ranchers of South America and
outback Australia. As equine sports became profes-
sionalized and more rule-bound, regulations evolved in
different countries regarding the style, weight, and length
of the whips permitted in horse racing, trotting, dressage,
and polo. The Zair brothers prided themselves on being
able to supply national and local sporting bodies around
the globe with whips that met their specification.

Early proof that this approach was paying off came
with two international exhibitions in Australia, one at
Sydney in 1879 and the other at Melbourne in 1880. Zair

90
A horse's head in white metal forms the handle
to a Zair prize whip, presented to Australian
jockey Tom Clayton, probably on the occasion
of his riding Acrasia to victory in the 1904
Melbourne Cup. It is marked G & J ZAIR MAKERS.

sent a wide range of exhibits to both shows, ranging from everyday items to their finest quality pieces with specialist carvings and gold and silver mounts. They emphasized the specifically 'colonial' nature of their offerings and the fact that they had been designed or adapted to meet Australian needs. For their pains they were rewarded with a First Special Prize at the Sydney exhibition and First Prize at Melbourne, awards that they promptly featured in their regular advertisements in the Australian and New Zealand press. John Zair Jr also took the opportunity of the Melbourne exhibition to travel to Australia to assess for himself what promised to be a big market for the company. He was interested too in sourcing supplies, and it was not long after this that kangaroo skin became one of the most important leathers in their business. A Zair trademark featuring a kangaroo holding a whip was registered with the Patent Office shortly afterwards. It became one of the company's three principal trademarks. The other two were a stag's head, which Zair had been using since at least 1870, and the name Merle & Co., which they appear to have used from about 1898 onwards on whips that had silver-plated or nickel collars and handles. The name seems to have been taken from Merle Lodge, John Zair Jr's residence in Moseley. Solid silver ornamentation was usually marked G&J.Z, which was registered with the Birmingham Assay Company in 1884, although there were also some silver mounts marked G & J ZAIR MAKERS.

Unlike Swaine & Adeney, Zair also manufactured a lot of whips for local companies to sell abroad under their own names. Companies they supplied included Brace, Windle & Blyth, saddlers of Walsall; John Birch & Sons Ltd, harness manufacturers, also of Walsall; William Middlemore, saddler of Birmingham; Hill Hartridge Dimsdale & Co., hardware manufacturers of Birmingham and London; and Ullathorne & Co., shoemakers and leather good merchants of Birmingham. Between them, these companies were selling Zair's whips branded as their own manufactures in Argentina, Australia, Brazil, Canada, Chile, New Zealand, South Africa, the United States, and the West Indies. Zair also made whips branded for overseas retailers, such as Henrich Baer of Zurich, Greatrex of Johannesburg, and the Kopf Manufacturing Company of New York. By the early twentieth century this all-encompassing approach to whip-making ensured that Zair held a commanding place in the industry. But unlike Swaine & Adeney they did not diversify into the manufacture of other goods, so that they were vulnerable to the erosion of the demand for whips by the rise of the motor car. Moreover Swaine & Adeney's dominance of the market for elite hunting and sporting whips gave Zair little room to expand the quality end of their production. There are hints of these pressures just before the First World War. On 29 January 1909, Zair's employees presented George Zair with a beautifully illuminated testimonial to mark his 70th birthday. The sentiments they expressed were apparently heartfelt ones from long-serving workers:

> We desire to take this opportunity of expressing to you our sincere appreciation of the many kindnesses we have received at your hands during our long association together, and of the interest you have invariably shewn in our welfare; and we trust that the kindly feeling which has always existed between us may ever remain unchanged.

Significantly, however, there were only thirty-five names on the testimonial, down from the forty-five who were employed in the 1890s. The wage books confirm this reduction in number of employees and show that it continued after the war. George did not live to see the huge changes ahead. He died on 23 March 1914, aged 75. He was a wealthy man, leaving a personal estate of

91
Zair apparently reserved their Merle brand for whips with silver-plated or nickel ornamentation. Many Merle & Co. whips survive today and they frequently come up at auction, but it is rare to find a collector or dealer who knows that this was one of Zair's brands.

92
The marks from a lady's riding crop by Zair, dated 1935. The G&J.Z mark was registered with Birmingham Assay Company in 1884.

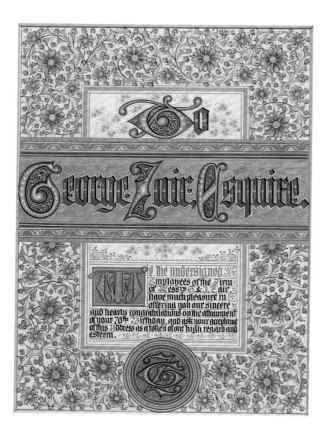

The opening page of the testimonial from Zair's workers to George Zair on his 70th birthday, 29 January 1909. It was produced by Edward Morton (c.1849–1913) of 17, Bennett's Hill, Birmingham, who billed himself as an illuminating artist. From at least 1878 until his death in 1913, he produced these elaborately decorated testimonials for a range of recipients, from retiring vicars and school headmasters to daughters of the landed gentry embarking on married life. At the behest of a number of town jubilee committees, he also produced several addresses to Queen Victoria on the occasion of her golden and diamond anniversaries in 1887 and 1897. Judging from newspaper notices and advertisements, he was one of the last specialists in a craft that claimed quite a few practitioners in the middle of the nineteenth century.

almost £100,000. After his death, his son, George Percy Zair, took over the running of the company. George Percy steered it through the war and in 1924 registered it as a limited company, G. & J. Zair Ltd, in which he and his widowed mother Fanny held most of the shares. By the close of 1926 they had decided to sell up to Swaine & Adeney, whereupon George Percy accepted an annual salary of £600, plus a share bonus, to stay on as manager of the Birmingham factory. He also became a director of Swaine & Adeney Ltd.

Swaine & Adeney kept the Zair name alive and continued to make whips at Birmingham, along with sporting seat-sticks and some of the Swaine & Adeney luggage items. More whips, too, appear to have been made for other companies and outlets to sell under their own name. Zair's archive records the dies they needed for impressing brand names into the metal pins embedded in whip handles. In the 1930s the dies included Callow, Harrods, and Whippy, all of London; Boyce & Rogers, H.W. Hill, and Gilbert, all of Newmarket; Watt of Edinburgh; and J. Salter & Sons of Aldershot, polo specialists. At the same time, some Zair products acquired a London provenance, and whips began to be marketed with the branding 'G & J Zair Makers London'.

Innovation continued at the Birmingham factory too. In 1953, Zair successfully applied to patent a whip with 'a flexible and resilient core ... formed by longitudinally-arranged glass fibres which are permanently bonded together ... by a synthetic resin or plastic'. The novel materials involved were supplied by Imperial Chemical Industries, but the technology itself was the work of Douglas Arthur Boyd, Zair's then manager. Fibreglass offered Zair not only strength and resilience, but economy too, as it enabled them to cut back on the use of expensive whalebone in hunting crops and sporting whips. Whips with fibreglass cores were to be one of their staple manufactures for the remainder of their trading years.

After the sale of their company, George Percy Zair and his mother retained ownership of the Bishop Street building, leasing it to the new parent company for £275 a year. But in 1947, following George Percy's retirement, the building was sold to Sir Robert Gooch, Bt, of Benacre Hall in Suffolk. His family trust already owned all of the land surrounding it. He leased it to G. & J. Zair Ltd until 1965, when Swaine Adeney Brigg decided to concentrate their manufacturing at their Great Chesterford premises and to discontinue active use of the Zair name. Thus the last whip was made at the Bishop Street factory a century after it was built for that purpose in 1865. Happily, however, the sense of the building's origins has not been entirely lost; today the factory accommodates a number of light industrial units that are known collectively as the Zair Works.

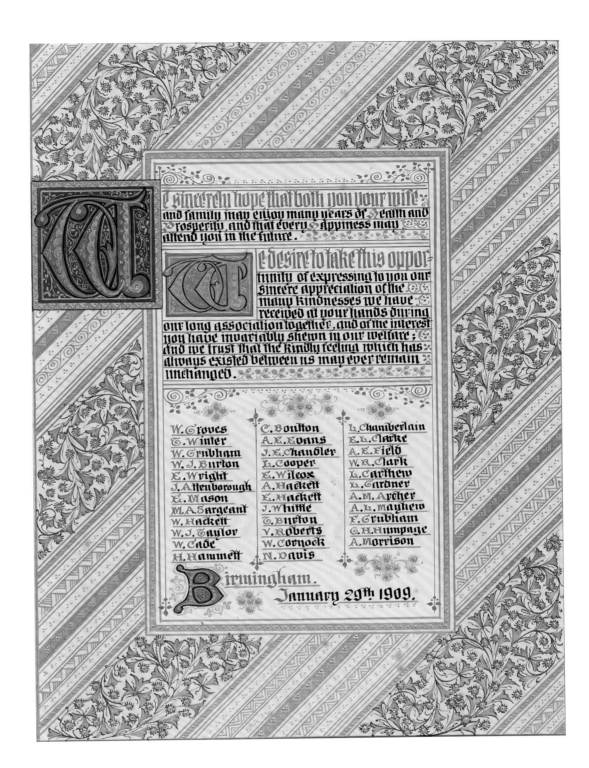

94
The second page of George Zair's 70th birthday
testimonial lists the following employees' names:
W. Groves, T. Winter, W. Grubham, W.J. Burton,
E. Wright, J. Attenborough, E. Mason,
M.A. Sargeant, W. Hackett, W.J. Taylor, W. Cade,
H. Hammett, C. Boulton, A.E. Evans, J.E. Chandler,
L. Cooper, E. Wilcox, A. Hackett, E. Hackett,
J. Whittle, T. Burton, V. Roberts, W. Cornock,
N. Davis, L. Chamberlain, E.L. Clarke, A.E. Field,
W.R. Clark, L. Carthew, L. Gardner, A.M. Archer,
A.L. Mayhew, F. Grubham, G.H. Humpage,
and A. Morrison.

4

Thomas Brigg & Sons
Royal Umbrella-Makers

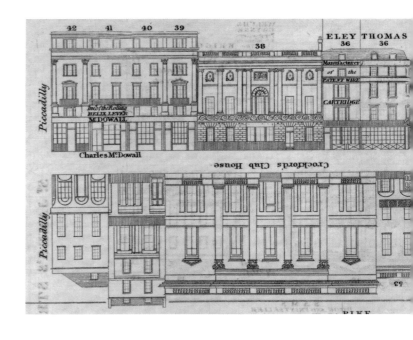

95
A detail of John Tallis's view of St James's Street, published as No. 14 in his *London Street Views* in 1838. When this plan was published, Thomas Brigg had already been trading at No. 23 for ten years, since 1828, but the company later came to believe that it had been founded in 1836.

ON 16 APRIL 1943, THE FRONT PAGE OF *THE TIMES* featured the following classified advertisement:

> SWAINE and ADENEY and THOS. BRIGG and SONS have amalgamated in order to conform to the Government's suggestion. They will do their utmost to maintain the reputation for quality for which both firms have been famous for so long. They are now trading as SWAINE, ADENEY, BRIGG and SONS, LTD., at 185 Piccadilly, W.1.

The agreement to merge Thomas Brigg & Sons with Swaine & Adeney had been signed two months earlier, on 9 February 1943. The firm of Brigg was London's leading maker of quality umbrellas. Like Swaine & Adeney, it had been struggling with the trading difficulties imposed by the war. It had also suffered the loss of its flagship showroom in Paris when Germany invaded France. The coming together of the two companies made good sense; both were St James's stalwarts and their product lists complemented each other and, in quite a few cases, overlapped. Moreover, Brigg's history was hardly any shorter or less illustrious than that of Swaine & Adeney.

The story begins with Charles Brigg, who was born on 24 November 1783 in the parish of St Gregory by St Paul in the City of London. He was the eldest of the five children of Thomas Brigg and Mary Stockwell who had married in the same church a few weeks before his birth. His father's occupation is unknown, but as a boy Charles trained as a plumassier or feather-maker. This trade involved the cleaning, dyeing, and styling of feathers into plumes and flowers for decorating hats, dresses, and fans. In this era, many of the feathers for flower-making came from domesticated poultry species, but plumes for court and military dress were often made from exotic birds, such as African ostriches and American egrets. Charles's speciality, initially at least, was in supplying plumes for the military, for in 1809 he appeared on an insurance record as 'Brigg, army feather maker'. This was at 3, Little Warwick Street (now Warwick House Street), behind Cockspur Street and just off Charing Cross. By 5 December 1817, according to an advertisement in the *Morning Chronicle*, he had moved around the corner to 63, Charing Cross. This was opposite the King's Mews (the future site of Trafalgar Square), and he remained trading there for the rest of his life. Besides the military plumes, he early branched out into women's fashion accessories, thanks in no small part to his wife Elizabeth, whom he had married in about 1804. An advertisement that she placed in the *Morning Post* on 31 May 1826 reveals her contribution to the business:

> Lace and veils cleaned and mended, Pinking Flounces for Ladies' Dresses on a short notice, Fans Mounted and Repaired, Court and Dress Plumes Cleaned and Mounted, by Mrs. Brigg, 63, Charing Cross. A fashionable assortment of Feathers and Flowers. Ladies' orders from the country punctually attended to. Shawls cleaned twice a week.

The accessories trade had plenty of tasks for small hands, and Charles and Elizabeth's six children were brought up to work in the business. The eldest, Thomas Edward, was born on 29 March 1805. In 1828 he opened a separate

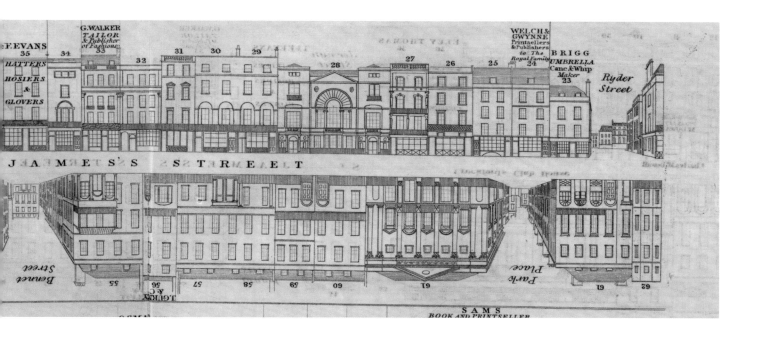

outlet of the family business at 23, St James's Street. The building stood on the corner of St James's Street and Ryder Street, just two blocks north of St James's Palace, which at the time housed several of the Prince Regent's younger brothers. No. 23 was to be the home of Brigg for the next 115 years.

One of Thomas's early advertisements, in the *Morning Post* of 21 May 1828, shows that in branching out on his own he had added the sale and repair of parasols to his services:

> Birds of Paradise, Fashionable Dress Plumes, French and Ball Hat-flowers, elegant Summer Parasols, in great variety, at BRIGGS' Manufactory, 23, St. James's-street, corner of Ryder-street. Feathers dressed, Parasols new covered, Fans repaired, &c., &c.

This new branch may have been established in consequence of Thomas's marriage on 16 February 1828 to Fanny Grellier of Chelsea. She was the descendant of Huguenot silk merchants of Spitalfields, and some of her relations may have supplied Brigg with the silk used to cover parasols. But it seems that her new husband and his father initially overreached themselves, for in August 1828 Charles Brigg appeared before the Court for Relief of Insolvent Debtors. The notice of his petition to the Court, published in the *London Gazette*, described him as:

> Brigg, Charles, late of No. 63, Charing-Cross, also at the same time of Little Chelsea, and also after that of Davies-Place, Great Chelsea, all in Middlesex, formerly a Plumassier and Florist, and lately an Umbrella-Manufacturer and Plumassier.

Then, in November, Thomas Edward Brigg, feather-manufacturer, was ordered to appear before the Bankruptcy Commissioners; on 9 January 1829 the *London Gazette* reported that he too had been registered bankrupt. But somehow the debts of father and son were satisfactorily adjusted and the creditors placated, for both the Charing Cross and the St James's Street branches of Brigg continued to trade. In August 1829 a respectable young lady was sought for an apprenticeship at St James's Street, where, it was promised, she would be trained up in 'two lines of business' (*The Times*, 3 August 1829). This seems to have been a reference to the traditional Brigg undertaking in the feather trade and the new line of making umbrellas. The umbrellas were obviously of increasing importance, for in April 1830, when an ailing Charles Brigg wrote his will, he described himself as an umbrella-maker. He died a few weeks later and was buried on 7 June 1830, aged 46, at St Martin-in-the-Fields. He left the Charing Cross business to his three daughters, Jane, Fanny, and Julia. The elder two, Jane and Fanny, ran the Charing Cross branch of Brigg for at least another decade.

Meanwhile, Thomas's business at 23, St James's Street flourished. Unsurprisingly, however, given the shop's location amid the gentlemen's clubs of White's, Boodle's, and Brooks's, his trade switched from feminine fripperies to men's accessories. This happened quite quickly. In 1838, only ten years after Thomas had founded his business, John Tallis published a pictorial plan of St James's Street detailing its individual traders. No. 23 was labelled 'Brigg – Umbrella, Cane & Whip Maker', indicating that Thomas had already shifted his focus to the essential trimmings of a gentleman's dress. Curiously, the letterpress accompanying Tallis's drawing of St James's Street also listed Brigg as a hairdresser. Confirmation of this is lacking, but it ties in with evidence from newspaper advertisements of a slightly later date that Thomas was retailing shaving accessories and toilet kits. Also, an account of a trial for theft published in the *Morning Post* of 13 March 1852 shows that by that date he had taken over a neighbouring shop to sell sponges. Nonetheless, in spite of all this diversification, it is clear that umbrellas continued to form the core of Thomas's business.

The rise of the umbrella in the Brigg family business mirrored its triumph as the essential water-proofing accessory in British society. In the 1780s when Charles Brigg was a boy this revolution in personal dress was far from complete. A portable, personal canopy, usually carried by an underling, had been a symbol of secular or sacred rank in many world civilizations, from the ancient Egyptians to the first Hindus. It appeared in a similar guise in Europe in the Middle Ages and by the fifteenth century lavishly decorated canopies hovered above the heads of popes and doges alike. In so far as they served a practical purpose, the canopies were sunshades, and both of the English-language terms for them reflect this

origin: parasols protect against the sun, while umbrellas (from the Latin *umbra*) create shade. It was as sunshades that their use spread in wider society, especially among upper-class women. Early supplies came largely from China, where the various East India trading companies supplemented their cargoes of tea with luxury crafts, including parasols with carved ivory sticks and painted silk or lacquered paper covers. By the mid-seventeenth century, however, the French were making their own parasols and they had also devised a more appropriate name for the version that kept off the rain – the *parapluie*. As early as 1715 a Monsieur Marius advertised a folding *parapluie* that he promised would fit into a pocket when not in use. This may have been the world's first telescopic umbrella, but sadly no examples of it survive to judge its effectiveness.

The British were slower to adopt umbrellas, and indeed they never adopted France's rain-specific label. 'Parasol' remained the term for a sunshade, while 'umbrella' was pressed into service for a rain shield, possibly because victims of the British climate had no trouble in associating shade with clouds. The parasol was still something of a novelty for women in the 1730s, when it appeared as a fancy-dress accessory in portraits of society ladies wearing Oriental costumes. But by about 1780 it had become part of the arsenal of a fashionable lady's wardrobe, serving as both a shield for her milk-white complexion and a formidable aid to flirtation. For the next one hundred and fifty years parasol fashions were to change with bewildering rapidity, providing a seemingly limitless market for the craftsmen and women who made and recovered them.

Umbrellas took a little longer to make headway in British society. Snobbery played a part here. Whereas a woman twirling a parasol was advertising her fair skin and her independence from the world of work, someone of either sex carrying an umbrella was effectively admitting that they could not call upon a sedan chair or carriage in inclement weather. The umbrella was also deemed a foreign and effeminate affectation; John Bull was quite sure they were the sort of thing that French dancing masters and Italian opera singers bandied about. The traveller and philanthropist Jonas Hanway (1712–1786) is credited with being the first man to use an umbrella in London, in the 1750s. He was apparently excused his behaviour on the grounds of his long exposure to foreign eccentricities. Otherwise, for a long time, only doctors and clergymen were permitted the indulgence. For the latter an early version of the golf umbrella was one of the tools of the trade, looming dolefully over the vicar's head at wet funerals. But gradually the umbrella won over its detractors. Evidence of their proliferation comes in the 1780s, when they first appear in court records as stolen goods. By the 1820s, satirists had begun to exploit their comic potential, particularly as markers of social distinction and manners. This was the best proof that they were establishing themselves as a staple of British life. Remarkably, within the space of a generation, carrying an umbrella went from revealing someone's lack of covered transport to announcing that they were not encumbered by shopping or the tools of their trade. Leap forward a century, to the interwar period, and it had become the height of vulgar behaviour for a gentleman 'in town' to carry anything but a neatly furled umbrella. As in so many other areas of British life, keeping dry had become a matter of class.

Thomas and Fanny Brigg had at least six children. Their first son, Thomas, died in infancy and it was his brother, William, born in 1831, who eventually took on the business from his father. He was working with his father by at least 1850, and it was probably soon after his twenty-first birthday that the company became known as

96
Three decorative parasols with carved ivory handles and lace and silk canopies, c.1860–85. All three are delightful instruments of coquetry, the delicacy (or absence) of their ferrules indicating that they were only ever intended to be twirled above a lady's head, rather than used in walking-stick mode. The central one of bobbin tape lace has a double lining; beneath the sober navy-blue silk lining the lace is a second inner lining of bright pink. This was a complexion-enhancing trick often used by parasol makers. In so far as onlookers only ever caught a glimpse of the pink, it was also remarkably suggestive. The parasols were originally part of the Swaine Adeney Brigg archive, which was unfortunately dispersed in the 1990s.

Premium ——— Par, & Discount ———

Brigg & Son. It became Thomas Brigg & Sons when a much younger son joined the team. This was another Thomas, a late baby born in 1845. Thomas Sr seems to have continued running the business until his sixties. He had retired, however, by the time of the 1871 Census. He died on 23 October 1881, aged 77. His sons William and Thomas Jr ran the business jointly as a partnership until February 1886, when young Thomas retired. He may have been forced out by ill health, for he died on 14 March 1888, aged only 43. His brother William remained at the helm until his retirement in 1898. The business still traded as Thomas Brigg & Sons, although for much of this latter period William was in partnership with his own two sons, William Henry Brigg (1858–1903) and Walter Alfred Brigg (1860–1950). After William Henry's death in 1903, Walter Alfred carried on the business, eventually making partners of two of his sons, Bertie Walter Brigg (1885–1972) and Guy Lenard Brigg (1890–1970). In these years the branding of goods was often simply 'Brigg & Sons' or just plain 'Brigg'. Walter retired in 1926. In 1931 Bertie and Guy turned the business into a limited company, Thomas Brigg & Sons, Ltd, in which they both held shares. Guy then withdrew from the day-to-day running of the business in February 1932. Thus it fell to Bertie, in the midst of the Second World War, to oversee the merger with Swaine & Adeney. In all, four generations of the Brigg family ran the company in the hundred and fifteen years of its independent existence, from 1828 when Thomas opened his shop in St James's Street, to 1943 when his great-grandson Bertie signed the merger agreement.

The second half of the nineteenth century was a period of consolidation, expansion, and refinement for the company. By 1898, when William retired, Brigg had evolved from a small concern covering and repairing everyday umbrellas and parasols to a recognizable name making top quality, unique umbrellas with an aristocratic clientele and prices to match. This transformation reflected changes in the umbrella-making industry as a whole and Brigg's reaction to them.

The adoption of umbrellas in Britain had been fostered by technological developments that made them more practical and effective. The earliest European examples had wooden frames and painted leather covers. They were unwieldy and heavy, which meant that the servants who lugged them around for their masters and mistresses were more than just a status symbol. The introduction of whalebone or cane ribs and oil-proofed silk or cotton covers reduced the weight considerably and made it feasible for a man or woman to carry one single-handedly. These lighter alternatives were readily available in Britain by 1800 and spawned a cottage industry of umbrella-makers who bought in the frames and stitched the covers for them. Judging from their advertisements in the 1820s, this was the level at which Charles and Thomas Brigg entered the industry.

97 (left)
Premium, Par & Discount, an etching made by George Cruikshank in 1822, satirizes the umbrella's role as a signifier of social status in Britain, from the furled elegance of the dandy, to the solid reliability of the Quaker paterfamilias, and the unfurled slovenliness of the man down on his luck.

98
A lady's parasol by Brigg, *c.*1900–1920, with red silk canopy, ivory tips and ferrule, and carved wooden handle in the form of a ladybird. While the silk is wearing thin at the folds, the 'Paragon' Fox frame remains in excellent order.

In the mid-nineteenth century the introduction of steel ribs made umbrellas lighter, sturdier, and slimmer still. In Britain many of the metal components for umbrella frames were made in the Midlands. Two of the biggest and most successful manufacturers were Henry Holland of Birmingham and Samuel Fox of Stocksbridge, near Sheffield. In 1840 Holland patented tubular steel ribs for umbrellas, giving a strong but lightweight frame, while in 1851 Fox patented the 'Paragon' frame, a system of U-shaped tempered steel ribs and stretchers that slotted inside one another, thus reducing the bulk of a furled umbrella. Parasol and umbrella manufacturers could purchase complete frames from suppliers such as Holland and Fox and then add their covers to them. Alternatively, they could purchase individual frame

components for assembly in their own workshops, accessorizing them with a variety of shafts, handles, ferrules, sliders, and rib tips, as well as the covers. Umbrellas produced in this way were unique, not only because of the accessorizing, but because it required skill and discrimination to achieve the correct tension in connecting the ribs to the chosen shaft and in shaping and inserting the wire spring mechanism in the shaft. Relatively early on, Brigg opted for this route of individualized umbrella production, buying their frame components from Fox Umbrella Frames Ltd. Fox's successor company, Hoyland Fox, still makes the frames today. Accordingly, craftsmen at the Swaine Adeney Brigg factory continue the art of wiring ribs and stretchers to

99

A brown silk parasol by Brigg, c.1895–1910, with nephrite knop and gilt-metal collar on a rosewood shaft. The hand-stitched canopy is in excellent condition and, when furled, the whole is barely 1½ inches wide. The length of the shaft (40 inches) and the metal ferrule help date the parasol to the late Victorian or Edwardian era when parasols increasingly doubled up as walking sticks. As walking sticks they were often grasped around the shaft, leaving the decorative knop on show.

a unique shaft and making by hand the springs to be slotted into it.

In the 1860s another technological revolution beckoned in the form of the sewing machine. For some years umbrella-makers boasted of providing the finest machine-sewn covers, but once the novelty wore off, high-end producers such as Brigg realized that machined covers had little to recommend them apart from speed of manufacturing. Brigg decided therefore to stick with hand-sewn covers, a tradition they continued until after the Second World War, when women with the necessary skill proved as scarce as fawn's feet for parasol handles. Today the covers are machine-sewn, but the gores

continue to be cut by hand and they retain the distinction of having turned and stitched edges on the seams instead of the selvedges seen in cheaper products.

Quite early on, as Tallis's 1838 plan of St James's Street shows, Brigg had decided to augment their umbrella range with a high-quality range of walking sticks. The walking stick had established itself as an accessory for English gentlemen in the seventeenth century, borrowing some of its authority from the staffs and maces traditionally wielded by kings and other holders of high office. With the rise of the dandy in the 1790s, it became an indispensable part of a stylish gentleman's wardrobe, the perfect finishing touch to a costume into which the wearer had poured all his aesthetic being. As a fashion accessory – a marker of style, rather than a mobility aid – the walking stick was always said to be 'worn', rather than carried. And, much as a man might have many neck-ties today, each one indicative of a particular mood or character that he might wish to convey, so the dandy had not one or two sticks, but dozens. In his memoirs, Captain Gronow recalled encountering the museum-like house of the fastidious Lord Petersham, which contained 'innumerable canes of very great value'. Gronow himself, a famously dandyish officer in the Welsh Grenadier Guards, was also known

100

Matters of Taste. No. 3. As regards, Walking Sticks, a lithograph by W. and J.O. Clerk, gently caricatures the diversity in walking sticks – and their wearers – at the beginning of Victoria's reign. The styles range from fine dress canes to sturdy day sticks to root-handled cudgels. In the centre of the lower strip a man draws a sword from his cane; to the far left of him, an itinerant stick-seller hawks his wares.

MATTERS OF TASTE, No 3.
As regards
WALKING STICKS.

Published at Rodgson's Wholesale Print Warehouse 111 Fleet Street

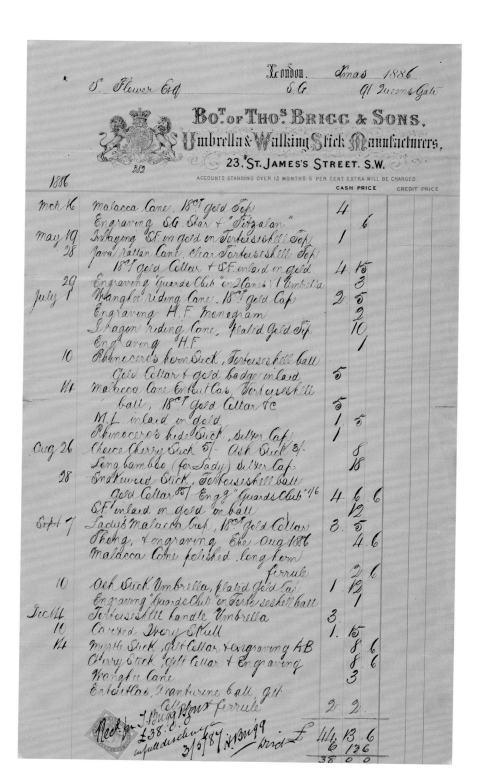

An invoice issued by Thomas Brigg & Sons to Severin Jephson Flower of 91, Queen's Gate, London, and Furze Down House, Tooting, for purchases covering the year to Christmas 1886. The invoice helpfully illustrates not only the range of sticks, whips, and umbrellas sold by Brigg in this era, but also the cost of the extras, such as engraving and gold-inlay work. The lady's Malacca crop which was engraved 'Eve Aug: 1886' appears to have been an eighteenth-birthday present for Severin's sister, Evelyn Jephson Flower (1868–1928). She was a keen hunter with a refreshing air of unconventionality about her. After her marriage in 1889 to a genteel but impoverished Scot, Ewen Cameron, she emigrated to America and took up ranching in Terry, Montana. She was also a pioneer photographer and is remembered today as a great documentary artist of rural life on the edge of the Montana Badlands.

102 (right)

The children of Philip and Elizabeth Flower, photographed by Edward Pattison Pett, c.1886. Evelyn, recipient of the lady's Malacca crop in the Brigg invoice (fig. 101), is the sturdy and determined-looking young woman standing at the back. Each of her brothers has a walking stick, an indication of the essential role they played in a gentleman's attire of the era.

for his walking sticks; the French journalist Hippolyte de Villemessant recalled that it was 'customary, in certain circles, to lay wagers that he slept with the top of his gold-headed cane between his lips'. 'He committed the greatest follies,' de Villemessant added, 'without in the slightest disturbing the points of his shirt collar.'

By the 1850s, when Brigg were selling sticks in quantity, there was a vast range of styles to choose from. Typically, walking sticks for day wear had lightweight wooden shafts, often of bamboo or cane, with handles that ranged from the discreet to the frivolously eccentric. Animal heads were a favourite. Walking sticks for evening dress were often made of ebonized hardwoods or expensive exotic materials such as tortoiseshell, with gold, crystal, or bejewelled knops. There was also a class of self-consciously rustic sticks for gentlemen to deploy when they retired to their country estates; these were usually slightly more artful than the genuinely rustic creations of country stick-makers. Brigg are often described today primarily as a retailer of these sticks,

but in fact they did a lot of the stick dressing themselves, as it duplicated skills they already employed in making umbrellas. They also commissioned decorative handles for sticks from craftsmen who worked especially for them. This was in contrast to many retailers who bought in readymade components, shafts and handles alike, from outside suppliers and merely joined them up. Thus, Brigg sticks quickly acquired a reputation as objects of quality and high finish.

The wisdom of Brigg's decision to concentrate on accessories for the discerning gentleman can be measured by a growing workforce. At the 1861 Census, Thomas Brigg was listed as an umbrella-maker at the St James's Street shop with five employees. Twenty years later, in 1881, Thomas Jr was listed in his father's stead, but with fifteen employees – eleven men and four women. His two nephews, William Henry and Walter Alfred Brigg, were by that stage working as salesmen for the shop, but most of the other employees would have been the craftsmen who assembled and completed the

103

A selection of walking-stick shafts illustrates the wide variety of woods used by Brigg and other stick-makers. The woods, from left to right, are cherry, hazel, bamboo, partridge cane, full-bark Malacca, and flowered or clouded Malacca. The cherry and hazel examples both retain their bark and in this form were most commonly used for sturdy day sticks. The bamboo too is a solid example, taken from the lower, thicker end of a stalk or culm. It is possibly Tonkin cane (*Arundinaria amabilis*), a tall, weighty bamboo from China that is today prized for natural fishing rods. The remaining three are finer woods, used for more fashionable canes, and all came from China or South East Asia. Partridge cane (*Rhapis excelsa*), also known as Annamite cane, was very popular around the turn of the twentieth century for both sticks and umbrella handles. It is very strong despite its narrow diameter and light weight. The evenly spaced nodes or rings in this example are an artificial conceit; the cane naturally has smooth sections sufficiently long to form a walking stick without nodes. Malacca cane (*Calamus scipionum*), more commonly known today as Semambu rattan, was and remains the king of canes for walking sticks. The best Malaccas are termed full-bark, which means that they have come from a long section between nodes that required no stripping to achieve a smooth, sleek finish. Canes that do contain a node are known as half-bark Malacca (if the node has been stripped and smoothed) or stepped Malacca (if the node has been retained as a feature). Another prized quality is the distinctive ridge that runs the full length of the cane, which in cross section is actually tear-drop shaped rather than round; the more prominent the ridge, the more desirable the cane. Flowered or clouded Malacca refers to a full-bark stick with a naturally occurring mottled finish. A good flowered Malacca was one of the most expensive sticks a gentleman could buy.

frames or dressed the sticks for the umbrellas and walking sticks. The women were probably employed in cutting out the gores for the umbrella covers, but the sewing of the covers, also a woman's job, was usually done off-site at piecework rates. Luxury handles and knops were also made off-site by a range of silversmiths and wood and ivory turners. These included standard designs, such as the heads of hares, donkeys, and ducks (beasts and birds with long ears, snouts, or beaks were a favourite as their protuberances made good T-shaped handles), and the silver or gold mounts used to fit antler and bone handles to a wooden shaft. But there were also special commissions, often fabulous creations carved from rock crystal or jasper and embellished with gemstones, gold, and enamels. Some of the silver and gold handles hid whisky flasks or push-button cologne sprays. Others were articulated toys made just for the fun of it - monkeys that poked out their tongues, ducks that quacked, or rabbits that flapped their ears. By the 1880s Brigg had a number of skilled craftsmen providing these elaborate finishing touches for their umbrellas and sticks. They included the silversmiths Charles Cooke of Frith Street, Soho, who worked as the chief mounter of umbrellas and sticks for Brigg from 1888 until his death in 1914; James Damant of City Road, who also had his own business making walking sticks; Charles Henry Dumenil of Golden Square, Soho; and Thomas and Maria Johnson of Bedford Row. Their makers' marks are frequently found on Brigg umbrellas and sticks. Stylistic evidence suggests that the Czilinsky family of ivory and wood carvers were also producing handles for Brigg products as well as for Swaine & Adeney.

104
A bamboo dress cane by Brigg, with 9-carat gold collar and solid tortoiseshell knop inlaid with gold coronet and monogram, the collar engraved 'FROM MISS AUNTIE/16 JUNE 1896'. The collar is hallmarked for London 1896 and bears the mark C C for Charles Cooke.

105
The maker's mark for Charles Cooke, who was the chief stick-mounter for Brigg from about 1888 until his death in 1914. Charles Arthur Cooke was born in Marylebone in 1860, the son of a tailor, Joseph Cooke, and his wife Anne. His older brother, John Robert (1856–1916), was apprenticed as a cane and whip-mounter at age 14, and went on to work as an umbrella-maker in Beckenham, Kent. By the time of the 1881 Census, Charles was himself working as a silversmith and ten years later, at the 1891 Census, his occupation had been refined to that of stick-mounter. He was already producing work for Brigg by that time, and had registered his C C mark with the London Assay Office in 1888, although the one shown here is from a later registration in 1898. He had several addresses in Soho during the 1890s, but early in the new century relocated his workshop to 4 Ridgmount Street, Bloomsbury. He evidently shared this space with Brigg, for after his death on 14 November 1914, his son Charles Arthur John Cooke (b. 1883) appears on the electoral roll there throughout the 1910s and 20s, along with Walter Alfred Brigg and his son Bertie. Charles Arthur John Cooke also continued to use his father's mark, which is why the mounts on Brigg sticks and whips are often attributed to Charles Cooke Sr many years after his death.

106

An evening cane by Brigg with an ebonized hardwood shaft and ivory handle depicting a bat and mongoose, *c.*1880. The carving is Japanese, in the style of netsuke work, and is stamped BRIGG near the base; the mount is unmarked. Such handles are commonly found on British sticks and umbrellas from this era, but they were not necessarily bought in job lots from Japanese workshops. Writing about whips in *Baily's Magazine* in 1900, Godfrey Bosvile reported that plain ivory handles were sent to Japan and were returned in a finished state within a year. The practice perhaps applied to sticks as well and may mean that companies such as Brigg and their mounters were matching ivory pieces to particular shafts prior to having them carved or lacquered to order by Japanese craftsmen.

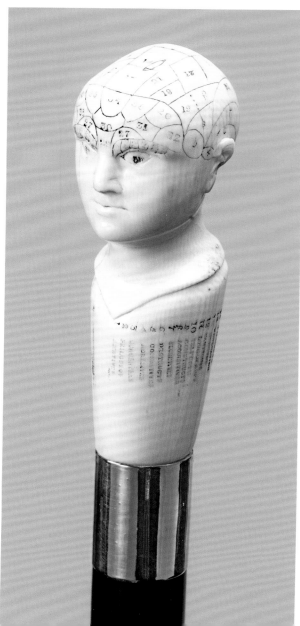

108

A horse-measuring stick by Brigg with an ivory horse's head handle mounted with a silver collar on a bamboo shaft. The collar is engraved WILLIAM CHAPMAN but is otherwise unmarked and the stick is only identifiable as a Brigg piece by the stamp on its measure (see fig. 109). The stick is of unusually fine quality; most horse-measuring sticks were more workmanlike objects, with the measure inserted into a hollowed-out shaft of hazel or cherry with an integral crook handle. The use of bamboo here, which is naturally hollow, produces a lighter, more elegant stick. The style of the carving and the lack of hallmarks on the collar, typical of Brigg's early sticks, suggest a date of c.1870–85.

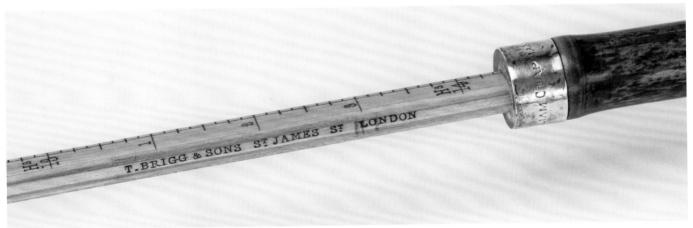

107 (left)

An evening cane by Brigg with ebonized hardwood shaft and ivory handle carved in the form of a phrenological head, c.1860–80. The pseudoscience of phrenology, which presumed to identify character traits according to the shape and formation of the skull, peaked in Britain in the first half of the nineteenth century. Accordingly, the ivory head here copies a drawing originally published in 1830 by the Scottish phrenologist George Combe in his *System of Phrenology*. But Combe's illustration was reprinted throughout the nineteenth century and it is likely that the craftsman used a later reprint as his model. In common with other early Brigg sticks, the mount is unmarked except for a stamp BRIGG LONDON.

109

The boxwood measure in the ivory horse-headed stick (fig. 108). The rule, marked in inches, centimetres, and hands, has a swivel arm housing a spirit level at the top. Similar measures appeared in all sorts of sticks until at least the Second World War, the only difference being the stick manufacturers' names stamped on them. They were presumably the work of a specialist company such as John Rabone and Sons, Birmingham.

A bamboo cane with a tau handle of fluted silver in twisted-rag style mounted by Thomas Johnson for Brigg and hallmarked for London 1896. The base of the handle is engraved CLAUDE de CRESPIGNY / 2ND LIFE GUARDS. Crespigny (1873–1910) was a keen polo player, veteran of the South African War, and aide-de-camp to Lord Curzon, Viceroy of India.

111

An evening cane by Brigg with a duck-headed
handle of carved horn mounted with a 9-carat
gold collar on an ebonized hardwood shaft.
The collar is stamped BRIGG and is hallmarked
for London 1899 with the mark of TJ for
Thomas Johnson.

112

The maker's mark for Thomas Johnson from
the Brigg duck-headed cane of 1899 (fig. 111).
This particular mark with the central full-point
was registered with the London Assay Office in
1891, following earlier London registrations by
Johnson dating back to 1877. Thomas Johnson
was born in Newcastle-upon-Tyne around
1840, the son of William Johnson, a mason. He
may have trained as a silversmith in London,
for he was living in Shoreditch when he married
there, on 28 April 1862, Maria Samson, the
daughter of Edward Samson, a local carpenter.
By the time of the 1871 Census, he was working
as a silversmith back in Newcastle, but the
family had returned to London by 1877 when
he registered his first maker's mark. In 1883
Thomas and Maria's daughter Elizabeth
married a trainee accountant, Robert Thomas
Ainsworth, and the following year she gave
birth to a son, Arthur Thomas Ainsworth.
Thomas Johnson died in the late 1890s, whereupon the silver business was continued in the
name of his widow, Maria Johnson, whose MJ
mark was registered with the London Assay
Office in 1904. But in the 1901 Census she
described herself as a widowed clothier, so it
seems that it was her young grandson, Arthur
Thomas Ainsworth, who was only 16 in 1901 but
already listed as a silversmith, who was carrying
on the family business. The arrangement
continued for over twenty years, for Brigg sticks
with the MJ mark dated for 1922 have appeared
at auction. Maria died on 8 May 1932, aged 90,
at which time Arthur Thomas Ainsworth was
still reported to be working as a silversmith.

113

An ivory rabbit's head automaton mounted with a silver collar on a bamboo shaft. The collar is stamped BRIGG and hallmarked for London 1898, with the maker's mark CC for Charles Cooke. As with the donkey-headed automaton, the carving of the rabbit was almost certainly done by a member of the Czilinsky family.

114, 115 (right)

Two views of an ivory donkey's head automaton mounted with a silver collar on a bamboo shaft. The collar is stamped BRIGG and hallmarked for London 1898, with the maker's mark CC for Charles Cooke, Brigg's chief stick-mounter. But while Cooke was responsible for mounting the stick, he did not make the donkey's head. Judging by the style and quality of the carving and painting, this was almost certainly a product of the Czilinsky family of ivory and wood carvers. The view on the left shows the donkey in 'down' position; pressing the button on the silver collar raises its ears and opens its mouth, revealing a set of delicately carved teeth and a long pink tongue.

The Dumenil Family of Silversmiths and Stick- and Pipe-Mounters

A number of Brigg umbrellas and walking sticks bear the maker's mark CD for Charles Henry Dumenil stamped on the grip or collar. They are mostly high-quality items with decorative knops in silver or gold, often taking the form of hares, swans, and ducks. A fair proportion of the surviving examples are what are now called gadget or system canes and umbrellas, with concealed pencils, flasks, atomizers, and other trickery. The gadgetry was very popular in the late Victorian and Edwardian eras and there was lively competition between manufacturers to produce mechanisms that were ever more intricate and intriguing. Dumenil was in the forefront of these developments, and in February 1894 he patented 'An Improved Combination of a Match Box or the like with a Walking Stick, an Umbrella, or the like'. Later the same year, jointly with William Henry Brigg, he patented 'Improvements in the Combination of Pencils and the like with Walking Sticks and the like'. The joint patent with Brigg was significant. Although a few non-Brigg canes by Dumenil survive from the 1880s, from 1889 onwards nearly all of his handles and knops appear on canes and umbrellas stamped with Brigg's retail mark. It is likely therefore that he had entered into an agreement to supply them exclusively. This line of work seems to have dried up with the onset of the First World War, so that most of his pieces for the company can probably be dated to the quarter century between 1889 and 1914.

Dumenil came from a family of London craftsmen whose livelihoods revolved around the gentlemen's accessory market. The family may have been of Huguenot descent; certainly they were members of the Anglican rather than the Catholic Church. Charles's father, Etienne Alexandre Duménil, was born in Whitechapel in about 1827. It is probable that he was the son of Alexandre François Jean-Baptiste Duménil and Harriet Towsey Graves, who were married at St Pancras Parish Church on 4 April 1825. By the time of the 1851 Census he was working as an ivory turner and carver at Queen's Head Court in St James's. Later the same year he married Elizabeth Baldwin, with whom he was to have four sons and several daughters. Charles was the second of these sons. Etienne Alexandre died in 1874, aged 47, whereupon his eldest son, also Etienne Alexandre, took over his business.

The younger Etienne Alexandre Dumenil (1852–1941) had a lengthy, chequered career. Unlike his father, he was trained to work primarily in metals, and by 1880 he was listed in *Kelly's Directory of the Watch and Clock Trades* as a gold and silver mounter at 74, Berwick Street, Soho. The business was at least moderately successful, as the 1881 Census recorded him as having a man (probably his brother Frederick), two youths, and one boy in his employ. In 1884–5 he registered two designs for walking stick and umbrella handles, so it is possible that he too did some work for Brigg. In late 1885 he handed over the business to Frederick and emigrated to Australia, setting up as a silversmith at 44, Little Bourke Street in Melbourne. Disaster struck eighteen months later, in April 1887, when he was arrested on suspicion of receiving jewellery stolen from a nearby shop. At his trial he pleaded that he had acted in good faith, but it was not a winning defence; he had been caught melting down the pieces only a few hours after the robbery and the thief was detained in a back room of his premises. On 5 May 1887 Melbourne's *Argus* reported that he had been sentenced to three years' imprisonment with hard labour. The term must eventually have been commuted, as the *Victoria Police Gazette* records his release from gaol on 21 August 1889. During his imprisonment, his wife Charlotte kept the family going back in London by working as a seamstress, while his two boys, Etienne Alexander (1881–1953), and Sydney Sylvester (b. 1883), trained as mounters

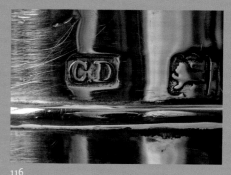

116
The maker's mark for Charles Henry Dumenil from the Brigg crook-handled pencil cane of 1897 (fig. 117). Dumenil registered this particular mark with the middle full-point at the London Assay Office in 1890; after his death in 1921 his sons continued to use a variation of the mark until 1937, when C.H. Dumenil Ltd went into liquidation.

and repairers of tobacco pipes. This was another specialist niche in the world of gentlemen's accessories. After his release, Etienne returned to London and at the time of the 1901 Census was working as a self-employed stick-mounter in St Pancras. His wife died the following year, whereupon he headed back to Little Bourke Street in Melbourne and set up as a tobacco-pipe manufacturer. He was still going strong, aged 80, when, on 10 December 1932, the *Argus* published a very respectful interview with him about his 'almost 50 years' in the pipe-making business. His conviction had apparently long been forgotten. He died in Melbourne in 1941, and was survived by his sons, who had also settled in Australia.

Meanwhile, the third son, Frederick Arthur Dumenil (1855–1894), had picked up the reins of the family business at 74, Berwick Street. He had worked initially as a whip- and stick-mounter, but after Etienne's departure he specialized in mounting pipes and it was probably he who trained up Etienne's sons in this work. He registered the maker's mark FD in 1885, but he died at an early age in 1894, whereupon the business passed to the fourth and youngest brother, Robert Victor (1862–1945), who also worked as a pipe-mounter. He registered the maker's mark R D in 1895, and examples of it can occasionally be found on pipes today. He remained in business until the 1920s.

Charles Henry Dumenil (1853–1921) was the second of the four boys and ran a company independently of his brothers. He set up as a silversmith, first at 60, Poland Street, Soho, and then, from 1881, at 17, Great Pulteney Street. From about 1879 to 1898 he traded as Charles Henry Dumenil, and thereafter as an incorporated company, C.H. Dumenil Ltd. From 1895 Thomas Charles Pickard was a partner in the firm, becoming a director along with Charles at its incorporation. Charles registered his first maker's mark C D at the London Assay Office in 1879 and a variation of it continued to be used after his death by two of his sons, Charles Henry Frederick (1877–1963) and Robert Victor (1890–1972), who worked in the business along with Thomas Pickard and his son Rowland Pickard. A fair amount of Dumenil silver work appears at auction today. Besides the cane and umbrella

handles for Brigg, it includes toilet sets and vanity cases, dressing-table mirrors, picture frames, trinket boxes, manicure sets, writing accessories, and a wide range of carriage clocks. The business was a healthy one, with turnover peaking at £124,000 in 1919, and when Charles died in 1921 he left a personal estate of over £27,000. But his sons and the Pickards struggled to maintain this success, particularly as the gentleman's cane fell out of fashion. They continued to produce silver boxes and grooming accessories, often with elegant tortoiseshell insets. But sales of these were hard hit by the Depression and by 1934 turnover had dropped to £13,000. The company may also have found it difficult to adapt Charles's ornate fin-de-siècle style to the sleek modernism of the post-war years. On 31 December 1937 the *London Gazette* reported that C.H. Dumenil Ltd had entered voluntary liquidation. It was subsequently absorbed by Padgett & Braham Ltd. An obituary for the company, from which the turnover figures above have been taken, was published in the *Watchmaker, Jeweller, and Silversmiths' Trade Journal* in April 1938.

117
A pencil cane by Brigg, with a silver crook handle mounted on a green-stained shaft. The handle and pencil mechanism are the work of Charles Henry Dumenil, and both bear his maker's mark C D and are also hallmarked for London 1897. The handle is additionally stamped PATENT BRIGG, a reference to the patent Dumenil registered jointly with William Henry Brigg in 1894 for 'improvements in the Combinations of Pencils and the like with Walking Sticks and the like'.

118
A pencil cane by Brigg with a tau handle in fluted silver in twisted-rag style mounted on an ebonized shaft. The pencil is spring-loaded and pops up on pulling the loop at the base of the handle. The handle is marked C D for Charles Henry Dumenil, hallmarked for London 1892, and stamped BRIGG PATENT. It uses a version of the mechanism that Dumenil created for matchboxes in walking sticks, but as it predates his patent for that, it was perhaps something of a prototype. The 'expelling spring', as he called it in the patent application, operates rather too energetically in this example.

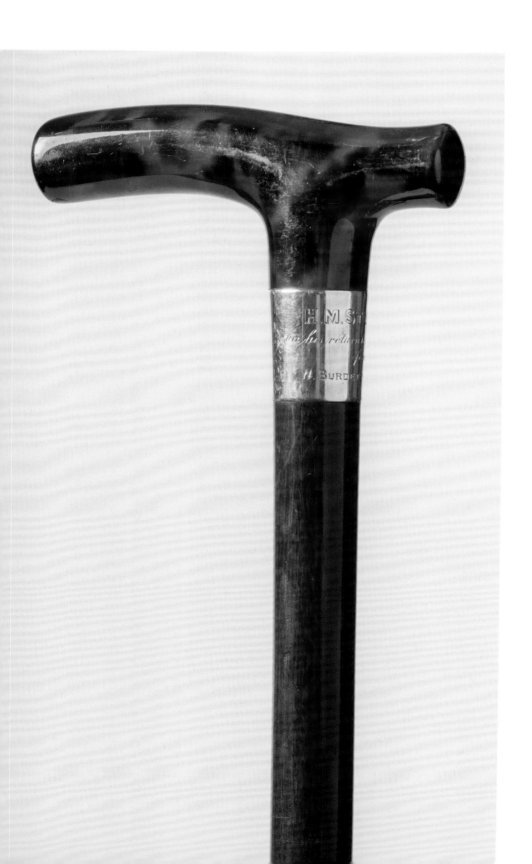

A walking stick by Brigg comprising a tau handle of solid tortoiseshell mounted with an 18-carat gold collar on a snakewood shaft. The collar is stamped BRIGG and engraved: H.M. STANLEY / On his return to England 1890 / from / W. BURDETT-COUTTS. It records the friendship between the Welsh journalist and adventurer, Henry Morton Stanley (1841–1904), and the American-born William Burdett-Coutts, who was the Tory MP for Westminster from 1885 until his death in 1921. Burdett-Coutts presented the stick to Stanley on the latter's return from the controversial private mission to 'rescue' Emin Pasha, a German doctor who had a tenuous claim to the governorship of Equatoria in southern Sudan. The stick is a fine example of Brigg's understated elegance. Snakewood (*Piratinera guianensis*) is a rare and beautifully figured hardwood from South America; it was one of the most expensive and sought-after woods for walking sticks.

120
A root-handled bamboo walking stick by Brigg, with a 9-carat gold collar mounted by Charles Cooke. The date stamp is rubbed, but an inscription on the collar dates it to 1907 or before. It reads: FROM / H.R.H. THE PRINCE OF WALES / XMAS 1907 / TO J.W. JONES / INDIA. SANDRINGHAM. The identity of the recipient is unclear, but given the future George V's passion for philately, it was possibly the well-known London stamp-dealer John W. Jones. A long-serving manager of Messrs Stanley Gibbons, he set up in business for himself around 1900 at 444, Strand, where he advertised himself as a specialist in 'Colonials'.

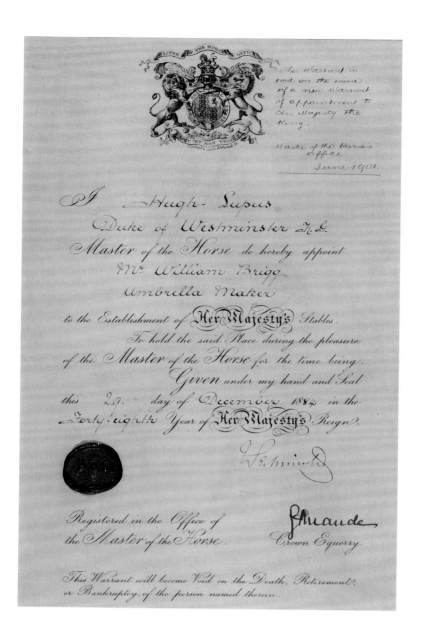

121
The Duke of Westminster, Queen Victoria's Master of the Horse, appoints William Henry Brigg 'Umbrella Maker to Her Majesty's Stables' on 29 December 1884.

Brigg's emphasis on fine craftsmanship and artistry brought significant rewards. In December 1884 they won their first royal warrant as umbrella-makers to Queen Victoria, the first time that an umbrella-maker had been so honoured. In December of the same year, Walter Brigg named his first-born son Bertie, possibly as a tribute to Victoria's own Bertie, the future Edward VII. In 1899 Brigg opened a showroom in Paris, at 33, avenue de l'Opéra. This shop became their window onto the Continent and brought them more royal patrons, including the King and Queen of Spain, the King and Queen of Portugal, the Queen of Norway, and the Duchess of Sparta. In 1908 they carried off the Grand Prix for umbrellas at the Franco-British Exhibition in Paris. By 1914 they had established an extensive network of outlets across the world, and, besides London and Paris, a Brigg umbrella could be bought from an approved retailer in Nice, Biarritz, Brussels, Florence, Palermo, Rome,

Naples, Vienna, Berlin, Barcelona, Madrid, and Buenos Aires. The extensive range of French and Italian outlets had an irony about it given that it had been the Italians and French who had first adopted the umbrella in Europe. Now they were buying them from the British.

This trend was consolidated in 1919 when Brigg bought up the goodwill and stock of Messrs Betaille, a leading French parasol manufacturer who traded at 20, rue Royale in Paris. One French admirer was the Modernist painter Amédée Ozenfant, who as a young man during the First World War had pined for an umbrella he saw in Brigg's Paris shop window. It had a handle formed from a superbly gnarled root and, desperate to own it, he paid the seemingly impossible price of 35 francs for it, only to suffer the ultimate umbrella nightmare: he left it in the Métro the very next day. Writing his memoirs half a century later, the woeful story of his *parapluie perdu* was still fresh in his mind.

122

A crook-handled pencil stick in full-bark Malacca by Brigg, with a gilt-metal collar and horn ferrule, formerly owned by the artist Augustus John (1878–1961). The collar is engraved: AUGUSTUS JOHN / 28, MALLORD STREET / CHELSEA. Although the pencil does not appear to have been used for any spur-of-the-moment sketching, John evidently used the stick a lot; the dark patch on the inside of the crook shows where the bark has been worn away by frequent handling. The collar is stamped BRIGG LONDON but has no other identifying marks. A crook-handled full-bark Malacca stick was a rare and expensive accessory because of the extra length needed between the plant's nodes to form the crook.

123

Augustus John, seen here in 1925 with the sculptors Constantin Brancusi and Frank Dobson, grasps a crook-handled pencil stick similar – or identical – to the one shown in fig. 122.

124 (left)
A detailed view of the Brigg sword stick (fig. 125) shows the decoration and manufacturer's brand on the blade. Malacca cane was ideally suited to sword sticks, as a skilled stick-dresser could split the cane in two, clean out the pith to leave a hollow tube for the blade, and then re-glue the halves together with no trace of the join. The lightness of the cane prevented the finished stick and blade from weighing too much for ordinary use.

125 (below)
A crook-handled sword stick in full-bark Malacca with horn ferrule. The collar, in 12-carat gold, is stamped BRIGG LONDON and bears the mark of Charles Cooke and the stamps for London 1918. It is engraved with the initials R.M.T.T. The three-sided steel blade (see fig. 124 for detail) was made by Cook & Co. of Clifford Street and Bond Street, London. The stick is the epitome of discretion; when closed there is nothing to indicate that it is anything other than a fine quality Malacca walking stick. The ferrule is unusually long for a stick of this late date; it suggests that the stick was made for an environment where pavements were not the norm, possibly an outpost of Empire.

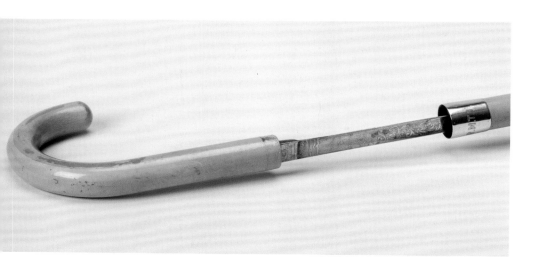

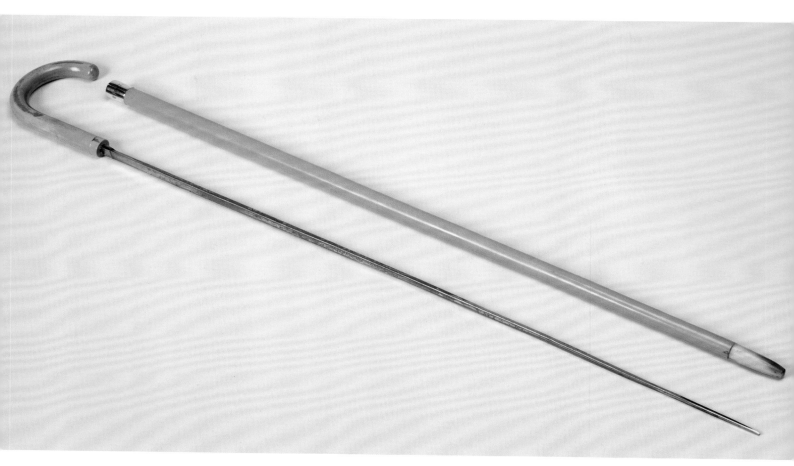

A trademark used by Brigg in the early twentieth century puns on the nautical homophone of the company's name. This example comes from a walking stick with a silver whistle mounted by Charles Cooke in 1910. It is not certain why and when Brigg used this mark; it is relatively uncommon and its use may have been limited to the dozen years or so before the First World War.

Much like Swaine & Adeney, Brigg's reputation and commercial success depended on keeping pace with the times as well as upholding standards of craftsmanship. Before the First World War they developed an early form of canopy for the motor car, a large umbrella with a hinge which allowed the canopy to be folded flat against the shaft and swivelled to head off rain and wind from a number of directions. This type of hinge was called a marquise and was in fact one of the oldest tricks in the umbrella world. The original marquise had been invented in France in the early eighteenth century as a way of making a stiff-framed umbrella more portable. Brigg also branched out into multiple-use objects. The first of these, in the 1880s, was the *en-tout-cas*, a British invention with a French name, which was both umbrella and parasol, and being neither too heavy nor too frivolous could be used in all weathers. Brigg were not the only makers of these, but they were one of their big sellers, especially with women. Another Brigg innovation was the 'Perfect', a shooting-stick that combined walking cane, silk umbrella, and pigskin seat in one. Brigg's French catalogue promised that the stick offered maximum elegance and comfort for minimum weight and advertised themin men's and women's sizes as the ideal accoutrement for hunters, golfers, fishermen, and artists. They continue to be sold today in a form barely modified from the early twentieth-century version. There was also the 'Brigson', a telescopic shooting-stick.

One big change after the First World War was the disappearance of the walking stick as an accessory for the urban man. Rustic sticks for country use were still in demand, but otherwise the market for gentlemen's canes dried up. This may have been partly because of the new taste for motoring as a leisure activity for the well-to-do, but possibly too because the stick had so obviously become a vital mobility aid for the war's casualties. With so many crippled veterans in the public eye, there may have been something faintly shaming about twirling a stick for appearance's sake only. Fortuitously for Brigg, however, the walking stick's decline was countered by the rise of the umbrella as a gentlemen's accessory. In 1930s London, it was inconceivable that a professional man could appear in public without a furled umbrella. It was a walking stick in all but name.

At this time, Brigg had few rivals for the quality of their umbrellas, or indeed the illustrious nature of their client list. In 1936–7 they proudly celebrated what they believed was the centenary of their shop at 23, St James's Street. It is not clear why or how 1836 had become lodged in the company's memory as its founding date, for, as Thomas Brigg's early advertisements in the *Morning Post* reveal, this was at least eight years after the fact. Nonetheless, 1836 had long held a talismanic status for the company. To mark the occasion they rolled out a new gentleman's umbrella – the ultra-slim 'Centenary'. Much as electronics companies today strive to design ever smaller, slimmer gadgetry, so Brigg constantly sought ways of streamlining the profile of a furled umbrella. The goal was an umbrella that was barely a whisker thicker than the displaced walking stick. Advertisements for the 'Centenary' proudly proclaimed that it 'rolls much smaller' and that its newly invented neckless tips were

127 (left)
A hazel walking stick by Brigg with integral handle carved in the form of a tiger's head, c.1920–40. A tiger is an exceedingly rare subject matter for a walking stick and it is likely that this piece was made to order for one of Brigg's customers, possibly someone with Indian connections. Although unsigned, the carving and painted decoration are of a calibre that the work can safely be attributed to the Czilinsky family.

128 (right)
A splendid pair of bloodhound walking sticks, each carved from a single piece of full-bark hazel and probably made in the 1920s or 30s. The sticks, which are stamped BRIGG, are subtly different and appear by their relative sizing to represent a hound and a bitch; they were possibly portraits of individual dogs carved to order from photographs. They can be attributed to the Czilinsky family, possibly Emil (1874–1949); Emil's grandson recalls that he had a particular fondness for bloodhounds. The rusticity of these sorts of sticks means that they survived longer as an accessory than gentlemen's dress and evening canes, which fell out of fashion after the First World War.

129 (below)
The Brigg stamp on the smaller of the bloodhound sticks (fig. 128). This is a particularly clear example of the branding, but in many animal-head hazel sticks the stamp is faint and can easily be missed. Other sticks have no branding at all, which seems rather remarkable now in view of the quality of their carvings.

not only neater but 'preserve an almost unbroken line from the handle onto the silk, and ... do not wear ugly rings around the surface of the cane'. This was clever design and marketing from a company whose umbrellas were famous for not wearing out. All Brigg umbrellas were things of beauty, but this one was sleeker and more covetable than all the others that had gone before it. Any stylish gentleman was bound to want one, even if he had several Briggs already.

At the end of the centenary year there was an even more novel event – Brigg's first ever sale. This was something they could legitimately claim was a-once-in-a-lifetime happening, and they accompanied their advertising with a portentous warning: 'It is not antici-pated that the opportunity will occur again before 2037.' In fact the sale was little more than a special centenary reduction of ten per cent on normal prices; Brigg were not about to go chasing customers with large seasonal reductions. But observers were nonetheless delighted with this sign of unbending in such a stalwart of St James's Street. News of the phenomenon was relayed to such faraway places as Adelaide, South Australia, where the *Advertiser* of 13 March 1937 reported that the sale had 'caused eyebrows to be raised in wonderment'.

One gentleman's umbrella in particular achieved world fame – this was Neville Chamberlain's black silk which he took with him to talks with Adolf Hitler at Munich in September 1938. The world, holding its breath in hope of peace, looked on in amazement as photographs emerged of Chamberlain's immaculately furled umbrella claiming a starring role in the proceed-ings. A few months later, in January 1939, the same umbrella twirled its way to Rome, when Chamberlain paid a visit to Benito Mussolini. Newspapers devoted column inches to this unlikely symbol of hope, with one or two of Brigg's salesmen providing discreet insights into the great man's brolly behaviour. Every few years, they reported, Chamberlain personally brought his umbrella into the St James's shop to be recovered. While it was being examined, he would while away the minutes admiring and fondling the more flamboyant styles on display, but he was never tempted to buy another, and always ordered simply that his old one be recovered. According to Viscountess Elibank, his wife had given it to him in 1899 and he refused therefore to countenance its replacement. It was a heavy black silk affair, with a Malacca cane handle, seven-eighths of an inch thick, spliced onto a Tonkin cane shaft, with a gilt collar. One of Brigg's insiders reported that it had originally cost £2 17s 6d, but that if the collar had been of solid gold the price would have been six guineas. It was smart but not showy. 'It's what one might call a Rolls-Royce of an umbrella,' the insider added. 'Natty but quiet; solid, but light – er, the sort of umbrella which becomes part of a man, if

130
The British Prime Minister Neville Chamberlain sports his famous 'umbrella of appeasement' at talks with Benito Mussolini in Rome in January 1939.

131 (far right)
The Brigg stand at an unknown trade fair, probably in the 1930s. It shows a near equal division between umbrellas and parasols on the right, and sticks and whips on the left. Interestingly, the ladies' umbrellas with the animal-head handles in the lower right-hand corner appear identical to the 'Tom Thumb' umbrellas retailed by Swaine & Adeney around the same time. This suggests that the two companies' eventual merger was the only feasible response to an increasingly overlapping product range.

I may say so.' The repair men recovered it each time, but they could not help but notice that it had not been opened since they had last ironed its hand-stitched gores into pristine pleats. Chamberlain had most recently brought it in just before he flew to Munich. This press reportage seemed to confirm Chamberlain's reputation as a sober and restrained politician, not given to rash decisions. In the United States the fascination with Chamberlain's prop prompted articles on the style and deportment of a true gentleman and kicked off a local revival in umbrellas and parasols. In July 1939 *Life* magazine devoted an article to the 'umbrella of appeasement', which was not yet a derogatory term for most people. For a few short months, umbrellas were no longer associated with soggy gloom, but were wielded in a spirit of hope and optimism. For his part, Hitler, who had

resented being forced into a diplomatic conference of 'equals' at Munich, could barely contain his scorn for 'umbrella politicians'.

At the time all this fuss must have seemed like magnificent publicity for Brigg. Indeed, the shop men could not have spoken to the press without the blessing of Brigg's management. But ultimately, of course, it was an ironic prelude to the ending of the company's independence. A few months later, the war that Chamberlain had tried to avert erupted, and soon afterwards Brigg lost their Paris showroom. The merger of Thomas Brigg & Sons with Swaine & Adeney followed in February 1943. When the war was over, a new era of economic austerity and political levelling ensured that the art of making and selling quality umbrellas would never again be quite the same.

5

Herbert Johnson
Hatters of New Bond Street

132
An early trade card from Herbert Johnson, issued after the move to 38, New Bond Street, in about 1895.

IN 1996 SWAINE ADENEY BRIGG BOUGHT ONE OF England's oldest surviving hatters, Herbert Johnson of New Bond Street. The company had not long since celebrated its centenary but had experienced considerable upheaval during the 1980s. The 1996 deal, bringing together two highly respected names in the world of accessories, was the beginning of a more assured future for Herbert Johnson.

The company takes its name from Herbert Lewis Johnson, who was born in the parish of St James's, Westminster, on 14 November 1856. His father, William Johnson (c.1822–1889), was a hatter from Newcastle-upon-Tyne who had moved to London as a young man and found work with the pioneering hat manufacturers Lincoln, Bennett & Co. of Piccadilly. By 1861 he was managing their business at 1, Sackville Street, and he remained one of the firm's managing partners until his death in 1889. On 2 October 1850, he married Sarah Spriggs. The daughter of William Spriggs, a London hatter and haberdasher, she worked as a hat trimmer. Herbert was the second of their four sons. He was educated at Mount Pleasant House, a preparatory school in Sunbury, and while many of his fellow pupils were destined for public schools, Herbert was instead apprenticed in 1872 to Lincoln, Bennett & Co. By the time of the 1881 Census he was lodging at 16, Duke Street, St James's, and working as a commercial traveller for them. Duke Street is not far from St James's Palace and it may have been while he was living there that he had his life-changing encounter with Albert Edward, Prince of Wales. According to company lore, Herbert was taking a stroll when he saw the prince's hat swept off by a gust of wind. Leaping to retrieve it, he smoothed its battered surface with a professional hand. The prince was impressed and advised his eager helper to open his own hat shop, promising to send his friends along to support the venture. It is unknown whether Herbert really did take inspiration from such a happy accident, or whether

he was already thinking of branching out for himself, but the story is a good one and it would be a pity to dismiss it entirely, especially as the prince did indeed lavish patronage on him.

On 10 June 1889 William Johnson died at his Regent's Park home, 26, Ulster Place. He left £500 to Herbert, who probably put it towards the hat shop he opened that year at 45, New Bond Street. Further financial and practical assistance came from a young man named Edward John Glazier (1864–1939). He was the first son of John Thomas Glazier (1828–1915), a funeral furnisher of Tottenham Court Road, and his wife, Emma Aste. The value of Edward's contribution may be indicated by his father's comfortable position in life. John Glazier was a wealthy man who lived well; in the 1891 Census the enumeration of his household at Croydon included five servants.

In 1890 Herbert took out a full-page advertisement for his hat shop in the 6th edition of *London of To-day*. Written by Charles Pascoe, this was a guide book for wealthy and style-conscious Americans. Herbert's patronage of the guide probably explains in part the fulsome write-up he received in its 'Shops for Gentlemen' chapter, but Pascoe seems also to have genuinely respected Herbert's abilities and those of his father before him:

> We may dismiss the subject of the Hat in a brief sentence. Go to Mr. Herbert Johnson (son of the late managing partner of Lincoln, Bennett, & Co., and himself for seventeen years with that firm), who has his place at 45, New Bond Street. His father was one of the best known and appreciated of leading West End tradesmen; always courteous and obliging; and the son is no less so. Mr. Herbert Johnson will inform you of all the latest shifts, curves, and shapes of the silk hat; and will make you one, or sell you one, of the most approved fashion, and as comfortable 'as they make them,' in silk, velvet, felt, cloth, straw, 'pith,' or other material suitable for all climates and all weathers.

133
The cover of a Herbert Johnson sales brochure from 1902 features the gossamer-bodied top hats for which the company became renowned.

134
Three trade cards advertising Herbert Johnson's distributors in St Petersburg, Yokohama, and The Hague, c.1905. The cards advertise the company's royal warrants from King Edward VII and George I, King of the Hellenes. Other cards in the series reveal that Herbert Johnson also had distributors in Kiev, Riga, Warsaw, Bucharest, Baden, Amsterdam, Haarlem, Palermo, Tokyo, Toronto, Montreal, and Johannesburg.

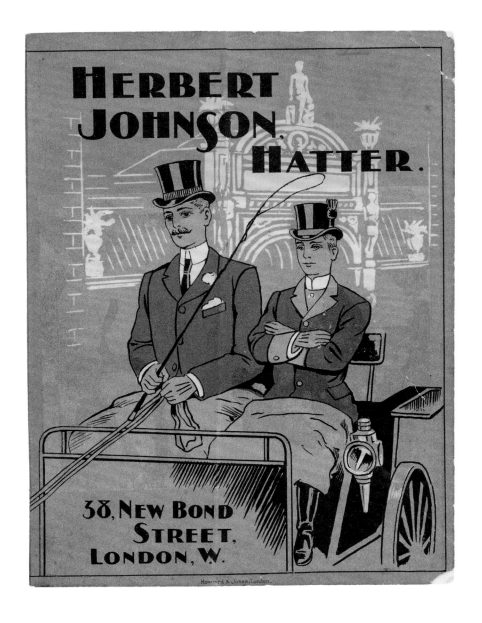

135
A Herbert Johnson top hat recovered from the wreckage of R M S *Titanic*. The hat is a collapsible silk one, intended for travelling. In spite of having spent almost a century under water, the hat's label remains legible.

Herbert's advertisement in Pascoe's guide helpfully tells us quite a bit about his fledgling shop. It had a number of what he called 'departments', which he listed as:

> Gentlemen's Velvet Napped and Silk Hats, in all
> the fashionable shapes
> Gentlemen's Hunting Hats, fitted with safety pads
> Velvet Hunting Caps
> Crush Hats, for the Opera and Theatre
> Felt Hats in all colours
> Tweed Shooting and Fishing Caps
> Tweed Caps of newest designs
> Club Caps in Silk and Tweed materials
> Youths' Silk and Felt hats
> Ladies' Silk and Felt Riding Hats
> Clerical Hats
> Livery Hats
> Hat Cases

With an eye to the guide's readership, he concluded with a promise that the 'requirements' of American ladies and gentlemen would be very carefully attended to.

The 1901 Census recorded Herbert Johnson's profession as 'Hatters' Shop Keeper'. This is a useful reminder of the work that he and Edward Glazier actually did. They made relatively few hats themselves. Instead they designed and commissioned a range of headgear from the small hat-making workshops that were dotted around London and also in the hatting centres of Luton and Stockport. The hats made to their specification were branded as Herbert Johnson creations, and such was their care in choosing only the best materials and working with only the finest craftsmen that this soon became a respected name in the retail trade. The Prince of Wales also came good with his promise of patronage. In 1901 he ascended the throne and Herbert Johnson was promptly

rewarded with a warrant of appointment as Hatter to HM The King Edward VII. The warrant was renewed for every year of Edward's reign and then continued into the reigns of subsequent sovereigns. After 1952 the company was routinely referred to in the press as 'the Queen's Hatters'. Other crowned heads of Europe followed Edward's example; in the early twentieth century patronage and warrants of appointment flowed from Nicholas II, Tsar of Russia; George I, the Danish King of the Hellenes; and Wilhelm II, Emperor of Germany.

Herbert and Edward supplied all manner of hats, but their shop became known for several lines in particular. Herbert Johnson silk-velvet top hats are eagerly sought at auction today as some of the finest surviving examples of a structured hat made with a 'gossamer body'. This is the name given to a tough but lightweight shell that is formed from fine muslin or cambric coated with shellac. The finished product was much lighter than the old beaver hats, and much less given to oozing undesirable substances in the heat than hat bodies proofed with glues, resins, and oils. Lincoln, Bennett are credited with developing the technology in the mid-nineteenth century, and it is likely that Herbert Johnson's father had a hand in its perfection; certainly Herbert himself would have known it well from his years with the company. He and Edward probably sourced many of their hats from his former employer, Lincoln, Bennett.

Buying a silk hat, however, was not just a question of choosing a quality item. There was also the matter of knowing when to wear it and what to wear with it, and, indeed, even what to call it. It was apparently in these matters that Herbert Johnson excelled himself. Charles Pascoe did not think a man could have a better guide:

HERBERT JOHNSON – HATTERS OF NEW BOND STREET

As for your hat, which you will do well to consult Mr. Herbert Johnson upon (his address is 45, New Bond Street, and he is *au fait* of all pertaining to the Hat), let no consideration of mere personal comfort ever tempt you to appear in any other but the orthodox 'silk-hat' – the 'tall-hat' vulgarly so-called – when suitably dressed for the promenade. The low-crowned felt hat and short walking- or shooting-jacket if you will; but never the low-crowned felt hat and the frock coat. The low-crowned hat worn with the ill-balanced frock coat at once stamp the wearer as a 'cad.' Why? No one has yet been able authoritatively to determine; but the fact nevertheless remains, that the low-crowned hat is an article of dress to be cast aside immediately the frock coat is assumed.

One of the earliest surviving – and most poignant – silk hats by Herbert Johnson is an 'extra quality', collapsible one retrieved from the wreckage of RMS *Titanic*, which sank in the North Atlantic on 14 April 1912. The address on the label is 38, New Bond Street, the shop to which Herbert and Edward relocated just before the turn of the century. It had been previously occupied by the well-known violin-making company, W.E. Hill & Sons, who moved across the road to 140, New Bond Street in 1895. Herbert Johnson was to trade at No. 38 until 1975. The label on the *Titanic* hat also shows the key elements of the Herbert Johnson logo, a crest featuring an antelope and, underneath, the Johnson family motto of 'Nunquam non paratus', which translates as 'Never unprepared'. In the *Titanic* example, these sit above a shield with the Herbert Johnson name and address, and although the wording on the shield varies over the years this basic combination has survived as the company's logo until today. The crest itself probably represents a visual pun. Depending on whether it is printed on a hat lining or stationery, the colouring varies, but in heraldic terms it is blazoned as antelope sejant argent, billetté sable, ducally gorged and lined or. This means a seated antelope, coloured silver or white, marked with black billets, with a ducal coronet around its throat and an attached cord reflected across its back, both coloured gold. In the

stamped version used on hat linings, the whole is usually printed in gold or black, and on bills and letterheads the black billets are often printed in red. The crest most closely resembles that used by branches of the Bagnall family in Staffordshire, Worcestershire, and Wales, but they are not the only family to have an antelope sejant in their crest. A more likely source of inspiration for a hatter – especially one with a sense of humour – was the antelope sejant in the crest of the *Capps* families of Norfolk and Kent.

The gossamer body of the silk hat readily lent itself to protective headgear for equestrian activities, with the result that the Herbert Johnson brand appeared on an increasing number of hunting hats, polo hats, and cavalry helmets. In the early years, most of their hats for women were of this nature – specialist riding and hunting hats. They did not stock the fashionable feathered and frothy hats that were to be found in a ladies' millinery shop.

Another specialist line which emerged more gradually was hats for the military. Herbert did not mention them in his 1890 advertisement, but by the time of the First World War this had become a big part of the shop's business. It was necessarily boosted during the war, not simply because of the dramatic expansion of the armed forces, but because the new style of warfare required different forms of headgear. In response to calls from army officers for a cap that would be both practical and comfortable for field operations, Herbert devised a new soft-topped cap with what became known as a 'floating bevel' top, rather than the stiff-edged fixed top of before. This field cap was later adapted for the dress caps of many regiments. Meanwhile, in the cramped confines of the armoured tank, it was quickly realized that the traditional peaked khaki cap was an awkward bit of uniform. After the war, Herbert worked with General Sir Hugh Ellis, Commandant of the Royal Tank Corps, to produce a dress cap in the style of a beret made of black Astrakhan wool with a feather hackle. The provision of military hats remains a major part of Herbert Johnson's work today and the company is the official hatter to almost ninety

136
An advertisement from 1950 for the 'Jauntie', a go-anywhere, emergency hat for women caught out by social niceties. Except during the 1990s, when the company briefly ventured into fashionable millinery, Herbert Johnson have always concentrated on making hats for women engaged in outdoor pursuits, such as riding, hunting, shooting, and motoring.

per cent of British Army regiments, as well as units in the Royal Navy, Royal Marines, and Royal Air Force.

Both Herbert Johnson and Edward Glazier had personal knowledge of the conditions in which their military customers found themselves fighting. Herbert had married Mary Eliza Geden in 1884; in 1915 their son, William Geden Johnson (1889–1953), was commissioned as a Lieutenant with the Royal Engineers and sent to France. Edward too had a son of fighting age. He had married Margaret Emily Jones in 1897, and their first son, Geoffrey John Glazier, was born in 1899. Geoffrey trained as a pilot and was commissioned as a 2nd Lieutenant in the Royal Flying Corps in November 1917. Edward himself, despite being in his early fifties, joined the Surrey Volunteers as a 2nd Lieutenant in 1917.

After the war, Herbert continued to run the shop until 1928, when he retired, aged 72. (He died on 3 August 1942 at Sutton in Surrey.) As his son William had pursued a career as a civil engineer, Herbert sold his interest in the shop to Edward Glazier. Edward turned it into a private limited company, registering it on 17 June 1929 as Herbert Johnson (Bond Street) Limited. Hats that bear this labelling (or an abbreviated version of it) can be dated to after the incorporation. If they also bear the address 38, New Bond Street, they can be dated to between 1929 and 1975.

Edward Glazier remained at the helm of Herbert Johnson until his death on 16 May 1939, describing it proprietorially in his will as 'my firm'. But in the 1930s

much of the day-to-day running of the company fell to his two sons, Geoffrey John Glazier (1899–1950) and Maxwell Henry Glazier (1907–1984). Besides his majority shareholding in Herbert Johnson, Edward also owned a chunk of shares in Battersby & Co. Ltd, one of the big hat-making firms of Stockport, Cheshire. He clearly valued these (forbidding his trustees from selling them while his widow remained alive), and thus it is likely that in the 1920s and 30s at least some of Herbert Johnson's hats were being made by Battersby's. These were most probably the felted hats, which were a speciality of the Stockport industry.

In the 1920s and 30s the company began to develop new lines which, much like Swaine & Adeney's innovations of the same era, reflected the new dominance of the motor car. Motoring caps became popular, including special models for women with integral tie-scarves for restraining their hair. But the biggest innovation was Herbert Johnson's development of the first crash helmets for motor sports. In the early 1930s the celebrated racing driver Lieutenant-Colonel Goldie Gardner approached Geoffrey Glazier to design a protective hat for his speed runs. Geoffrey employed the gossamer-body technology to design a tough but lightweight helmet that fitted snugly around the temples but sat high on the head, leaving a cushion of air between the head and the shell of the hat. The basic shell was lined with cork and could be coloured according to preference and accessorized with canvas neck protector, leather chin strap and peak, and

celluloid wrap-around visor. The finished product was undeniably stylish and there were few racing drivers in the 1940s and 50s who did not covet one. But they were not cheap. In the 1950s, the basic shell cost £7 10s, while the extras cost another 30 shillings. The legendary British driver Sir Stirling Moss recalled that when he was starting out he could only afford one, a white model with the full set of leather and canvas accessories. He was wearing it when he won the British Grand Prix at Aintree on 20 July 1957 and, four weeks later, the Italian Grand Prix at Pescara. He subsequently sold it to the British Oxygen Company. They covered it in gold leaf and used it as the Golden Helmet Trophy for the British Formula Ford Championships, which they sponsored in the early 1970s. When the helmet, complete with gold leaf, came up for auction at Bonhams in 2009, it fetched a staggering £23,000. Moss meanwhile had become so nostalgic for his lost Herbert Johnson that in 1996 Geoffrey Glazier's son, Timothy, introduced him to the veteran hat-maker Ray Corne of Patey's. The Corne family of hatters had made the original Herbert Johnson

137
The British racing driver Stirling Moss celebrates his victory in the Italian Grand Prix at Pescara, on 18 August 1957, with Tony Vanderwell, designer of his winning Vanwall. Moss is wearing his white Herbert Johnson racing helmet.

138
A shellac racing helmet with visor by Herbert Johnson, c.1935–40. The box is addressed to 'J.G. Talbot, High Beeches, Peterley, Gt Missenden, Bucks'. This was a residence of the Chetwynd-Talbot family and suggests a link with the famous Talbot marque of racing cars, which was launched in 1903 by Charles Chetwynd-Talbot, 20th Earl of Shrewsbury, and the French motoring pioneer Adolphe Clément-Bayard.

helmets and Ray was able to make Moss a replica of his early one, using the original form and gossamer-body technology. It took some special pleading on Moss's part, but eventually he won a dispensation from the British racing authorities permitting him to wear the helmet when taking 1950s cars for a spin.

Moss's original helmet has not been the only one to appear at auction. Other recent examples include that worn by F.W. Carr who drove MG racing cars at Brooklands in Surrey in the 1930s; this came up for auction at Bonhams in 2010. Also the helmet worn by Major Tony Rolt in his winning drive in the Le Mans 24-Hour Race in 1953 was sold by Bonhams in 2009 for £11,500. Less exalted examples of the helmet sell for smaller sums, often with their original Herbert Johnson box. In the late 1950s Herbert Johnson conformed to new safety regulations introduced by the Royal Automobile Club and the British Standards Institution and began retailing fibreglass helmets. These were made by E.W. Vero Ltd, with the addition of Herbert Johnson's

140 (right)
Arthur Lowe in character as the pompous but essentially decent Captain Mainwaring of the BBC television series *Dad's Army*, c.1975. He wears one of Herbert Johnson's floating-bevel soft-topped military caps, originally developed for army use during the First World War.

141 (far right)
Tom Baker is incarnated as the fourth Doctor in the BBC science-fiction series *Doctor Who*, 1974. Along with his ever-lengthening scarf, the Doctor's floppy Herbert Johnson fedora was an integral part of his character. Its colour changed over the years; this first one was in brown.

139
One of the last of Herbert Johnson's shellac racing helmets, with silver-painted finish, and its original box, which is postmarked 1952.

traditional, high-end extras. But these new models never had the cachet of the original gossamer-body helmet and Herbert Johnson soon left them to other retailers.

Racing drivers provided one form of celebrity advertising for Herbert Johnson after the Second World War. Another, largely unexpected form emerged with the take-off of British television drama in the 1950s and 60s. Gradually Herbert Johnson became a principal port of call for television producers and their costume designers. In *The Avengers* Patrick Macnee's Steed not only twirled a Brigg umbrella; he also sported a Herbert Johnson bowler hat. Like the umbrella it was a weapon in disguise; the grey felt version used in the 1968/9 series purported to contain a lethal steel brim. Meanwhile, in *Dad's Army*, Arthur Lowe's Captain Mainwaring glowered from beneath a Herbert Johnson floating-bevel peaked khaki cap, while in the 1970s a whole host of Benny Hill's comedic creations maniacally filled the small screen in Herbert Johnson tweed flat caps and felt trilbys. Also in the 1970s, Tom Baker made a floppy Herbert Johnson fedora an integral part of his Byronic portrayal of Doctor Who. That hat had several incarnations, moving from brown to green to burgundy over the course of his tenure as the Doctor. He was not the only fan of the fedora; other Herbert Johnson models in velour were sported by Jimi Hendrix and Mick Jagger. Hendrix's was a purple model trimmed with a snakeskin hat band; it came up for sale at Christie's in 1994. At the more rarefied end of the cultural scale, Sir Roy Strong, Director of the Victoria and Albert Museum from 1973 to 1987, often strode about in a greenish-brown Herbert Johnson felt fedora. He subsequently donated it to the V&A, where it very possibly sits in the store alongside a similar one given by Sir Cecil Beaton.

Much of this broadening of Herbert Johnson's appeal in the 1960s and 70s can be attributed to Geoffrey Glazier's son, Timothy (1934–2009). He was the third generation of the Glazier family to go into the business and after his father's death in 1950 brought a younger eye to hat design and marketing. Under his inspired leadership, the concept of a 'groovy Herbert Johnson hat' on sale in Todd's, Gary Craze's achingly trendy hairdressing salon in the King's Road, somehow sat quite happily with the reputation that came from providing headgear for the Queen and Army Chiefs of Staff. Something of this atmosphere was captured in Robert Kane's book *London A to Z* (1974), which described Herbert Johnson in tones of admiring wonder as 'surely the most off-beat merchant ever to hold a royal warrant'.

Tim Glazier was also responsible for extending the company's costuming range from the small to the big screen. One of the first starring roles for a Herbert Johnson hat in a motion picture was Inspector Clouseau's trilby in *A Shot in the Dark* (1964), the second of Blake Edwards's *Pink Panther* series. An initial felt one later gave way to the tweed version that Peter Sellers made an inseparable part of the Inspector's bumbling character, an ironic nod to his pretensions to style and panache. Sellers himself referred to it as his 'lucky hat'. In *White Hunter, Black Heart* (1990), Clint Eastwood donned a high-crowned cotton twill trilby, while Jack Nicholson wore a purple felt fedora as the Joker in *Batman* (1989). But the most famous movie exposure for the company was indubitably the first three instalments of Steven Spielberg's *Indiana Jones* series starring Harrison Ford. Richard Swales was the chief designer at Herbert Johnson in 1980 when Spielberg and Ford visited the shop and asked for assistance in devising a hat for Indiana Jones's

142
Peter Sellers stars as Inspector Clouseau, complete with a Herbert Johnson tweed trilby, in Blake Edwards's *The Return of the Pink Panther*, 1975.

143
A Herbert Johnson advertisement, *c.*1950, for felt hats, high-crowned and broad brimmed, of the sort that inspired Indiana Jones's iconic headgear.

first outing in *Raiders of the Lost Ark*. He recalled that a wide-brimmed, high-crowned hat called the Poet was chosen, in a shade of sable rabbit felt. The design had been in production since the 1890s, and was only slightly modified for the film, trimming the brim into an ellipse to avoid difficulties with camera angles and narrowing the ribbon to give the sense of an even taller crown. Forty-five hats were supplied for the first film alone, with some sized to fit stunt men and doubles rather than Ford; all were initialled 'IJ' inside. *Raiders'* costume designer, Deborah Nadoolman, has a slightly different version of the story, saying that it was a modified version of Herbert Johnson's Australian design that was selected and that the crown had actually to be lowered, not heightened. 'Indy' fans have been debating the merits and authenticity of the hats ever since, devoting literally thousands of web pages to the accuracy of Richard Swales's recall. But as far as Herbert Johnson are concerned, it was the Poet that they supplied for *Raiders* and it is the Poet that they still sell today.

Tim Glazier was not at Herbert Johnson when the Indiana Jones hats were commissioned. He left the company in the early 1970s to work as a freelance hat and clothing designer, subsequently branching out into corporate marketing. In 1975, not long after his departure, Herbert Johnson were forced by a proposed rent increase from about £3,500 a year to almost £35,000 to leave their old premises at 38, New Bond Street. The new shop was at 13, Old Burlington Street, where they remained until 1988, when they shifted back to New Bond Street.

In retrospect, these moves were symptomatic of a company that was struggling to define its purpose and market in the 1980s. In 1984 the company appointed Robin Benson as managing director and he embarked on an expansion programme designed to capitalize on the

HERBERT JOHNSON,
38, NEW BOND STREET,
LONDON – W. 1.

cachet of the Herbert Johnson name. This was not unlike the expansion moves at Swaine Adeney Brigg in the same decade, and risked concentrating too much attention on the brand rather than the product. Under Benson's management, the company began to market a branded range of outerwear and also a collection of ties, socks, and leather accessories. In June 1987 the textiles giant, John Crowther Group, paid £950,000 to buy both Herbert Johnson (Bond Street) Limited and its sister export company, Herbert Johnson (Sales) Limited, which had been set up in 1976. Crowther vowed to fund Benson's expansion plans, and as part of this plan they relocated the shop in May 1988 to 30, New Bond Street, a few doors from Herbert Johnson's original site. Once this was firmly established, the plan was to open more shops, both in Britain and abroad, and to develop a network of concessions within department stores. Through no fault of Herbert Johnson, however, these plans fizzled out as the over-optimistic decade came crashing to a recessionary end.

In the summer of 1988, just weeks after the move back to New Bond Street, Herbert Johnson's parent company Crowther was taken over by Coloroll, an aggressively ambitious home products group. Coloroll wanted the carpet companies in the Crowther group but not the clothing companies. They immediately sold these, including Herbert Johnson, to a management buy-out team who called themselves the Response Group. In December 1988 the Response Group announced that they would be selling off unwanted companies as soon as possible, with Herbert Johnson at the head of their disposal list. Thus, the company's centenary was not celebrated with quite the enthusiasm that it deserved.

In February 1990, as Coloroll teetered on bankruptcy and the Response Group went into receivership with

debts of £50 million, Herbert Johnson was sold to its own management. The driving force here was Anthony Marangos, who was named as the company's new chairman and managing director. He was a former managing director of Cartier's UK operations and of Laura Ashley in Europe who had been seeking a company of his own to mould for some years. He too had big plans for a network of overseas shops, but he was careful to refocus the company's activities on designing and selling quality hats. He brought in new designers, notably Sylvia Fletcher who revitalized the women's collection, and was rewarded with a much higher profile for the company in the fashion press. In 1993 the young American milliner Prudence also began designing women's hats for Herbert Johnson. But Marangos's tenure at Herbert Johnson was relatively short-lived. In 1996 the company was sold to Swaine Adeney Brigg, and it began to share manufacturing and retail premises with them. After a short time in Swaine Adeney Brigg's new premises at 10, Old Bond Street, Herbert Johnson moved with them to 54, St James's Street. The move heralded a return to Herbert Johnson's earliest trading identity. Women's decorative millinery was discontinued in favour of a focus on smart dress hats for gentlemen, sporting and hunting hats for both men and women, and hats for the military and other uniformed professions. This fitted well with Swaine Adeney Brigg's own approach, particularly with regard to their women customers. Swaine Adeney Brigg have always provided accessories for women who *do* things, whether it be whips and hats for women who ride or leather attachés for women who broker City deals. The emphasis today at Herbert Johnson remains on stylish functionality, for men and women alike.

6

'Pendragon perfection:
the skilled touch of craftsmen'

145 (overleaf)
Queen Elizabeth is presented with
a personalized trunk at the Travel Goods
Factory at Papworth, May 1962.

146 (right)
The first of many royal visits: Queen Mary
and her daughter Princess Mary are shown
around the fledgling Papworth Tuberculosis
Colony by Dr Pendrill Varrier-Jones in 1918.

IN 1997 SWAINE ADENEY BRIGG ACQUIRED THE travel goods division of Papworth Industries, the manufacturing arm of Papworth Village Settlement. Many aspects of the business fitted comfortably into the Swaine Adeney Brigg ethos. There was a passionate concern for quality craftsmanship and a proud history of royal patronage and award-winning design. There was also a history of one family's deep involvement in the business.

A tuberculosis colony founded in Cambridgeshire in 1915, Papworth Village Settlement was the brainchild of a Welsh surgeon, Pendrill Varrier-Jones (1883–1941). During the First World War he was appointed temporary County Tuberculosis Officer for Cambridgeshire and almost immediately began implementing his dream to achieve a more stable, hopeful future for tuberculosis sufferers. Before the antibiotic revolution of the 1940s, which enabled the disease to be cured, sufferers were doomed to a cycle of recovery periods in sanatoria followed by a return to full-time work, a relapse and, eventually, premature death. Tuberculosis was one of the biggest killers in early twentieth-century Britain and, owing to its infectious nature, it was a notifiable disease. But sufferers, especially men responsible for earning their families' upkeep, were fearful of declaring their symptoms because of the enforced unemployment that followed. They often disguised their failing health until the disease was fatally advanced, all the while increasing the risk of infection to people around them. Varrier-Jones's idea was to establish a self-supporting industrial colony, where sufferers could learn to live with the disease, while at the same time doing a level of work that would not aggravate their condition. He began in 1915 by buying a house at Bourn and installing the first few patients in airy wooden shelters. A few months later the Cambridgeshire Tuberculosis Colony won official backing. By early 1918, Varrier-Jones had raised almost £10,000 from donations to buy nearby Papworth Hall, a

neo-classical pile that had been built for Charles Madryll Cheere in 1808–10. In February 1918, twenty-five patients, many of them ex-servicemen, moved in.

Varrier-Jones was a man of extraordinary energy and determination, charming and persuasive when necessary, and at all times iron-willed. Almost immediately he secured royal approval for the venture, and on 9 October 1918 Queen Mary made the first of many royal visits. By then there were already two dozen wooden shelters for the more stable patients, sixty beds in the hall for the seriously ill, eight cottages for the patients' wives and children, and five separate industries: a carpentry and cabinet-making workshop, boot-repair workshop, poultry farm, orchard, and piggery. The industries were a key part of Varrier-Jones's vision. Patients in an improving state of health were gradually assigned paid work of a bearable nature for as many hours a day as they could safely do. The products and produce were sold at commercial rates on the open market to raise funds to make their employment self-funding. New industries were added in 1919, including a printing shop and bindery and a trunk-making workshop. This latter workshop was the origin of Pendragon Travel Goods.

The driving force behind the trunk workshop was a classic Papworth 'colonist'. James Alexander Box was born in London in 1890, the son of a saddler in Greenwich. He was trained up in the family business and had been working for his father when he enlisted in the army in December 1915. He was assigned as a Saddler to the Royal Field Artillery, but in 1918 he was diagnosed with tuberculosis and declared unfit for service. Sent to Papworth, he put his leatherworking skills to good use in establishing the trunk-making department. Surprisingly quickly, Papworth Industries trunks and cases began appearing in prestigious outlets in London, such as Selfridges department store. But because of the unpredictable nature of Papworth's labour force in the early days, there was a danger of orders not being met on time.

Box therefore suggested that Papworth form an alliance with his wife's family, the Charnocks, who owned a bag-making business in London. James Box had married Jane Charnock in 1915; her father George ran the family business with his sons, George Jr (1887–1936), Ernest (1891–1964), and Sidney (1902–1966). The original agreement with Papworth was that the Charnocks would finish off orders that Papworth's workers were struggling to meet. This arrangement worked well, but Dr Varrier-Jones thought it could be improved upon and by February 1923 he had persuaded the Charnocks to shift their business to Papworth. George Sr, who was nearing retirement, stayed behind in London to wind up things, but his three sons spent the rest of their working lives at Papworth and all, in turn, headed the trunk-making department.

With more machinery, experience, and skills, the department grew rapidly. In 1924 Papworth Industries won their first royal warrant as trunk and cabinet-makers to King George V. But in 1925, just as the staff were completing a set of samples for the British Empire Exhibition at Wembley, a fire broke out and the factory was burned to the ground. Very few of the goods or machines could be saved. There was no time to mourn the loss. Before the ashes were cold, Varrier-Jones had

despatched George and Ernest Charnock to London to buy more materials and tools, and the workers were knocking up a temporary factory. Production was underway again in 48 hours and the original orders lost in the fire were completed in a fortnight, including the show pieces for Wembley. Sidney Charnock remembered that the men worked desperately long hours without additional pay to pull off the recovery. It was probably not ideal from a medical point of view, but it proved Varrier-Jones's point about giving people something to live for.

In 1926 Papworth Industries opened a new trunk-making factory to replace the one lost in the fire. Sadly, this was also the year of James Box's death. In his place, George Charnock Jr became the manager of the new factory, which was very well equipped. There were all manner of sewing and cutting machines, a hydraulic press, an automatic platen cutter, and the largest power-operated guillotine in Britain. The workers, however, were still trained in traditional leatherworking skills, so that the factory was able to produce an enormous range of products, from utility fibre suitcases to unique, handcrafted leather folios and attachés. In this respect, the approach was rather like that of Zair's in the whip industry in the late nineteenth century. Papworth made goods at both ends of the market, from solid basics to expensive, luxury items. A section of the new factory was given over entirely to making fibre goods, such as canvas kit bags and vulcanized fibre cabin trunks.

Varrier-Jones was determined to avoid the stigma of the charity bazaar and insisted that the goods produced by Papworth Industries were of the highest standard possible. This approach was rewarded with repeated royal warrants. The 1924 warrant as trunk and cabinet-makers to George V was retained until his death. A new appointment from Edward, Prince of Wales, came in 1931, which was continued until his abdication. Both the new king, George VI, and his consort, Elizabeth, made Papworth their trunk and cabinet-makers; after a hiatus during the Second World War the appointment from Elizabeth was renewed until not long before her death in 2002. Papworth Industries also had a royal warrant from Queen Elizabeth II as travel goods maker from 1972 until the Industries' break up and sale in 1996. A more personal honour was bestowed on Dr Varrier-Jones when he was knighted in 1931.

147
Papworth Industries' original workshop for making trunks and portmanteaux, seen here in about 1920, was functional. After a fire in 1925, it was replaced with a modern and well-equipped factory.

148 (right)
The first royal warrant: George V appoints Cambridgeshire Tuberculosis Colony 'into the place and quality of Trunk Makers & Cabinet Makers to His Majesty' on 28 August 1924.

PENDRAGON PERFECTION

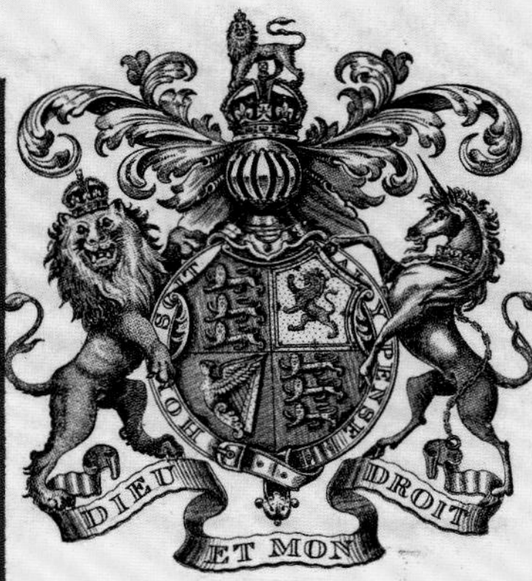

Cancelled on the death
of the holder.

Ulick Alexander
Keeper of the Privy Purse.
9th June 1941.

Privy Purse Office

These are to Certify that by command of

The King

I have appointed

The Cambridgeshire Tuberculosis Colony

into the place and quality of

Trunk Makers & Cabinet Makers

to His Majesty

To hold the said place so long as shall seem fit to The Keeper of the Privy Purse for the time being

This Warrant is granted to

The Right Hon: Sir Thomas Clifford Allbutt K.C.B. F.R.S.

Thomas Musgrave Francis Esq:

Philip Varrier-Jones Esq: M.A. M.R.C.S. L.R.C.P.

trading under the title of

The Cambridgeshire Tuberculosis Colony, Papworth Hall.

and entitles the holder to use the Royal Arms in connection with the Business but it does not carry the right to display the same as a flag or trade mark

It is strictly personal and will become void and must be returned to the Keeper of the Privy Purse on the Death Retirement or Bankruptcy of the person named therein

Given under my hand and Seal this 28th day of August 1924 in the 15th Year of His Majesty's Reign

Wm Parsadle

Keeper of the Privy Purse.

149 (left)
Workers selecting hides for cutting in the new trunk-making workshop built at Papworth after the fire of 1925.

150 (below)
What Papworth Says: a fundraising appeal from 1928. The appeal highlights the difficulties Pendrill Varrier-Jones faced in running a conventional business with unconventional financing. In quoting the leading economist John Maynard Keynes, it also shows the extraordinary level of support he was able to garner for his venture.

151 (right)
The Duke and Duchess of York (the future King George VI and Queen Elizabeth) chat with a patient on a visit to Papworth in 1929.

Varrier-Jones never stinted on money where he thought its investment would bring a good return. Thus Papworth's trunk-makers were backed up by an impressive array of sales representatives across England and Scotland. They emphasized Papworth's willingness to tailor items for particular needs, and thereby won many orders for scientific-instrument cases, salesmen's sample cases, and other custom-made luggage. After the initial showing at Wembley, Papworth also had regular stands at the British Industries Fair and through this medium established contacts with overseas buyers. In the 1930s Papworth cases were being sold in the United States, the Netherlands, France, and Ireland. George Charnock was delighted when the buyer from Saks Fifth Avenue paid a visit to Papworth to select in person the lines for sale in the famous New York store. By this date many of the goods were being marketed under the trademark of Pendragon, which had been Sir Pendrill's nickname as a child. The logo showed an Arthurian dragon with a quill pen. Sir Pendrill was a formidably articulate man, and this may have alluded to his conviction that the pen was mightier than the sword.

The numbers and scale of the trunk-making department's operations exceeded expectations. By 1937 Papworth Industries were producing thirty thousand pieces of luggage a year and the new factory that had seemed so spacious in 1926 was bursting at the seams. Varrier-Jones and his governors therefore committed £20,000 to building a new Travelling Goods Factory, with

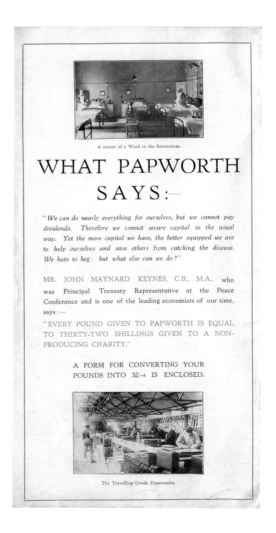

A corner of a Ward in the Sanatorium.

WHAT PAPWORTH SAYS:—

"*We can do nearly everything for ourselves, but we cannot pay dividends. Therefore we cannot secure capital in the usual way. Yet the more capital we have, the better equipped we are to help ourselves and save others from catching the disease. We hate to beg: but what else can we do?*"

MR. JOHN MAYNARD KEYNES, C.B., M.A., who was Principal Treasury Representative at the Peace Conference and is one of the leading economists of our time, says :—

"EVERY POUND GIVEN TO PAPWORTH IS EQUAL TO THIRTY-TWO SHILLINGS GIVEN TO A NON-PRODUCING CHARITY."

A FORM FOR CONVERTING YOUR POUNDS INTO 32/-s IS ENCLOSED.

The Travelling Goods Department.

30,000 square feet of workshop space, overhead power plugs, and mobile machinery. George Charnock did not live to see the new factory, however; he died in 1936 and his brother Ernest succeeded him as departmental manager. Ernest's background was similar to that of James Box; as a skilled leatherworker he had served in the First World War as a Saddler in the Royal Field Artillery.

The new factory was completed exactly a month before the outbreak of the Second World War in September 1939. It was fortuitous timing, for the trunk-making department was superbly placed for switching production from leisure and business travel goods to wartime needs. The regular lines were shelved and by early 1940 the department had two hundred and fifty employees working fulltime on military contracts. The range of goods produced was mind-boggling, from fibre attaché cases for the Admiralty to canvas covers for Spitfire, Halifax, and Stirling aircraft. New technology was developed on the job, such as applying heat to mould the fibre attachés into shape. Production runs were enormous too: in one week the factory turned out a thousand canvas suitcases and five thousand attachés. The war also brought an unexpected boost to the factory's leatherworking capacity. In mid-1940, just after the evacuation from Dunkirk, Papworth Industries won an emergency subcontract to produce thirty thousand sets of leather personal equipment for infantrymen. Each set contained eleven pieces, including belt and braces, utility pouch, cartridge carrier, and mess-tin carrier. Papworth called it the Dunkirk Order, and Sidney Charnock looked back on it as the crowning achievement of the department's wartime service. The men were divided into shifts so that work could continue around the clock. Much to everyone's amazement, they met the first order on time, and then went on to manufacture another thirty-five thousand sets. In all they made seven hundred and fifteen thousand pieces of leather kit in a matter of weeks, an achievement all the more remarkable given that many of the workers not only were suffering from tuberculosis but also were engaged in the Home Guard, Special Police, and other civil defence forces.

The war witnessed another major change at Papworth. On 30 January 1941, Sir Pendrill Varrier-Jones died of heart failure. It was a tragically early death and many Papworth people feared that the settlement had taken a fatal blow, but his legacy was secure. At the war's end Papworth Village Settlement had hospital and sanatorium accommodation for three hundred and fifty men and women undergoing treatment. There were another two

152, 153

The front cover and detail from the *Pendragon Travel Goods Catalogue* of April 1951. The artist's impression of a Highland setting with railway evokes all the stylishness of travelling by steam train. Specializing in goods made in leather, canvas and fibre, Papworth Industries prefaced their catalogue with an invitation to their 'friends at Home and Abroad' to visit the Pendragon Travel Goods Factory at Cambridge, claiming that it was one of the largest in the country.

The inside detail shows a vulcanized fibre suitcase 'specially designed for easy packing'. The coat hangers in the lid enabled two ladies' or men's suits 'to be carried without fear of creasing'.

154

A Papworth Industries catalogue from 1957 uses the imagery of aeroplanes and advanced railways to illustrate the company's determined modernization after the war.

hundred former patients housed in hostels and cottages, along with their spouses and children. Papworth Industries, which were staffed and managed by former patients, employed an average of four hundred people daily, at full trade union rates, and had an annual turnover of £430,000.

Inevitably, there were big changes at Papworth after the war. On 5 July 1948 its hospital and surgical units were brought under state control as part of the new National Health Service. Their management, however, remained in the hands of the local governing committee. In time, Papworth Hospital went on to become a world leader in heart surgery and in 1979 it was the scene of Britain's first successful heart transplant. This was sadly ironic given Varrier-Jones's own death from heart failure, but it was a natural extension of Papworth's skills. The surgeons he had gathered together necessarily became experts in lung surgery and it was but a short step from there to cardio-thoracic medicine.

Meanwhile, antibiotics began to make dramatic headway against tuberculosis and there was a welcome falling off in new admissions to the settlement. In 1957 the governing body decided to admit people with other disabling conditions, but the philosophy of the settlement remained much the same as before. Papworth was not offering a magical cure; it was offering a way of living with a disability and of earning a meaningful living.

For the trunk-making department, returning to civilian production after the war was a major challenge. Production methods, supplies, and the market had changed dramatically. There was a shortage of hides, and those available were of variable quality, supplies having been diminished by wartime demand. Air travel posed new challenges too, as luggage needed to be lightweight and robust, which meant changes both to shape and to construction materials. Out went square corners and full-grain leather, and in came rounded corners, plywood frames, and moulded bases rather than individually constructed ones. An experimental department was set up to develop new lines and exploit new materials, such as tubular aluminium case frames and the rapidly increasing range of plastic fabrics. But plastic and vinyl, Papworth soon discovered, were words that the public distrusted; so the trunk-making department named their versions Dragonhide and Lionide. Plastics were particularly helpful in developing soft-bodied luggage, such as foldable suit bags. At Papworth, this form of 'hanging wardrobe' was christened the Pendrobe.

None of these changes was particularly easy for the trunk-making department, and many of the older

nest material

Model 218 C.C. Hide Suitcase (above)
Please see page 9 for specification.

Model 228. Hide Moulded Suitcase
Golden colour aniline hide or coach hide on a special moulded aero-ply foundation. Good nickel plated fittings. Centre clip (except on 24"). Drill lining and web straps in body. A very light case yet with maximum capacity. Model 228 D.—Made in Dragonide fabric, with chestnut, golden or Rawhide effect. Gent's and ladies' models available.
Sizes : 24" × 15" × 8", 26" × 16" × 8½", 28" × 17" × 9", 30" × 17½" × 9½".

workers resented the introduction of new styles and materials and increased mechanization. But the department never lost touch with its roots in hand-made leather goods. While the mass market seemed to lose interest in hand-stitched cases, there was still a rare breed of client willing to pay for full-grain leather suitcases and attachés made exactly as they had been since before the war. And to meet this demand, Papworth Industries continued to apprentice new workers in the old craft sections whenever possible. At the time no one foresaw the rise of cheaper, rival manufactures from Taiwan and Japan, but ultimately the trunk-making department was to be saved by this decision to preserve the old skills alongside the new.

In 1950 the old skills were put to good use in a new marketing venture, when the department began to develop suites of products that could command by themselves a full-page advertisement or an entire window display. The first of these was a set of luggage comprising six pieces for women and three for men. The woman's range had a make-up case, hat box, weekender, suitcase, two-suiter case, and a full-sized wardrobe that held up to nine dresses. The set was made of contrasting golden and buff full-grain hides, with hand-tooled effects, and each piece was lined with tartan moiré silk. But beneath the traditional exterior was a lightweight aluminium and plywood frame. It was a top-of-the-range set and won Papworth considerable publicity. England's favourite ballerina, Margot Fonteyn, was one of the first customers.

The Charnocks continued to steer the trunk-making department through the interesting post-war years. Ernest remained in charge until his death in 1964, aged 72. At that point, Sidney, the youngest of the three

155 (left)
Making suitcases at Papworth Industries, July 1960. The rounded corners and lightweight construction point to the increasing popularity of air travel but also to a post-war world in which porters and servants were increasingly scarce.

156 (right)
A Papworth Industries advertisement aimed at the upper end of the travel goods market from 1961. Ultimately, Papworth's trunk-making department was saved by the decision to preserve quality hand-finished production alongside cheaper lines.

157 (above)
Another version of the Pendragon Travel Goods trademark (see p. 135). It has recently been adopted by Swaine Adeney Brigg for their recently revived Pendragon brand of luggage and leather goods.

1st class travellers

PENDRAGON luggage offers something for every journey.
Models illustrated here :
719 D.E. Hatcase ; 41a Train Case
(*in Luxan or Vaumol hide*).
719 D.E. Zip Valises
(*in Luxan or Vaumol hide*).

Papworth Industries

Papworth Everard CAMBRIDGE *Telephone :* CAXTON 271

SHOWROOMS **LONDON** : 26 FITZROY SQ. W1 *EUSTON 3295* **GLASGOW** : 5 DIXON ST. C1 *CENTRAL 6054*

LEATHERGOODS, October 1961   49

brothers, took the helm. One of his first acts was to write a short history of the department, from which much of the information in this history has been taken. But he died not long after his brother, in 1966, and this brought to an end the Charnock family's 43-year association with Papworth Industries.

As a whole Papworth Industries continued to flourish into the 1970s. Some of their best-known products came from a coach-building workshop established in 1962, which won contracts to build bright yellow Post Office vans and the iconic Green Goddess fire engines. By the middle of the decade, turnover was £2 million, with a surplus of some £150,000. Papworth Village Settlement was a charity set up as a company limited by guarantee. As such it had no shareholders, only members. Being part of Papworth Village Settlement any surpluses made by Papworth Industries were ploughed back into the charity for further staff training and improvements to the facilities. The trunk-making department in the mid-1970s had about a hundred employees. This was down on the wartime peak and indicated a trend towards fewer workers concentrating on more high-value lines.

When Tim Eiloart from the *New Scientist* visited Papworth in 1976 he was pleasantly surprised by the quality of the products. 'In Travel Goods', he noticed, 'there were leather attaché cases, tool cases, they even make the velvet lined boxes which hold a lord's regalia. There were a number of 'seconds' that looked like firsts to me.' The Industries' administration manager, Bert Dearson, explained the philosophy behind the strict rule on seconds:

> We cannot tell people to lower standards. This one probably failed because of that little dent in the leather there . . . It's the same here everywhere. We can't build Defence vehicles to the toughest military specs and then say, 'OK relax the standards a bit' for the next batch of lorries.

In fact the future of travel goods at Papworth Industries lay in this approach. As cheap foreign imports weakened Papworth's hold on the popular luggage market, production turned towards smaller volumes of high-quality items. There were also investments in design, and in 1983 Papworth's Yuki Collection of handbags, overnight

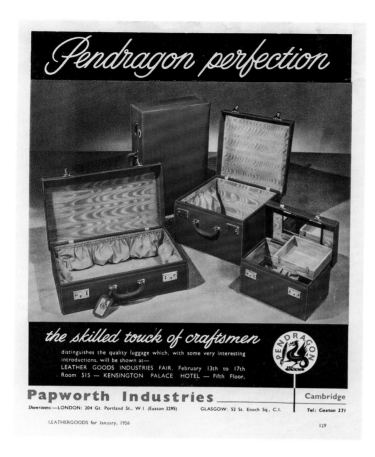

158
Pendragon perfection: an advertisement for a woman's travelling set in red leather and moiré silk, 1956.

159
A travelling wardrobe trunk and matching travelling case made for Princess Margaret by Papworth Industries on the occasion of the royal family's tour to South Africa in 1947. One trunk each was made for the Princesses Elizabeth and Margaret and another for their mother. Each trunk was built to hold eighteen full-length dresses; large ball-bearings were slotted in the base to make them mobile. Of the commission, Sidney Charnock observed that: 'The privilege of making trunks for the Royal Family is without doubt a great honour, but behind the scene it is a harassing period, involving many a headache.'

160 (right)
Ballet dancer Margot Fonteyn embarks from the BOAC terminal at Victoria, London, on a tour of the USA and Canada in 1951. Her luggage is a personalized suite made by Papworth Industries.

bags, and briefcases won a coveted Design Council Award. But besides shifts in the market, there were also changes in society's attitudes to disability. In 1996, Papworth's governors decided to focus on helping people with disabilities acquire skills for living and working in the wider world, beyond the traditional sheltered environment of the settlement. As a consequence, Papworth's industries were sold off as separate, viable concerns. The travel goods business and the Pendragon brand were bought by Swaine Adeney Brigg in 1997. The Papworth and Pendragon names seem to have been somewhat interchangeable. By 2002, Swaine Adeney Brigg had dropped the Pendragon name in favour of Papworth Travel Goods. The new owners retained the original workforce, but shifted the manufacturing to Bar Hill just to the north-west of Cambridge, where they were soon after joined by Swaine Adeney Brigg's craftsmen from Great Chesterford. Even today, there are one or two workers who were born at Papworth, children of early colonists, who grew up listening to their parents' stories of the big war orders or reminiscences of the legendary Sir Pendrill Varrier-Jones. It is in honour of his vision and achievements that Swaine Adeney Brigg have recently revived his Pendragon brand of luggage and leather goods. The rigorous standards of production that he set for his workers, in spite of their poor health and the virulent prejudice they often faced from outsiders, remain an inspiration today.

7
Looking Ahead

THE WORLD ECONOMIC CLIMATE IS UNSTABLE AND threatening, and many good businesses may not live to see the next ten years. Swaine Adeney Brigg's ability to survive as a business and as a brand has always been grounded in craftsmanship and skill as well as in quality of materials and construction. It is the company's strongly held belief that customers, existing and future, will choose the long-lasting quality of Swaine Adeney Brigg products and hence ensure the company's continuing survival.

The resurgence of activity in the company's repairs department tells an important part of the story. It is not just a matter of cost-cutting by customers in hard times; there is a conscious decision not to renew. A cherished attaché case or item of travel luggage carries memories and value much as a piece of antique furniture does. This endorses the company's ethos of built-in longevity.

Swaine Adeney Brigg have now chosen to realize the full potential of their brands in leather goods, umbrellas, hats, clothing, whips, and sticks across the world. There are plans afoot to add new designs while maintaining their long-standing range of key products. At the same time they are seeking out more skilled workers as well as training young people through apprenticeships. When new products or businesses become available, they are ready to explore new opportunities. For example, they acquired the recently shut-down trench-coat production facility of Aquascutum in Corby, Northamptonshire, with a view to improving their productive capacity for umbrella covers, canvas bags, and light leather bags as well as making trench coats to complement their umbrellas. With staff numbers there expected to be around 25 to 30, skilled jobs that would otherwise have been lost to the Far East have been rescued.

161 (above)
Trimming a sheet of cowhide for hand-sewn attaché case handles.

162 (below)
Checking goods before despatch.

148

163 (left)
Sewing the canopy of an umbrella to
its frame at the Norfolk workshop of
Swaine Adeney Brigg.

164 (above)
A rack of umbrella sit-ups forms the backdrop
to a craftsman at his bench, where he is affixing
the stem to the stretchers of an umbrella.

165 (right)
Handles of finished umbrellas in
stripped ash, hickory, and cherry.

Modern retailing must embrace the internet as
a selling tool and Swaine Adeney Brigg continue to
develop online marketing with a view to reaching every
corner of the globe. But traditional retailing has not been
forgotten, for they have made a commitment to open
three new stores in London, one in their traditional
area of St James's, one in Mayfair and one in the City
of London. In this way they will reach and service all
of their traditional customers and further expose their
products to those who have yet to enjoy them.

Their tradition is to make any bespoke product that
their customers require. Recent output has included
a leather covered box to take a favourite tea set for an
American actress, a portmanteau for the principal of a
famous and exclusive London hotel, and a set of attaché
cases for all of the ministers of a sovereign state.

Their mission is always to give true service and
support to their customers throughout the world and
supply exclusive hand-made products using the finest
quality materials. This is how they define luxury.

166 (above left)
This craftsman, shown hand-stitching an attaché-case handle held in a spring-loaded vice, originally worked at the Great Chesterford works, near Saffron Walden.

167 (above right)
Beginning his career at Papworth Industries making items in leather and canvas in 1959, this craftsman is shown machine-stitching a leather case.

168 (left)
High-quality leather goods and umbrellas are worthy of repair, and refurbishment is very much part of Swaine Adeney Brigg's ethos. Here a well-loved briefcase has been dismantled to replace worn-out elements.

General events

1746   The King's Army defeats the Jacobites at the Battle of Culloden (16 April).

1750   The Jockey Club is founded in London; it relocates to Newmarket in 1752.

1753   Hugo Meynell, a pioneer of high-speed fox-hunting across open ground, becomes Master of the Foxhounds at the Quorn Hunt in Leicestershire.

1760   George II dies; his grandson succeeds as King George III.

1768   The first four-day royal race meeting is held at Ascot.

1781   An umbrella is listed among stolen goods for the first time in a trial at the Old Bailey in London.

1783   *Instructions for Ladies in Riding*, a short manual of horsemanship for women, is published by a London riding master named Carter.

1784   The first official mail coach runs from Bristol to London.

1793   War declared by Britain against Revolutionary France.

1796   George Bryan 'Beau' Brummell becomes a captain in the 10th Hussars and exerts a powerful influence on men's fashion, including fastidious attention to understated, elegant accessories.

1802   The short-lived Peace of Amiens begins.

1803   War with France resumes in May.

1811   George, Prince of Wales, becomes Prince Regent on the permanent incapacitation of his father, George III.

1814   After Napoleon's surrender in May, aristocratic social intercourse across Europe resumes in full with the celebrated Congress of Vienna.

1815   The Battle of Waterloo, 18 June, brings twenty-five years of almost continuous warfare in Europe to an end.

1820   George III dies; his son the Prince Regent succeeds him as King George IV.

1825   The Stockton and Darlington Railway opens; it is the first public steam-powered train service.

1829   George Shillibeer introduces the omnibus to London; the first route runs from the Yorkshire Stingo in Marylebone to the Bank of England in the City.

Swaine Adeney Brigg

1762   John Ross, a saddler probably of Scottish origin, opens a whip-making shop at 8, Marylebone Street, London, around this year.

1769   After a fire in Marylebone Street, John Ross moves his whip manufactory to 238, Piccadilly.

1769   Newspaper notices describe John Ross as whip-maker to the Duke of Cumberland; the Duke is a younger brother of George III, Prince Henry Frederick.

1782   James Swaine is apprenticed to Benjamin Griffith & Co., whip-makers of 322, High Holborn.

1786   John Köhler opens a horn and trumpet manufactory at 9, Whitcomb Street, London, around this year.

1798   John Ross sells his whip manufactory to James Swaine and Benjamin Slocock; the new company is called Swaine & Co. Swaine & Co. advertise themselves as 'Whip-Makers to His Majesty', George III.

1805   Charles Brigg opens a shop for military plumes at 3, Little Warwick Street, London, around this time; he subsequently shifts to 63, Charing Cross.

1818   Swaine & Co. provide the whips for the funeral of Queen Charlotte, consort of George III.

1822   Swaine & Co. move to 224, Piccadilly, about this year.

1825   Benjamin Slocock Sr retires from Swaine & Co.; William Isaac replaces him as a partner.

1828   Thomas Edward Brigg, son of Charles, opens a feather and umbrella manufactory at 23, St James's Street, London. He and his father are declared bankrupt, but continue trading.

1830   George IV dies; his brother succeeds him as King William IV. The first mail delivery by train takes place on the Liverpool and Manchester Railway.

1831   The Game Act establishes close seasons to protect grouse and other game birds from over-hunting.

1837   William IV dies; his niece succeeds him as Queen Victoria.

1840   Queen Victoria marries Prince Albert of Saxe-Coburg and Gotha. Henry Holland of Birmingham patents tubular steel ribs for umbrellas.

1846   The last mail coach departs from London.

1850   Side-saddles with a third pommel, offering more stability and comfort for women riders, become commercially available around this time.

1851   Samuel Fox of Stocksbridge patents the 'Paragon' umbrella frame with U-shaped steel ribs and stretchers.

1861   Albert, Prince Consort, dies and his widow Queen Victoria retreats from public life; their son Albert Edward, Prince of Wales, becomes a figurehead for equestrian sports.

1862   The 'Brighton Age' is the last truly commercial stage coach to depart from London; subsequent coaching revivals are oriented towards leisure and tourism.

1863   Albert Edward, Prince of Wales, marries Princess Alexandra of Denmark.

1869   The first polo match is played in England on Hounslow Heath between the 10th Hussars and the 9th Lancers.

1870   The Coaching Club is founded in London, with a mission to keep alive four-in-hand coaching as a leisure activity.

1875   The Hurlingham Polo Committee is founded in London and draws up the rules for the sport in England.

1885   Henry Somerset, 8th Duke of Beaufort, publishes *Hunting*, the first title in the *Badminton Library of Sports and Pastimes*.

1830   John Augustus Köhler, grand-nephew of the horn-maker John Köhler, opens an instrument-making shop at 35, Henrietta Street, Covent Garden.

1832   Swaine & Co. patent the Humane Safety Arab Whip, a riding whip with an inbuilt flywhisk.

1835   Swaine & Co. move to 185, Piccadilly; the company uses the name Swaine & Isaac from this date. John Zair founds a whip-manufactory in Birmingham around this time.

1837   James Swaine dies, aged 70; his son Edward runs Swaine & Isaac in partnership with William Isaac.

1845   James Adeney, nephew and son-in-law of Edward Swaine, becomes a partner in what is now called Swaine, Isaac & Adeney.

1848   William Isaac retires; the company is now called Swaine & Adeney.

1851   Swaine & Adeney win first prize at the Great Exhibition.

1852   Thomas Brigg's son William joins the family business around this time, which now trades as Thomas Brigg & Son.

1865   John Zair's sons, George and John Jr, take over the family whip-making business as Messrs. G. & J. Zair around this year, and build new premises at 111–19, Bishop Street, Birmingham.

1866   Thomas Brigg's youngest son, Thomas Jr, joins the family business around this time, which now trades as Thomas Brigg & Sons.

1872   Herbert Lewis Johnson is apprenticed to Lincoln, Bennett & Co., hat manufacturers of Piccadilly, where his father William is one of the managing partners.

1878   John Augustus Köhler dies; his son, Augustus Charles, switches manufacturing at J. Köhler & Son from keyed instruments to natural coach and hunting horns.

1879   Augustus Charles Köhler publishes *The Coach Horn: What to Blow, How to Blow it.* G. & J. Zair win First Special Prize for their whips at the Sydney International Exhibition. Charles Henry Dumenil registers C D as a maker's mark; it appears on many walking sticks and umbrella handles made for Thomas Brigg & Sons.

1880   G. & J. Zair win First Prize for their whips at the Melbourne International Exhibition.

1885   Thomas Brigg & Sons are appointed umbrella-makers to Queen Victoria. G. & J. Zair register G & J Z as a maker's mark.

1888 The first models of Karl Benz's Patent Motorwagen are sold in Germany and France; it is the first petrol-powered automobile.

1897 The Royal Automobile Club is founded in London.

1900 Genteel women riders begin to experiment with cross-saddle riding from around this time.

1901 Queen Victoria dies; Albert Edward, Prince of Wales, succeeds her as King Edward VII.

1902 Motors and Motor-Driving is the last book to be published in the Duke of Beaufort's Badminton Library of Sports and Pastimes.

1906 The Automobile Club de France organizes the first Grand Prix motor race on a purpose-built circuit at Le Mans.

1910 Edward VII dies; his son succeeds him as King George V.

1914 The Great War commences; it will be the last major conflict to rely on horses.
The last horse-drawn omnibus makes its run in London.

1918 The Great War ends; the walking stick acquires a new prominence as a mobility aid for injured veterans.

1924 The British Empire Exhibition opens at Wembley, showcasing products from all but two of the Empire's fifty-eight countries.

1929 A catastrophic crash in world stock markets and the ensuing panic usher in the Great Depression.

1935 Wallace Carothers invents nylon at the Dupont Experimental Station in Wilmington, Delaware.

1936 George V dies; his son becomes King Edward VIII; the new king abdicates in December of the same year and is succeeded by his brother as King George VI.

1939 The Second World War begins; by early 1942 the British Army's cavalry regiments are fully mechanized.

1889 Herbert Lewis Johnson and Edward John Glazier open a hat-retailing business at 45, New Bond St, London, under the name of Herbert Johnson.

1895 Herbert Johnson hatters move to 38, New Bond St around this year.

1899 Thomas Brigg & Sons open a showroom in Paris at 33, avenue de l'Opéra.

1901 Herbert Johnson are appointed hatters to Edward VII.

1902 Edward Swaine Adeney Jr registers ESA as a maker's mark.

1907 Swaine & Adeney buy horn-maker J. Köhler & Son; they concentrate future production on hunting horns.

1908 Thomas Brigg & Sons win the Grand Prix for umbrellas at the Franco-British Exhibition in Paris.

1910 Swaine & Adeney are registered as a limited company.

1915 Pendrill Verrier-Jones founds the Cambridgeshire Tuberculosis Colony.

1918 The Cambridgeshire Tuberculosis Colony moves to Papworth Hall and becomes known as the Papworth Village Settlement.

1919 Thomas Brigg & Sons buy the goodwill and stock of Messrs Betaille, a French parasol-maker.
James Alexander Box, a saddler suffering from tuberculosis, founds the trunk-making department at Papworth.

1923 The Charnock brothers, George, Ernest, and Sidney, move to Papworth to improve quality in the trunk-making department.

1924 G. & J. Zair are registered as a limited company.
Papworth Industries are appointed trunk and cabinet-makers to George V.

1926 Papworth Industries open a new trunk-making factory.

1927 Swaine & Adeney Ltd buy G. & J. Zair Ltd; they continue manufacturing at the Birmingham factory until 1965.

1928 Herbert Lewis Johnson retires and sells his share in the hat business to Edward Glazier.

1929 Edward Glazier registers his hat business as Herbert Johnson (Bond Street) Ltd.

1931 Thomas Brigg & Sons are registered as a limited company.

1931 Swaine & Adeney Ltd buy Frederick Bedford Smith Ltd, manufacturer of polo equipment.

1932 Herbert Johnson Ltd develop the gossamer-body crash helmet for the racing driver Lieutenant-Colonel Goldie Gardener around this time.

1936 Thomas Brigg & Sons celebrate their centenary, 108 years after the founding of the shop at 23, St James's Street.

1938 British Prime Minister Neville Chamberlain carries a Brigg umbrella to talks with Adolf Hitler in Munich.

1939 Papworth Industries open a new Travelling Goods Factory.

1940 Britain introduces an emergency Purchase Tax on goods deemed to be luxury items; it begins at the rate of 33⅓ per cent, rising to 100 per cent in 1943.

1945 The Second World War ends; rationing of foods and some manufacturing materials in Britain continues until 1954.

1946 Britain reduces its Purchase Tax on luxuries from 100 to 33⅓ per cent; it soon rises again and is levied throughout the 1950s at either 50 or 60 per cent.
The International Convention for the Regulation of Whaling is signed, marking an international effort to regulate commercial whaling and conserve whale stocks; this affects the supply of whalebone for whip-making.

1948 The Morris Minor debuts at the Earls Court Motor Show in London, promising affordable motoring to people on modest incomes.

1952 George VI dies; his daughter becomes Queen Elizabeth II.

1958 The British Overseas Airways Corporation (BOAC) opens a passenger jet service across the Atlantic; jet air travel begins to revolutionize the luggage industry.

1964 Mary Quant launches the miniskirt at her boutique on the King's Road in Chelsea, heralding a rapid relaxation in dress codes for both sexes.

1973 Britain joins the European Economic Community (EEC); the old Purchase Tax on luxuries is replaced by a more widely applied Value Added Tax of 10%.

1978 Deng Xiaoping, leader of the Chinese Communist Party, initiates market reforms that ultimately result in the emergence of China as a major importer of European luxury goods.

1987 Black Monday (19 October) sees world stock markets crash and brings a sudden end to the high spending 1980s.

1991 The Soviet Empire collapses; the liberalization of the Russian economy brings a new class of millionaire buyer to the luxury goods market.

2005 The Hunting Act 2004, which bans hunting with dogs, comes into force in England and Wales.

1940 Thomas Brigg & Sons lose their Paris showroom to the German occupation of France.
Papworth Industries fulfil the 'Dunkirk Order': 715,000 pieces of leather kit for infantrymen.

1943 Swaine & Adeney Ltd merge with Thomas Brigg & Sons Ltd to form Swaine, Adeney, Brigg & Sons Ltd.

1957 Racing driver Stirling Moss wins the British Grand Prix at Aintree wearing a Herbert Johnson crash helmet. Papworth Village Settlement admits people with disabling conditions other than tuberculosis.

1964 Swaine Adeney Brigg cease production at Zair's factory in Birmingham.

1968 Patrick Macnee's character of Steed in the British television series The Avengers dons a steel-rimmed bowler hat made by Herbert Johnson.

1975 Rent increases force Herbert Johnson to move to 13, Old Burlington St.

1980 Richard Swales, chief designer at Herbert Johnson, remodels the Poet, a wide-brimmed felt hat, for Harrison Ford's character Indiana Jones in Stephen Spielberg's Raiders of the Lost Ark.

1987 The John Crowther Group, a textiles conglomerate, buys Herbert Johnson (Bond Street) Ltd.

1988 Herbert Johnson move to 30, New Bond St.

1990 Herbert Johnson are sold to their own management under the leadership of Anthony Marangos.

1995 Swaine Adeney Brigg move to 10, Old Bond St.

1996 Swaine Adeney Brigg buy Herbert Johnson.

1997 Papworth's governing body close their sheltered workshops and sell off Papworth Industries; Swaine Adeney Brigg buy the travel goods division of Papworth Industries.

1998 Swaine Adeney Brigg move to 54, St James's St.

2009 Norfolk businessman Roger Gawn buys Swaine Adeney Brigg.

2011 Swaine Adeney Brigg make the postilion whips for the wedding of William, Duke of Cambridge, and Miss Catherine Middleton.

List of Illustrations

1 Invoice from John Ross to George Wyndham, 3rd Earl of Egremont, 1779. (West Sussex Record Office: PHA 8079. Courtesy of The Right Honourable Lord Egremont)

2 Crown Estates survey of Marylebone Street, 2 July 1771. CRES 39/124. (The National Archives)

3 *West Country Mails at the Gloucester Coffee House, Piccadilly*. Engraving by Christian Rosenberg, after James Pollard, 1828. (© The Trustees of the British Museum)

4 Crown Estates survey of six houses on the south side of Piccadilly, 1811. CRES 39/141. (The National Archives)

5 Invoice from James Swaine & Co. to Frederick Booth, Esq., 26 September 1798. Q/STB/121. (City of London, London Metropolitan Archives)

6 Trade card for Griffith & Son, Whip Manufacturers, engraved by Henry Thomas Green, c.1825–40. (© The Trustees of the British Museum)

7 Invoice from Swaine & Co. to Mr Hinton Kelly, November 1802. (SAB Archive/Photograph by James Austin)

8 Opening from a Swaine & Co. account book, 1818. (SAB Archive/Photograph by James Austin)

9 *His Majesty King Geo. III Returning from Hunting*. Etching with aquatint by Matthew Dubourg, after James Pollard, 1820. (The Royal Collection © 2012, Her Majesty Queen Elizabeth II)

10 Equestrian portrait of George IV when he was Prince of Wales. Oil painting by George Stubbs, 1791. (The Royal Collection © 2012, Her Majesty Queen Elizabeth II)

11 *A View near Petersham*. Etching by William Heath, 1823. (© The Trustees of the British Museum)

12 *Divers Drivers. A Cab. A Jarvey. A Long Trot. An Out & Outer*. Etching by William Heath, 1827. (© The Trustees of the British Museum)

13 Piccadilly, from John Tallis, *London Street Views*, no. 23, London, c.1838; detail. (Digital Collections and Archives, Tufts University)

14 Swaine & Isaac trade card, c.1837–40. (© The Trustees of the British Museum)

15 Piccadilly, from John Tallis, *London Street Views*, no. 23, London, c.1838; detail. (Digital Collections and Archives, Tufts University)

16 Swaine & Adeney riding crop with onyx knop given to Queen Victoria at Christmas, 1843; detail. (The Royal Collection © 2012, Her Majesty Queen Elizabeth II)

17 Two side-saddle whips by Swaine & Adeney, c.1860–1910. (SAB Archive/Photograph by James Austin)

18 Equestrian portrait of Queen Victoria. Oil painting by Alfred, Count d'Orsay, c.1846. (© Crown copyright: UK Government Art Collection)

19 Swaine & Isaac walking stick with carved coral knop and Malacca shaft, given by Queen Victoria to Prince Albert in 1845. (The Royal Collection © 2012, Her Majesty Queen Elizabeth II)

20 Prince Albert in riding costume. Watercolour by William Drummond, c.1839–40. (Photograph © Philip Mould Ltd, London/The Bridgeman Art Library)

21 Four prize whips made by Swaine & Adeney for international exhibitions, c.1851–62, formerly in the Swaine Adeney Brigg Archive. (Photograph by Peter Tebbit)

22 Swaine & Adeney whip mounts from Cassell's *Illustrated Exhibitor*, no. 27, 6 December 1851, p. 510. (SAB Archive/Photograph by James Austin)

23 *Case of Whips and Canes. Prize Medal. Messrs. Swaine and Adeney*. Engraving from the *Illustrated Exhibitor*, 20 September 1862, p. 144. 7957.ee.13. (© The British Library Board)

24 Edward Albert, Prince of Wales, in shooting costume. Oil painting by Frank William Dicey, 1875. (The Royal Collection © 2012, Her Majesty Queen Elizabeth II)

25 *Princess Alexandra's Arrival Procession Passing Temple Bar, 7 March 1863*. Watercolour by Robert Charles Dudley, 1863. (The Royal Collection © 2012, Her Majesty Queen Elizabeth II)

26 Swaine & Adeney trade card, c.1865. (SAB Archive/Photograph by James Austin)

27 Swaine & Adeney trade card, c.1889. (SAB Archive/Photograph by James Austin)

28 Swaine & Adeney blackthorn carriage whip made for the house of Rochefoucauld-Doudeauville, c.1880–1900. (© RMN/Thierry Ollivier)

29 Swaine & Adeney riding crop of plaited horsehair, presented by Queen Victoria to a grandchild in 1883; detail. (The Royal Collection © 2012, Her Majesty Queen Elizabeth II)

30 Floor plan of 185, Piccadilly, from a lease renewal, 1889. (SAB Archive/Photograph by James Austin)

31 *Fores's Contrasts. The Driver of 1832. The Driver of 1852*. Aquatint by John Harris, after Henry Alken, 1852. (Yale Center for British Art, Paul Mellon Collection, USA/The Bridgeman Art Library)

32 Shafts from hunting whips made by Swaine & Adeney and Zair, c.1900–35. (Courtesy of Mrs Lindsey Knapp, Victoria Gallery/Photograph by James Austin)

33 Two Swaine & Adeney walking sticks with gold match-holders, c.1906. (Courtesy of Michael German Antiques Ltd/Photograph by James Austin)

34 German-language Swaine & Adeney trade card, c.1895. (SAB Archive/Photograph by James Austin)

35 Köhler-pattern hunting horn in copper and silver by Swaine & Adeney, c.1907–30. (Courtesy of Mrs Lindsey Knapp, Victoria Gallery/Photograph by James Austin)

36 *The Meet*. Oil painting by Hermann Conrad Fleury, c.1910. (Private Collection/The Bridgeman Art Library)

37 *Hunt Servants' Whips and Other Requisites*. Sales catalogue by Swaine & Adeney, c.1907–10. (SAB Archive/Photograph by James Austin)

38 *Hunt Servants' Whips, Hunting Horns, Spurs, &c.* Sales catalogue by Swaine & Adeney Ltd, c.1910. (SAB Archive/Photograph by James Austin)

39 Gentleman's hunting whip with stag-horn handle and silver collar, with marks for Edward Swaine Adeney Jr, London 1935. (Courtesy of Mrs Lindsey Knapp, Victoria Gallery/Photograph by James Austin)

40 Page from Swaine & Adeney *Hunt Servants' Whips* catalogue, c.1907–10, advertising hunting accessories. (SAB Archive/Photograph by James Austin)

41 *Polo at Hurlingham*. Oil painting by Henry Jamyn Brooks, 1890. (Private Collection/Wingfield Sporting Gallery, London, UK/The Bridgeman Art Library)

42 Maker's mark for Edward Swaine Adeney Jr, registered in 1910. (Courtesy of Mrs Lindsey Knapp, Victoria Gallery/Photograph by James Austin)

43 SWAINE branding from a Swaine & Adeney hunting crop, c.1920. (Courtesy of Mrs Lindsey Knapp, Victoria Gallery/Photograph by James Austin)

44 Metal pin from a Swaine & Adeney hunting crop, c.1920. (Courtesy of Mrs Lindsey Knapp, Victoria Gallery/Photograph by James Austin)

45 Advertisement for the Eatanswill, from a *War Equipment* catalogue, c.1915–18. (SAB Archive/Photograph by James Austin)

46 Title page from '*Good Hands*' 1750–1927, published by Swaine & Adeney Ltd, c.1927. X.619/6107. (© The British Library Board)

47 Illustration of whip-making (p. 8) from '*Good Hands*' 1750–1927, published by Swaine & Adeney Ltd, c.1927. X.619/6107. (© The British Library Board)

48 Shop sign painted by William Nicholson for Swaine & Adeney, c.1900–30, formerly in the Swaine Adeney Brigg Archive. (Photograph by Peter Tebbit)

49 Swaine & Adeney hunting companion in pigskin case, c.1930; showing the original box. (Courtesy of Mrs Lindsey Knapp, Victoria Gallery/Photograph by James Austin)

50 Swaine & Adeney hunting companion in pigskin case, c.1930; showing the pigskin case opened out with contents. (Courtesy of Mrs Lindsey Knapp, Victoria Gallery/Photograph by James Austin)

51 Swaine & Adeney advertisement for walking sticks and umbrellas with carved animal heads, c.1910. (SAB Archive/Photograph by James Austin)

52 Hazel walking stick with a pheasant's head, probably a Czilinsky piece, c.1910–40. (Courtesy of Michael German Antiques Ltd/Photograph by James Austin)

53 Drawing from Ferdinand Czilinsky's British patent: 'Improvements in Pen and Pencil Cases for all Kinds of Walking, Umbrella and Sunshade Sticks', no. 16,624 of 1902. (SAB Archive)

54 Brigg walking stick with an ivory cockatoo's head automaton on a Malacca shaft, 1899; showing the crest down. (Courtesy of Michael German Antiques Ltd/Photograph by James Austin)

55 Brigg walking stick with an ivory cockatoo's head automaton on a Malacca shaft, 1899; showing the crest up. (Courtesy of Michael German Antiques Ltd/Photograph by James Austin)

56 Nilgiri cane walking stick with a fox terrier's head, probably made by August Czilinsky for Swaine & Adeney, c.1910–40. (Courtesy of Michael German Antiques Ltd/Photograph by James Austin)

57 Hazel walking stick with a Dalmatian's head, probably a Czilinsky piece, c.1910–40. (Courtesy of Michael German Antiques Ltd/Photograph by James Austin)

58 Hazel walking stick with a Scottish terrier's head, probably a Czilinsky piece for Swaine & Adeney, c.1910–40. (Courtesy of Michael German Antiques Ltd/Photograph by James Austin)

59 Hazel walking stick with a hound's head, probably a Czilinsky piece, c.1910–40. (Courtesy of Michael German Antiques Ltd/Photograph by James Austin)

60 Swaine & Adeney oak hunting appointment holder with a 1931 sales catalogue. (Courtesy of Mrs Lindsey Knapp, Victoria Gallery/SAB Archive/Photograph by James Austin)

61 Advertisement for the Swadeneyne seat stick, 1931. (SAB Archive/Photograph by James Austin)

62 Swaine & Adeney boot pulls with foxhound handles, c.1930–60, with detail. (Courtesy of Mrs Lindsey Knapp, Victoria Gallery/Photograph by James Austin)

63 Swaine & Adeney whip-holder in the form of a horse collar, c.1930–60, with hunting crops. (Courtesy of Mrs Lindsey Knapp, Victoria Gallery/Photograph by James Austin)

64 Photograph of Martins Bank, 23, St James's Street, Piccadilly, 1963. CRES 35/3767. (The National Archives)

65 Two propelling pencils in the form of hunting horns, c.1930 and 1957. (Courtesy of Mrs Lindsey Knapp, Victoria Gallery/Photograph by James Austin)

66 Swaine Adeney Brigg hunting canteen, c.1950. (Courtesy of Mrs Lindsey Knapp, Victoria Gallery/Photograph by James Austin)

67 Hazel walking stick with a fox's head, probably a Czilinsky piece, c.1910–40. (Courtesy of Michael German Antiques Ltd/Photograph by James Austin)

68 Bernard Lee, Sean Connery, and Desmond Llewelyn in a still from *From Russia with Love*, 1963. (© Everett Collection/Rex Features)

69 Publicity still of Patrick Macnee in character as John Steed of *The Avengers*, c.1965. (SAB Archive)

70 Robert Adeney, the last of the family owners of Swaine Adeney Brigg, c.1986. (SAB Archive)

71 Princess Anne examines a riding crop at Swaine Adeney Brigg's Piccadilly shop, October 1986. (SAB Archive)

72 *The Woman who Backed a Winner with Her Brigg Umbrella*. Drawing by Claire Minter-Kemp, c.1990. (© Claire Minter-Kemp)

73 Swaine Adeney Brigg shop at 185–6, Piccadilly. Watercolour by Claire Minter-Kemp, c.1986. (© Claire Minter-Kemp/SAB Archive/Photograph by James Austin)

74 Making briefcases at Swaine Adeney Brigg's factory at Bar Hill, March 2012. (Photograph by James Austin)

75 Carriage procession of the Duke and Duchess of Cambridge to Buckingham Palace after their wedding on 29 April 2011. (Photograph by Dimitar Dilkoff/WPA Pool/Getty Images)

76 Bill from John Köhler for a trumpet sold to the Earl of Egremont's Troop of Sussex Yeoman Cavalry, 1 May 1795. (West Sussex Record Office: PHA 6638. Courtesy of The Right Honourable Lord Egremont)

77 Trumpet in F, by John Augustus Köhler, c.1838. (The Joe R. and Joella F. Utley Collection of Brass Instruments, National Music Museum, University of South Dakota)

78 Trumpet in F, by John Augustus Köhler, c.1838; detail showing the signature plate. (The Joe R. and Joella F. Utley Collection of Brass Instruments, National Music Museum, University of South Dakota)

79 Trumpet in F, by John Augustus Köhler, c.1838; detail showing the garland. (The Joe R. and Joella F. Utley Collection of Brass Instruments, National Music Museum, University of South Dakota)

80 *Drags of the Four-in-Hand Club Passing the Five Bells Tavern, New Cross*. Oil painting by Samuel Henry

Alken, c.1860–5. (© The Berger Collection of the Denver Art Museum, USA/The Bridgeman Art Library)

81 Coaching horn owned by General Sir Edwin Alderson, c.1900. (SAB Archive/Photograph by James Austin)

82 Köhler hunting horn and leather case, c.1876. (Courtesy of Mrs Lindsey Knapp, Victoria Gallery/Photograph by James Austin)

83 Köhler hunting horn and leather case, c.1876; detail showing the maker's signature. (Courtesy of Mrs Lindsey Knapp, Victoria Gallery/Photograph by James Austin)

84 Coaching whip owned by General Sir Edwin Alderson, c.1900. (SAB Archive/Photograph by James Austin)

85 Front cover of The Coach Horn: What to Blow, How to Blow It, 5th edition, c.1907. 7890.a.64. (© The British Library Board)

86 Zair Works, Bishop Street, Birmingham, 2009. (Photograph © Andrew Clayton)

87 Floor plan of Zair's factory, Birmingham, from an insurance document, 1930. (SAB Archive/Photograph by James Austin)

88 Advertisement for G. and J. Zair's Whips, from the Queenslander, Brisbane, 30 December 1871, p. 12. (National Library of Australia)

89 Zair's Kangaroo Brand trademark, from a sales catalogue, c.1920. (SAB Archive/Photograph by James Austin)

90 Zair prize whip with horse-head handle, c.1904; detail. (Courtesy of Charles Leski Auctions, Melbourne, Australia)

91 Zair's Merle & Co. trademark, from a sales catalogue, c.1920. (SAB Archive/Photograph by James Austin)

92 Marks from a lady's riding crop by Zair, dated 1935. (Courtesy of Mrs Lindsey Knapp, Victoria Gallery/Photograph by James Austin)

93 Opening page of a workers' testimonial to George Zair on his seventieth birthday, illuminated by Edward Morton of Birmingham, 1909. (SAB Archive/Photograph by James Austin)

94 Second page of a workers' testimonial to George Zair on his seventieth birthday, illuminated by Edward Morton of Birmingham, 1909. (SAB Archive/Photograph by James Austin)

95 St James's Street, from John Tallis, London Street Views, no. 14, London, c.1838; detail. (Digital Collections and Archives, Tufts University)

96 Three parasols with carved ivory handles, c.1860–85, formerly in the Swaine Adeney Brigg Archive. (Photograph by Peter Tebbit)

97 Premium, Par & Discount. Etching by George Cruikshank, 1822. (© The Trustees of the British Museum)

98 Brigg parasol with red silk canopy and ladybird handle, c.1900–20. (Courtesy of Michael German Antiques Ltd/Photograph by James Austin)

99 Brigg parasol with brown silk canopy and nephrite knop, c.1900–10. (Courtesy of Michael German Antiques Ltd/Photograph by James Austin)

100 Matters of Taste, No. 3. as Regards Walking-Sticks. Lithograph printed by W. and J.O. Clark, c.1835–40. (© The Trustees of the British Museum)

101 Invoice issued by Thos. Brigg & Sons to S. Flower, Esq., Xmas 1886. SC/GL/TCC/OS/A-CAK. (City of London, London Metropolitan Archives)

102 The children of Philip and Elizabeth Flower. Photograph by Edward Pattison Pett, c.1886. Evelyn Jephson Cameron Collection of Personal Photographs, PAC 90-87 A2, page 2. (Montana Historical Society Research Center, Archives)

103 Selection of walking-stick shafts. (Courtesy of Michael German Antiques Ltd/Photograph by James Austin)

104 Brigg dress cane with tortoiseshell knop on bamboo shaft mounted by Charles Cooke, 1896; detail. (Courtesy of Michael German Antiques Ltd/Photograph by James Austin)

105 Maker's mark of Charles Cooke from a donkey-headed automaton stick mounted for Brigg in 1898. (Courtesy of Michael German Antiques Ltd/Photograph by James Austin)

106 Brigg evening cane with a Japanese ivory handle depicting a bat and mongoose, c.1880. (Courtesy of Michael German Antiques Ltd/Photograph by James Austin)

107 Brigg evening cane with an ivory phrenological head, c.1860–80. (Courtesy of Michael German Antiques Ltd/Photograph by James Austin)

108 Brigg horse-measuring stick with carved ivory horse's head, c.1870–85. (Courtesy of Michael German Antiques Ltd/Photograph by James Austin)

109 Brigg horse-measuring stick with carved ivory horse's head, c.1870–85; detail showing the boxwood rule. (Courtesy of Michael German Antiques Ltd/Photograph by James Austin

110 Brigg cane with a silver tau handle mounted by Thomas Johnson, 1896. (Courtesy of Michael German Antiques Ltd/Photograph by James Austin)

111 Brigg evening cane with carved horn duck's head mounted by Thomas Johnson, 1899. (Courtesy of Michael German Antiques Ltd/Photograph by James Austin)

112 Brigg evening cane with carved horn duck's head mounted by Thomas Johnson, 1899; detail showing Johnson's mark. (Courtesy of Michael German Antiques Ltd/Photograph by James Austin)

113 Brigg walking stick with an ivory rabbit's head automaton mounted by Charles Cooke, 1898. (Courtesy of Michael German Antiques Ltd/Photograph by James Austin)

114 Brigg walking stick with an ivory donkey's head automaton mounted by Charles Cooke, 1898; views showing the ears down. (Courtesy of Michael German Antiques Ltd/Photograph by James Austin)

115 Brigg walking stick with an ivory donkey's head automaton mounted by Charles Cooke, 1898; view showing the ears up. (Courtesy of Michael German Antiques Ltd/Photograph by James Austin)

116 Brigg pencil cane with a silver crook handle mounted on a green-stained shaft by Charles Henry Dumenil, 1897; detail showing Dumenil's mark. (Courtesy of Michael German Antiques Ltd/Photograph by James Austin)

117 Brigg pencil cane with a silver crook handle mounted on a green-stained shaft by Charles Henry Dumenil, 1897. (Courtesy of Michael German Antiques Ltd/Photograph by James Austin)

118 Brigg spring-loaded pencil cane with a silver tau handle mounted by Charles Henry Dumenil, 1892. (Courtesy of Michael German Antiques Ltd/Photograph by James Austin)

119 Brigg walking stick with a tortoiseshell tau handle and snakewood shaft, presented by William Burdett-Coutts to Henry Morton Stanley in 1890. (Courtesy of Michael German Antiques Ltd/Photograph by James Austin)

120 Brigg root-handled bamboo walking stick, presented by George V, when Prince of Wales, to J.W. Jones, 1907. (Courtesy of Michael German Antiques Ltd/Photograph by James Austin)

121 Warrant appointing William Henry Brigg umbrella-maker to Queen Victoria, 1884. (SAB Archive/Photograph by James Austin)

122 Brigg full-bark Malacca pencil stick, the collar engraved with the name and address of the artist Augustus John. (Courtesy of Michael German Antiques Ltd/Photograph by James Austin)

123 Augustus John; Constantin Brancusi; Frank Owen Dobson, by unknown photographer, vintage press print, c.1925. (© National Portrait Gallery, London)

124 Brigg sword stick in full-bark Malacca mounted by Charles Cooke, 1918; detail of the blade. (Courtesy of Michael German Antiques Ltd/Photograph by James Austin)

125 Brigg sword stick in full-bark Malacca mounted by Charles Cooke, 1918. (Courtesy of Michael German Antiques Ltd/Photograph by James Austin)

126 Brigg trademark of a brig between the letters B and S, from a whistle stick mounted by Charles Cooke in 1910. (Courtesy of Michael German Antiques Ltd/Photograph by James Austin)

127 Hazel walking stick with a carved tiger's head, probably a Czilinsky piece for Brigg, c.1920–40. (Courtesy of Michael German Antiques Ltd/Photograph by James Austin)

128 Pair of hazel walking sticks with carved bloodhound heads, probably Czilinksy pieces for Brigg, c.1920–40. (Courtesy of Michael German Antiques Ltd/Photograph by James Austin)

129 Pair of hazel walking sticks with carved bloodhound heads, probably Czilinksy pieces for Brigg, c.1920–40; detail showing the stamp BRIGG on the smaller of the sticks. (Courtesy of Michael German Antiques Ltd/Photograph by James Austin)

130 Neville Chamberlain walks with Lord Halifax and Benito Mussolini in Rome, 31 January 1939. (© Daily Mail/Rex Features)

131 Brigg stand at an unknown trade fair, c.1935. (SAB Archive/Photograph by James Austin)

132 Trade card from Herbert Johnson, c.1895. (SAB Archive/Photograph by James Austin)

133 Herbert Johnson sales brochure, 1902. (SAB Archive/Photograph by James Austin)

134 Three from a series of fifteen trade cards advertising Herbert Johnson's international outlets, c.1910. (SAB Archive/Photograph by James Austin)

135 Herbert Johnson top hat recovered from the wreck of RMS Titanic, and shown on display at Titanic:

The Artefact Exhibition, London, November 2010. (Ilpo Musto/Rex Features)

136 Herbert Johnson advertisement for the 'Jauntie', a women's crushable hat, 1950. (SAB Archive/Photograph by James Austin)

137 British racing driver Stirling Moss celebrates victory in the Italian Grand Prix at Pescara with Tony Vanderwell, designer of his winning Vanwall, 18 August 1957. (Photograph by Keystone/Getty Images)

138 Shellac racing helmet and visor by Herbert Johnson, with original box, c.1935–40. (Bonhams Automobilia Department)

139 Shellac racing helmet, with silver-painted finish, and original box, by Herbert Johnson, c.1952. (Bonhams Automobilia Department)

140 Arthur Lowe in character as Captain Mainwaring in the BBC television series Dad's Army, c.1975. (Moviestore Collection/Rex Features)

141 Tom Baker stars as the fourth Doctor in the BBC television series Doctor Who, 1974. (Photograph by Michael Putland/Getty Images)

142 Peter Sellers stars as Inspector Clouseau in Blake Edwards's Return of the Pink Panther, 1975. (Everett Collection/Rex Features)

143 Herbert Johnson advertisement for men's felt hats, c.1950. (SAB Archive/Photograph by James Austin)

144 Harrison Ford stars as Indiana Jones in a still from Steven Spielberg's Raiders of the Lost Ark, 1981. (©Lucas film/Everett/Rex Features)

145 Queen Elizabeth is presented with a trunk at the Travel Goods Factory at Papworth, May 1962. (Cambridgeshire Archives: Papworth Village Settlement, 1140/5/17/76. © The Times)

146 Queen Mary and Princess Mary at Papworth, accompanied by Dr Pendrill Varrier-Jones, 1918. (Cambridgeshire Archives: Papworth Village Settlement, 1140/25/1/234)

147 Trunk and portmanteau-makers at Papworth, c.1920. (Cambridgeshire Archives: Papworth Village Settlement, 1140/25/1/22)

148 Warrant appointing the Cambridgeshire Tuberculosis Colony trunk- and cabinet-makers to George V, 1924. (Cambridgeshire Archives: Papworth Village Settlement, 1140 31/1)

149 Hide room in the trunk-making workshop at Papworth, c.1929. (Cambridgeshire Archives: Papworth Village Settlement, 1140/25/1/15)

150 What Papworth Says: a page from a fundraising appeal, 1928. (Cambridgeshire Archives: Papworth Village Settlement, 1140/5/1/2, p. 8)

151 The Duke and Duchess of York chat with a patient at Papworth, 1919. (Cambridgeshire Archives: Papworth Village Settlement, 1140/25/1/243)

152 Pendragon Travel Goods Catalogue, April 1951. (SAB Archive)

153 Pendragon Travel Goods Catalogue, April 1951. (SAB Archive)

154 British Craftsmanship combined with Finest material: a spread from a Papworth Industries travel goods catalogue, 1957. (SAB Archive/Photograph by James Austin)

155 Making suitcases at Papworth Industries, July 1960. (Cambridgeshire Archives: Papworth Village Settlement, 1140/40/6/29. Photograph by E. Leigh)

156 1st class travellers: an advertisement from Papworth Industries, 1961. (SAB Archive/Photograph by James Austin)

157 Pendragon Travel Goods trademark. (SAB Archive)

158 Pendragon perfection: an advertisement from Papworth Industries, 1956. (SAB Archive/Photograph by James Austin)

159 Travelling wardrobe trunk and matching case made by Papworth Industries for Princess Margaret, 1947, with a Hermès black-leather travelling case. (© Christie's Images/The Bridgeman Art Library)

160 Margot Fonteyn embarks from the BOAC terminal at Victoria, London, on a tour of the USA and Canada, 13 August 1951. (Keystone/Getty Images)

161 Trimming a sheet of cowhide. (SAB Archive/Photograph by James Austin)

162 Checking goods before despatch. (SAB Archive)

163 Sewing a cotton umbrella canopy. (SAB Archive)

164 Umbrella-maker at his bench. (SAB Archive)

165 Umbrella handles. (SAB Archive/Photograph by James Austin)

166 Hand-stitching an attaché-case handle. (SAB Archive/Photograph by James Austin)

167 Repairing a briefcase. (SAB Archive)

168 Machine-stitching a leather case. (SAB Archive/Photograph by James Austin)

169 The Duchess of Cambridge on board the royal barge Spirit of Chartwell at Her Majesty The Queen's Diamond Jubilee on 3 June 2012. (Photograph by Dylan Martinez/WPA Pool/Getty Images)

A Note on Sources

Few early company records survive at Swaine Adeney Brigg. Many of the royal warrants have been preserved, along with some scattered invoices and advertisements from the early nineteenth century, and one account book for Swaine & Co., which covers the years 1818-25. Until recently there was a substantial archive of old records, prize manufactures, and shop fittings, but this was sadly dissipated, c.1994-2003. This means that, apart from G. & J. Zair and Papworth Travel Goods, none of the companies that make up the Swaine Adeney Brigg family has a long run of extant records. The history in this book has therefore been pieced together from a wide range of paper archives, digitized records, and published material. The most important of these sources are listed below.

ONLINE SOURCES
Most of the genealogical information has been sourced from parish registers, census records, and the wills of the Prerogative Court of Canterbury, which are held by either the London Metropolitan Archives or the National Archives and which are accessible in digital format through their web partner Ancestry, at *ancestry.co.uk*. Post-1857 wills have been sourced from the Probate Department of Her Majesty's Court Service in High Holborn, London.

The *London Gazette*, England's paper of record, is an invaluable source of information about business partnerships, bankruptcies, and royal warrants; relevant notices have been consulted from its digital archive at *www.london-gazette.co.uk*

Another valuable historical source is The Proceedings of the Old Bailey, at *www.oldbaileyonline.org*, which includes transcripts and digital images of reports of criminal trials held at the Old Bailey from 1674 to 1913. The trials contain a perhaps unexpected amount of information on the working practices of London businesses and crafts.

The historical British newspaper advertise-ments and articles have been accessed via the British Library's Burney and 19th Century digitized newspaper collections, as well as their British Newspaper Archive, *www.britishnewspaperarchive.co.uk*. Australasian advertisements and stories have been accessed through the National Library of Australia's digitized collection, *http://trove.nla.gov.au/newspaper*, and the National Library of New Zealand's Papers Past,*http://paperspast.natlib.govt.nz*.

Some information about patents has been sourced from newspaper advertisements; from the mid-nineteenth century many can be found on Espacenet, the worldwide patent database maintained online by the European Patent Office: *http://www.epo.org/*.

Reportage in *The Times*, *Financial Times*, *Observer* and some American newspapers has been helpful for telling the more recent story of Swaine Adeney Brigg. This has been accessed through the commercial digital archives of Newsbank and Gale NewsVault, both available at the British Library.

The online archives of the auction houses Christie's, Sotheby's, and Bonham's have been invaluable in tracking noteworthy manufactures, especially whips, umbrellas, walking sticks, and Herbert Johnson hats and crash helmets. There are competent summaries of the debates about the Herbert Jones hats worn by Harrison Ford in the Indiana Jones movies at *www.indygear.com* and Jean-Michel Sorin's *www.jones-jr.com*.

ARCHIVAL SOURCES
Documents consulted include, at the London Metropolitan Archives, the Records of the Sun Fire Office (MS 11936A-MA15034), the London Aged Christian Society (A/LAC), and the Over-sized Trade Card Collection (SC/GL/TCC/OS/A-CAK).

The West Sussex Record Office at Chichester is the caretaker of the Petworth House Archives, which include several early invoices from John Ross and John Köhler. The author is grateful to the Rt. Hon. Lord Egremont for permission to access and reproduce these documents.

The paving rate and watch rate books for the St James's area of the City of Westminster are held at Westminster Archives; relevant volumes consulted on microfilm include D627-32 and E1715-22. St James's Parish Records have also been consulted there on microfilm.

The Crown Estate records at the National Archives include early survey reports for the shops owned by John Ross and James Swaine; see, in particular, CRES 39/124 and CRES 39/141.

The Charles Booth Collection at the London School of Economics contains the notes of George Duckworth's interview with James Adeney in 1893 and related material (Notebooks A15 and B97).

A very large run of company records for G. & J. Zair is held by Birmingham Archives (MS 160), while the company records for Papworth Industries are contained in the business section of the Papworth Village Settlement Archive at Cambridgeshire Archives (K/1140/C).

REFERENCE WORKS
Publications quoted in the text have usually been identified by their author or title, but much of the background information draws heavily on key reference works. The book could not have been written without the research made available in the following publications:

G.B. (Godfrey Bosvile), 'Whips', *Baily's Magazine of Sports and Pastimes*, Issue 489, 1 November 1900, pp. 315-24

Sidney Charnock, *Papworth Trunk-Making Department, 1921-1959*, Papworth Everard, 1965

T.S. Crawford, *A History of the Umbrella*, Newton Abbot, 1970

John Culme, *The Directory of Gold and Silversmiths, Jewellers and Allied Traders, 1838-1914: From the London Assay Office Registers*, Woodbridge, 1987

Catherine Dike, *Cane Curiosa: from Gun to Gadget*, Paris and Geneva, 1983

— *Les Cannes à système. Un Monde fabuleux et méconnu*, Paris, 1982

— *Walking Sticks*, Oxford, 1990

Jeremy Farrell, *Umbrellas and Parasols*, London, 1985

Amanda Murray, *All the Kings' Horses: Royalty and Their Equestrian Passions from 1066 to the Present Day*, London, 2006

Jane Rees and Mark Rees, *The Rule Book: Measuring for the Trades*, Lakeville, 2010

Swaine & Adeney Ltd, *'Good Hands' 1750-1927*, London, c.1927

Joseph Sheldon, *The Founders and Builders of Stocksbridge Works*, Stocksbridge, 1922

Hazel Stansfield, *Samuel Fox & Company Limited, 1842-1967*, Stocksbridge, 1968

Lance Whitehead and Arnold Myers, 'The Köhler Family of Brasswind Instrument Makers', *Historic Brass Society Journal*, 2004, vol. 16, pp. 89-123

Index

accounts 15, 16–18, 26, 68, 70
Adeney, Edward Swaine, Jr 44, 48–52, 56, 63, 65, 68, 72, 153
Adeney, Edward Swaine, Sr 41, 44, 49
Adeney, Gilbert Lattimer 63, 65, 68
Adeney, James 35–6, 41–3, 44, 152
Adeney, Mary Ann 35
Adeney, Robert Edward John 49–50, 68, 69, 70–1, 72
Adeney, William 27, 35
Adeney, William Henry 49
Adeney, William James 41
advertising 12–14, 36–8, 43, 44, 49, 55, 66, 70, 84, 86, 92, 93, 124–6, 128, 131, 132, 142–6
aeroplanes 141, 142
agents 49, 62, 140
    Eldrid Ottaway & Co. Ltd 62
    Everard Kerlen 62
    Gordon & Gotch Ltd 62
    Jabez Cliff & Co. Ltd 62
    Thomas, Pavitt & Co. 62
    William Banks & Co. 62
Ainsworth, Arthur Thomas 107
air travel 142–3, 153
Albert, Consort of Queen Victoria 31, 34, 41, 152
Alderson, General Sir Edwin 79, 80–1
Alexandra, Consort of Edward VII 34–5, 36, 38, 44, 152
Alken, Henry 39
Alken, Samuel Henry 78
alligator hide 50, 56, 62
animal-head carvings 56–61, 66–7, 101, 105, 107–9, 118–19
Annamite cane
    See partridge cane
Anne, Princess 69
antibiotics 136, 143
apprenticeships 14, 15, 34, 43, 72, 93, 124, 144, 152
Aquascutum 148
Arundinaria amabilis
    See Tonkin cane
ash 45, 48, 50, 149
attaché cases 141, 145
Australia 25, 35, 38, 50, 86–7, 110, 120
automatons 58–9, 108–9
Automobile Club de Paris 153
Avengers, The 66, 69, 131, 153

Badminton Library of Sports and Pastimes 152, 153
Bagnall family 127
Baily's Monthly Magazine of Sports and Pastimes 38–41
Baker, Tom 130–1
baleen 16, 28, 33
    See also whalebone
bamboo 16, 40–1, 42, 45, 48, 50, 85, 101, 102, 103, 105, 106, 108–9, 113
    See also whangee
bankruptcy 93, 152
Baptist Missionary Society 84
bark 60–1, 102, 115
Batman 131
Battersby & Co. Ltd 128
Baynard Press 51
Beaton, Sir Cecil 131
Beaufort, 8th Duke of (Henry Somerset) 79, 152, 153

Benson, Robin 132–3
Benz, Karl 153
Berkeley, Colonel William (1st Earl Fitzhardinge) 20, 21
Berkeley Hunt 20
Betaille, Messrs 114, 153
Bethlehem Hospital Governors 25, 39
Birmingham 43, 62, 63, 68, 84–5, 88, 97, 152, 153
Birmingham Assay Company 49, 50, 87
Birmingham Central Literary Association 84
Blackburn, Fanny 85, 88
Blackburn, James 85
Blackman, Honor 66
blackthorn 37, 50
Bolton 46
Bond, James 66, 68
Bonhams 129, 130
Boot, Caroline 35
Booth, Charles 41
Booth, Frederick 13
Bosvile, Godfrey 104
Box, James Alexander 136–7, 141, 153
boxwood 105
Boyd, Douglas Arthur 88
braiding machines 14–15, 41, 43
Brancusi, Constantin 115
branding 28, 35, 46–7, 50, 58, 59, 61, 66, 86–7, 96, 118
Brewers' Company 15, 35–6
Brigg, Bertie Walter 63, 65, 96, 103, 114
Brigg, Charles 92, 93, 94, 96, 152
Brigg, Fanny 93
Brigg, Guy Lenard 96
Brigg, Thomas Edward 92–4, 95–6, 101, 152
Brigg, Thomas, Jr 96, 101, 152
Brigg, Walter Alfred 96, 101, 103, 114
Brigg, William 95–6, 152
Brigg, William Henry 96, 101, 110, 114
Brigg & Sons, Thomas 56, 62, 63, 65, 92–121, 152, 153
Bright, John 84
British and Foreign School Society 27
British Empire Exhibition 137, 153
British Industries Fair 140
British Oxygen Company 129
Brooks, Henry Jamyn 48–9
Brummell, 'Beau' 18, 152
Brune, Monsieur 18
Burdett-Coutts, William 112
Buxton, Eliza 81
Byng, Frederick 'Poodle' 18

Calamus scipionum
    See Malacca cane
Cambridge, Duchess of 73, 160
Cambridge, Duke of (Prince Adolphus) 15, 16–17, 18
Cambridge, Duke of (Prince William) 73
Cambridgeshire Regiment of Militia 76
Cambridgeshire Tuberculosis Colony 136, 153
Cameron, Ewen 100
Cameron, L.C.R. 81
cane 40–1, 50, 96, 101, 102, 111

    See also bamboo, Malacca, Nilgiri, Tonkin
canes
    See walking sticks, dress canes
Capps family 127
Carothers, Wallace 153
Carr, F.W. 130
catalogues 44–5, 46, 48, 50, 51, 55, 62, 63
Chamberlain, Neville 120–1, 153
Charlotte, Consort of George III 18, 152
Charnock, Ernest 137, 141, 144, 153
Charnock, George, Jr 137, 140, 141, 153
Charnock, George, Sr 137
Charnock, Jane 137
Charnock, Sidney 137, 141, 144–5, 146, 153
Cheere, Charles Madryll 136
cherry 102, 105, 149
Chetwynd-Talbot, Charles 129
China 95, 102, 153
Christie's 131
Clayton, Tom 86
Clément-Bayard, Adolphe 129
Clerk, W. and J.O. 99
Coach Horn, The 78, 81, 152
coaches 12–13, 20–1, 39, 152
coaching 20–1, 39, 41, 78–81
Coaching Club 79, 152
coachmen 17, 20–1, 39, 54–5
cockatoos 58–9
Coloroll Group 133
Combe, George 105
Connery, Sean 66
Cook & Co. 116
Cooke, Charles Arthur 59, 103, 108, 113, 116
Cooke, Charles Arthur John 103
Cooke, John Robert 103
coppicing 56
Corne, Ray 130
Courtney, Rohan 72
craftsmanship 49, 51–3, 65
crash helmets 128–31, 153
Craven Chapel 27
Craze, Gary 131
Crespigny, Claude de 106
crests 127
crocodile skin 63
Cruikshank, George 96–7
Cumberland, Duke of (Prince Ernest Augustus) 15, 18
Cumberland, Duke of (Prince Henry Frederick) 10, 19, 152
customization 52, 66, 68, 140
Czilinsky, Alfred Augustus 59
Czilinsky, August 56, 58–9, 61
Czilinsky, Emil Lorenz 58, 118–19
Czilinsky, Ferdinand, Jr 58
Czilinsky, Ferdinand, Sr 58–9
Czilinsky family 56–61, 66–7, 103, 108, 118–19

Dad's Army 130–1
Damant, James 103
dandyism 20, 34, 66, 96–7, 99
de Bruyne, John 72
de Bruyne, Tracey 72
Dearson, Bert 145

DeCenzo, David 72
Design Council 146
Dicey, Frank William 34
Dickens, Charles 50
disability 143, 146
Dissenters 27, 34
Dobson, Frank 115
Doctor Who 130–1
dogs 45, 46, 56, 60–1, 64, 101, 118–19
Doudeauville, duc de (viscomte Sosthène II de la Rochefoucauld) 37
Dozenal Society 65
drag racing 79
Dragonhide 143
dress canes 99, 101, 103, 104–5
Drummond, William 31
Dublin 18, 38
Dubourg, Matthew 17
Duckworth, George 41–4
Dumenil Ltd, C.H. 111
Duménil, Alexandre François Jean-Baptiste 110
Dumenil, Charles Henry Frederick 111
Dumenil, Charles Henry 103, 110–11, 152
Duménil, Etienne Alexandre, Jr 110
Duménil, Etienne Alexandre, Sr 110
Dumenil, Frederick Arthur 110
Dumenil, Robert Victor, Jr 111
Dumenil, Robert Victor, Sr 111
Dumenil, Sydney Sylvester 110
Dumenil, William Henry 111

East, Alfred Ernest 50
Eastwood, Clint 131
ebonized hardwood 104–5, 107, 111
ebony 50, 58
Economist 65
Edward VII 44, 125, 126, 153
    as Prince of Wales 34–5, 38, 41, 114, 124, 126, 152
Edward VIII 138, 153
Edwards, Blake 131
Egremont, 3rd Earl of (George Wyndham) 10, 76
Eiloart, Tim 145
Elibank, Viscountess 120
Elizabeth II 134, 140, 146, 153
Elizabeth, Consort of George VI 138, 141
Ellam, Benjamin 34–5
Ellis, General Sir Hugh 127
employees 14, 41–3, 49, 72, 85, 87, 89, 101–3, 143, 145
    women 41, 43, 72, 85, 99
    Zair, named 89
Ensign Trust 70
en-tout-cas 117
European Economic Community 153
Evangelical Magazine and Missionary Chronicle 34, 41
exhibitions 32–3, 36–8, 80, 86–7, 114, 121, 137, 152, 153

factories 10, 63, 68, 70, 71, 72, 84–5, 153
    trunk-making 137, 138, 140, 141, 153
fashion
    men's 18, 20, 31, 93, 99–101, 111, 126–7, 152
    women's 28, 70, 92, 93, 95, 153

feathers 92, 93
fedoras 130-1
fibreglass 48, 88, 130-1
Field, Abraham 36
Field, The 38
First World War 49-50, 51, 85, 117,
    127, 128, 130-1, 136, 141, 153
Fitchew, William 31
Fleming, Ian 66
Fletcher, Sylvia 133
Fleury, Hermann Conrad 45
Flower, Evelyn Jephson 100-1
Flower, Severin Jephson 100-1
Fonteyn, Margot 144, 147
Ford, Harrison 131-2, 133, 153
Formula Ford Championship 129
Fortnum and Mason 24, 25
Four-Horse Club 20, 79
Four-in-Hand Club 79
Fox umbrella frames 56, 97-8, 152
France 49, 58, 92, 95, 140, 153
Franco-British Exhibition, 1908 114
Frederick Bedford Smith Ltd 56, 153
French, Margaret 14
Fukusuke Corporation 71
Fundamentals of Management 72

Gardner, Lieutenant-Colonel Goldie
    128, 153
Gawn, Roger 7, 72, 153
Geden, Mary Eliza 128
gentlemen's clubs 25, 93
George I, King of the Hellenes 125, 126
George III 10, 15, 17, 18, 25, 152
George IV 25, 41
    as Prince of Wales and Regent
    10, 15, 16-17, 18, 19, 20, 152
George V 52, 113, 137, 138, 153
George VI 138, 141, 153
Germany 43, 92, 153
Glazier, Edward 128
Glazier, Edward John 124, 126, 153
Glazier, Geoffrey John 128
Glazier, Maxwell Henry 128
Glazier, Timothy 129-30, 131, 132
gloves 52
Gooch, Sir Robert 88
'Good Hands' 1750-1927 51-3
gossamer-body headgear 126, 127,
    128, 130-1, 153
Grand Prix motor racing 129, 153
Graves, Harriet Towsey 110
Great Exhibition, 1851 33, 36-7, 78,
    80, 152
Green Goddess fire engines 145
Green, Henry Thomas 14
Grellier, Fanny 93, 95
Grenadier Guards 76-7
Griffith, Benjamin 14, 152
Griffith, Charles 14
Griffith, Thomas 14
Griffith & Son 14
Gronow, Captain 18, 99-101
gun shop 70
gut 16, 43, 48

hairdressing 94, 131
handbags 52, 65, 145
Hanway, Joseph 95
Harper, Thomas 78
Harris Watson Holdings PLC 72
Harris, John 39
hats 124-33
    felted 126, 127, 128, 131-2
    gossamer-body 125, 126-7,
    128-30, 153
    military 127-8, 130-1
    sporting 126, 127, 128-31, 133
    top 125, 126-7
    women's 127, 128, 133

hazel 50, 56-7, 59, 60-1, 66-7, 102,
    105, 118-19
headgear, equestrian 13, 127
    military 92, 127-8, 130-1
heart surgery 143
Heath, William 20, 21
Hendrix, Jimi 131
Herbert Johnson hatters 72, 124-33,
    153
Herbert Johnson (Bond Street) Ltd
    128, 153
hickory 149
Highways and Horses 79
Hitler, Adolf 120-1, 153
Holland umbrella frames 97-8,
    152
holly 16, 41, 50
horn 28, 56, 107, 116
horns 76-81, 152
    coaching 44, 78-9
    hunting 44, 76, 80-1, 153
    mail 79
    natural 78-81
Horse and Hound 38
horse racing 10, 18, 41, 48, 86, 152
horse-drawn transport 13, 20-1, 39,
    44, 50, 62, 152, 153
horsemanship 19, 20, 52, 152
horse-measuring sticks 62, 105
Hoyland Fox Ltd 98
Huguenots 93, 110
hunting 16, 17, 20, 28, 41, 44-5,
    46-7, 152, 153
hunting accessories 13, 28, 44-5, 48,
    55, 62-3, 64, 66
Hunting Act, 2004 153
Hunting Horn, The 81
Hurlingham Club 48-9, 152

Illustrated Exhibitor 33, 36-7, 38
Imperial Chemical Industries 88
India 38, 50
Indiana Jones 131-2, 133, 153
invoices 10, 12-14, 15, 100
Ireland 18, 80, 140
Isaac, William 16, 21, 25, 35, 152
ivory 26, 41, 50, 56, 58-9, 76, 78, 94,
    95, 97, 104-5, 108-9, 110

Jacobites 152
Jagger, Mick 131
Japan 104, 144
Jockey Club 152
Johannesburg 87, 125
John, Augustus 115
John Crowther Group 133, 153
Johnson, Herbert Lewis 124, 126,
    128, 152, 153
Johnson, Maria (née Samson) 103,
    107
Johnson, Thomas 103, 106, 107
Johnson, William 124, 126, 152
Johnson, William Geden 128
Jones, J.W. 113
Jones, Margaret Emily 128
Jones, W. Milward 80

Kane, Robert 131
kangaroo hide 40-1, 46-7, 48,
    50, 56, 86
kapok 50
Kelly, Hinton 15
Kent, Duke of (Prince Edward) 15
Keynes, John Maynard 140
Knowland, Thomas 11
Köhler, Augustus Charles 78-9,
    81, 152
Köhler, Elizabeth 76
Köhler, John, Jr 76
Köhler, John, Sr 76

Köhler, John Augustus 76-8, 80,
    152
Köhler, John Buxton 76, 81
Köhler & Son, J. 44, 76-81, 152, 153

lancewood 26
Le Mans 130, 153
Lea, James 85
Lea, Lister 85
Lea, Montague Percy 85
Leadenhall Press 36
leather 16, 17, 40-1, 43, 44, 46, 48,
    50, 56, 80, 96, 140, 141, 142, 143
    See also alligator, kangaroo,
    lizard, pigskin, shagreen
leatherworking skills 44, 45, 50, 52,
    68, 136, 137-8, 141, 144
Lesser, Guy 72
Liberals 84, 85
Lincoln, Bennett & Co. 124, 126, 152
Lionide 143
lizard skin 56, 62, 63
loaded sticks 50
London 10-12, 27, 84, 88
London A to Z 131
London Aged Christian Society 27
London Assay Office 49, 50, 58, 103,
    107, 111
London Missionary Society 27
London of To-day 124
Longmate, Barak 13
losses 70, 71
Louis Philippe, King of France 36
Lowe, Arthur 130-1
luggage 44, 50, 52, 68, 72, 88, 136-47
    canvas 142
    fibre 137-8, 141, 142
    military 50, 141
    motoring 44, 52
    soft-bodied 143
    women's 144-5, 146-7
luggage suites 136-7, 143, 144-5,
    146, 147
Luton 126

Macnee, Patrick 66, 69, 131, 153
Mainwaring, Captain 130-1
Malacca cane (*Calamus scipionum*)
    31, 48, 50, 56, 59, 100, 102, 115,
    116, 120
Manners, Lord (John, 5th Duke of
    Rutland) 18
Marangos, Anthony 133, 153
Margaret, Princess 146
Marius, Monsieur 95
marketing 18, 44-5, 62, 68, 140,
    144, 149
markets, colonial 25, 38, 86, 87
    international 36, 43, 50, 51, 68,
    70-1, 86-7, 114, 125, 140, 153
Markov, Georgi 68
marquise hinge 117
Martins Bank 65
Marx, Karl 58
Mary, Consort of George V 136-7
Mary, Princess 137
Maudslay, Athol 79
Melbourne 86-7, 110, 152
Memoirs of a Fox-Hunting Man 55
Merchant Navy Pension Fund 71
Merle & Co. 87
Merle Lodge 87
mess tin 50, 51
military canes 50
military headgear 92, 127-8, 130-1
millinery 92, 127, 128, 133
Minter-Kemp, Claire 70, 71
Mitchell, Elizabeth 59
Mitthofer, Elizabeth Sarah 78
Montana 100

Morton, Edward 88
Moss, Sir Stirling 122, 129-30, 153
motor cars 44, 79, 81, 87, 117,
    128, 153
    accessories 44, 52, 117, 128
    motor racing 129-31, 153
Munich 120-1, 153
musical instruments 76-8
Mussolini, Benito 120-1
Myers, Arnold 76, 78

Nadoolman, Deborah 132
National Health Service 143
New Zealand 86, 87
Newmarket 88, 152
Nicholas II, Tsar of Russia 126
Nicholson, Jack 131
Nicholson, William 54-5
Nilgiri cane 50, 59, 61
Noirit, Albert 62
Noirit, Juan Emilio 62
Nonconformism 27, 84
nylon 48, 66, 153

Old Bailey 14, 21, 24, 58
omnibuses 152, 153
Orsay, Count Alfred d' 26-8
otter hunting 45
Ozenfant, Amédée 114

Padgett & Braham Ltd 111
Papworth Hall 136, 153
Papworth Hospital 143
Papworth Industries 72, 136, 137,
    138, 140-1, 143, 144, 145, 150, 153
Papworth Travel Goods 146, 153
Papworth Village Settlement 136, 141,
    143, 145, 153
Paragon umbrella frames 97, 152
parasols 93, 94-5, 96-7, 98, 114, 153
Paris 18, 36, 38, 58, 63, 92, 114,
    121, 153
Paris Jockey Club 37
partridge cane (*Rhapis excelsa*) 102
Pascoe, Charles 124, 126-7
patents 49, 50, 56, 58-9, 62, 63, 88,
    110, 111, 152
Patey Hats 130
pear wood 58
pencil umbrellas 56
pencil walking sticks 58, 66, 110-11,
    115
pencils 66
Pendragon Travel Goods 136, 140,
    142-3, 145, 146
Pendrobe 143
Percival, Thomas 76
Petersham, Lord (Charles Stanhope,
    4th Earl of Harrington) 18, 20, 99
Pett, Edward Pattison 100-1
pheasants 56-7
Philadelphia 38
philanthropy 27, 31, 34, 41, 84, 85
phrenology 104-5
Piccadilly 12-14, 22-5, 69
Pickard, Rowland 111
Pickard, Thomas Charles 111
Pictology Ltd 71
piecework 43, 49, 85
pigskin 16, 50, 55, 56, 62, 63
Pink Panther 131, 132
pipe-mounters 110-11
Piratinera guianensis
    See snakewood
plastics 143
plumes 92, 93
Poet hat 132
Pollard, James 12-13, 17
polo 45-9, 56, 86, 127, 152, 153
postilions 20, 73, 153

INDEX

premises 84
  8, Marylebone Street 10–12, 152
  10, Old Bond Street 72, 153
  23, St James's Street 63, 65, 92–4, 117, 152
  54, St James's Street 72, 153
  63, Charing Cross 92–3
  185, Piccadilly 22–5, 38–9, 70–1, 152
  224, Piccadilly 25, 152
  238, Piccadilly 12–14, 18, 25, 152
  Bar Hill 72, 146
  Brigg's 63, 65, 92–4, 114, 152
  Great Chesterford 68, 71, 72, 85, 88, 150
  Herbert Johnson's 124, 125, 127, 132, 133, 153
  Köhler's 76, 78, 81, 152
  Newbury Street 63, 68
  Paris 114, 153
  Zair's 84–5, 88, 152, 153
prices 46, 50, 55, 56, 120, 129
Prince Regent
  See George IV
Prudence 133
Punch 34–5
purchase tax 153

Quant, Mary 153
quills 16, 43

Raiders of the Lost Ark 131–2, 133, 153
railways 14, 39, 41, 44, 78, 79, 142, 152
rattan 48, 50
  See also cane, bamboo
religion 25, 27, 34
rent 39, 70, 71, 78, 132, 153
repairing 148, 150
Response Group 133
retailers 18, 88, 114
  Boyce & Rogers 88
  Brace, Windle & Blyth 87
  Callow 88
  Gibson 18
  Gilbert 88
  Greatrex 87
  H.W. Hill 88
  Harrods 88
  Henrich Baer 87
  Hill Hartridge Dimsdale & Co. 87
  J. Salter & Sons 88
  John Birch & Sons Ltd 87
  Kopf Manufacturing Company 87
  Ullathorne & Co. 87
  Watt 88
  Whippy 18, 88
  William Middlemore 87
Rhapis excelsa
  See partridge cane
rhinoceros horn 50, 56, 100
riding costume 19, 20, 29–31
Robbins, Stephen 72
Rolt, Major Tony 130
Rosenberg, Christian 13
Ross, John 10–14, 18, 19, 46, 52, 65, 152
Royal Automobile Club 130, 153
Royal College of Music 78
Royal Field Artillery 136, 141
Royal Flying Corps 128
Royal Lancashire Volunteers 76
royal patronage 10, 12–15, 18–19, 24, 25, 26, 27, 28–31, 36, 38, 41, 44, 52, 114, 124, 125, 126, 136–7, 138–40, 146, 152, 153
Royal Society of Arts 27

Royal Tank Corps 127
royal warrants 10, 114, 126, 131, 137, 138–40, 152, 153
rules 105

Sabson whips 66
saddlers 17–18, 34, 62, 84, 87, 136, 141
Saddlers' Company 14, 36
saddlery 68
Saks Fifth Avenue 140
sales 16, 17–18, 68, 70, 71
San Francisco 70
Sassoon, Siegfried 55
Scasebrook, Mr 16
Schnebbelie, Jacob 13
Scholefield, William 84
seat-sticks 52, 62, 63, 88
Second World War 62–3, 92, 121, 141–3, 153
Selfridges department store 136
Sellers, Peter 131, 132
Semambu rattan
  See Malacca cane
sewing machines 99, 137, 150
shagreen 17, 26, 56
Shamoon, Stella 68, 70
shaving accessories 94
Shaw, John 78
shellac 126, 129, 130
Shillibeer, George 152
shooting-sticks 117
shop sign 54–5
Shot in the Dark, A 131
side saddles 25, 28–30, 152
silk 56, 62, 65–6, 93, 94–5, 97, 98, 120–1
silversmiths 31, 43, 49, 66, 103, 107, 110–11
slavery 27, 84
Slocock, Benjamin, Jr 15–16
Slocock, Benjamin, Sr 12–14, 15–16, 21, 36, 152
Smithson, Alison and Peter 65
snakewood (*Piratinera guianensis*) 112
South Africa 87, 146
South America 86, 87
South Berkshire Hounds 62–3
Spielberg, Steven 131–2, 133, 153
sponges 94
Sporting Gazette 38
sports 20–1, 28, 34, 41, 44–9, 50, 56, 86, 127, 129–31, 152, 153
Spriggs, Sarah 124
St James's, Piccadilly 25, 27, 63, 72, 92–4, 124
stag horn 17, 28, 44, 46–7, 50, 64
Stanley, Henry Morton 112
Stanwell 14, 25
Steed, John 66, 69, 131, 153
stick-dressing 43, 45, 48, 85, 101–3, 116
stick-mounters 103, 107, 108–9, 110–11, 113, 117
stock market crash 153
Stockport 126, 128
Stocksbridge 56, 97
Strong, Sir Roy 131
Stubbs, George 19
suitcases 137, 141, 143–4
suppliers 16–17, 50, 62
  Buttons Ltd 63
  John Stych & Co. 62
Surrey Volunteers 128
Sussex Yeoman Cavalry 76
swagger sticks 50
Swaine, Ann 15, 27
Swaine, Caroline 35
Swaine, Edward 14–15, 27, 31, 34–6, 41, 84, 152

Swaine, James 12–15, 17, 18, 25–7, 28, 46, 52, 65, 152
Swaine, John, Jr 13, 14, 15, 17
Swaine, John, Sr 14
Swaine, Sarah 35
Swaine & Adeney 35–48, 76, 80, 81, 85
Swaine & Adeney Ltd 35, 48–56, 62–4, 84, 88, 153
  buy Zair 51, 88, 153
  merger with Brigg 56, 63, 92, 96, 121, 153
Swaine Adeney Brigg 10, 14, 71–2, 133, 148–9
  archive 26, 33, 37, 55, 95
  buy Herbert Johnson 72, 124, 133, 153
  buy the travel goods division of Papworth Industries 72, 136, 146, 153
Swaine, Adeney, Brigg & Sons, Ltd 63, 65–71, 92
Swaine Adeney Inc. 70
Swaine & Co. 12–20, 21, 25, 152
Swaine & Isaac 21, 22–4, 25, 26, 27, 28, 31, 34–5, 152
Swaine, Isaac & Adeney 35, 152
Swaine, Slocock & Swaine 15
Swales, Richard 131–2, 153
sword sticks 58, 62, 66, 99, 116
Sydney 86–7, 152
synthetic textiles 143

Taiwan 144
Talbot racing cars 129
Talbot, J.G. 129
Tallis, John 22–5, 92–3, 93–4, 99
television 66, 131
terrier bag 46
theft 12, 14, 94, 110
Tillotson & Son Ltd 46
Tinning, Mr 16
Titanic, RMS 126, 127
tobacco pipes 110–11
Todd's hairdressing salon 131
Tokyo 70, 125
Tonkin cane (*Arundinaria amabilis*) 102, 120
top hats 125, 126, 127
tortoiseshell 56, 100, 101, 103, 112
trade cards 14, 24, 36, 43, 124, 125
trademarks 86, 87, 117, 140, 145
Travelling Goods Factory 140–1, 153
trumpets 76–8
trunks 134, 136–41, 146, 153
Tryon, Anthony (3rd Baron Tryon) 72
tuberculosis 136, 141, 143, 153
Tuer, Andrew White 36

umbrellas 52, 56, 65, 92–9, 114, 117–21
  Brigg 66–7, 68, 90, 92, 93–4, 96–9, 114, 117–21
  frames 56, 96–8, 149
  history of 94–5, 96–9, 152
United States of America 87, 121, 140
Universal Federalist Council 58

value added tax 153
Vanderwell, Tony 122, 129
vanity cases 65, 146, 147
Vanwall racing cars 129
Varrier-Jones, Pendrill 136–40, 141, 146, 153
Vaughan, Richard ('Hell-Fire Dick') 21
Vero Ltd, E.W. 130–1
vesta walking sticks 42
Victoria and Albert Museum 131
Victoria, Queen 24, 25, 26, 27, 28–31, 34, 36, 38–9, 88, 114, 152, 153
Vienna 38
Villemessant, Hippolyte de 101
Villiers & Jackson 66

wages 41–3, 85, 87, 143
walking sticks 20, 26, 31, 42, 43, 44, 50, 56–61, 66–7, 78, 99–113, 115–19
  animal-head 56–61, 66–7, 101, 103, 105, 107–9, 118–19
  as fashion accessories 20, 99–101
  automatons 58–9, 103, 108–9
  Brigg 58–9, 100, 103–13, 115, 118–19
  history of 99–101, 117
  Swaine & Adeney 42, 61, 62
  Swaine & Isaac 31
  system 42, 58–9, 62, 78, 103, 105, 110–11, 115, 116, 117
Walsall 62, 84, 85, 87
War Damage Commission 63
war equipment 49–50, 51, 62, 141
Warren, Richard 10–11
Warwickshire Museum Service 76
Weaver, Major John 68
Welsh Grenadier Guards 99
Wembley 137, 140, 153
Westbrook, Sarah 35
Westbrook, Zachariah 35
whalebone 16, 28, 43, 45, 46–7, 48, 50, 53, 66, 88, 96, 153
whangee bamboo root 56, 66, 69
whip-holders 64
whip-making 10, 14–15, 16–17, 33, 41–4, 48, 53, 86, 88
  braiding 14–15, 28, 32–3, 37, 40–1, 43, 85
  materials 16–17, 28, 40–1, 50, 86
  mounts 27, 28, 32–3, 37–8, 41, 43
  stocks 10, 16, 43, 45, 48, 53, 86
  thongs 41, 43
  wirework 26, 43, 45
whips 10, 12, 14–17, 20–1, 25, 26, 27, 28–31, 32–3, 36–44, 46–7, 50–1, 53, 64, 86, 100, 104
  driving 15, 16, 20–1, 26, 37, 41, 43, 79, 80–1
  fibreglass 48, 88
  for women 24, 28–30, 37, 100
  hunting 28, 44, 46–7, 50, 64, 88
  nylon core 48, 66
  polo 48
  prize 32–3, 36–7, 41, 86
  riding 16–17, 25, 26, 27, 28–30, 32–3, 36, 38–9, 41, 43, 56, 69
  royal wedding 38, 41, 73
  side-saddle 28–30
  steel core 48, 56
  with flywhisks 25, 26, 37, 86, 152
White Bear Inn 12
White Hunter, Black Heart 131
Whitehead, Lance 76, 78
Wilhelm II, Emperor of Germany 126
William IV 25, 26, 41, 152
  as Duke of Clarence 15, 18
woods 16, 26, 43, 48, 50, 56–7, 58, 59, 60–1, 102
  See also individual wood types
Wyndham, General Sir Henry 41

York, Duke of (Prince Frederick) 15

Zair, Eliza 84
Zair, G. & J. 50, 51, 56, 62, 68, 84–9, 152, 153
  limited company 88, 153
  records 56, 59, 61, 85, 87, 88
Zair, George 82, 84–6, 87–8, 89, 152
  testimonial to 82, 87–8, 89
Zair, George Percy 51, 85–6, 88–9
Zair, John, Jr 84, 85–7, 152
Zair, John, Sr 84, 85
Zair, Mabel Lucy 85
Zair Works 84–5, 88